Psychological

Jurisprudence

SUNY series on New Directions in Crime and Justice Studies
Austin T. Turk, editor

Psychological Jurisprudence

*Critical Explorations
in Law, Crime, and Society*

Edited by
Bruce A. Arrigo

State University of New York Press

Published by
State University of New York Press, Albany

© 2004 State University of New York

For information, address State University of New York Press,
90 State Street, Suite 700, Albany, NY 12207

Production by Michael Haggett
Marketing by Susan M. Petrie

Library of Congress Cataloging in Publication Data

Psychological jurisprudence : critical explorations in law, crime, and society /
edited by Bruce A. Arrigo.
    p. cm. — (SUNY series in new directions in crime and justice studies)
Includes bibliographical references and index.
ISBN 0-7914-6151-3 (hardcover : alk. paper) — ISBN 0-7914-6152-1
(pbk. : alk. paper)
1. Forensic psychology. 2. Insanity—Jurisprudence. 3. Crime—Psychological
aspects. I. Arrigo, Bruce A. II. Series.
K2289.P79 2004
340'.19—dc22

                                        2004007830

10 9 8 7 6 5 4 3 2 1

Contents

Preface

OVERVIEW

The field of law and psychology (or law-psychology-crime more generally) emerged more than three decades ago committed to effecting meaningful, sustainable change for persons funneled through various systems of institutional control (e.g., the systems of criminal justice, mental health, social welfare, children and youth services). The belief was that the values and insights of psychology (and psychiatry) could humanize the experiences of people subjected to these (totalizing) apparatuses in ways that would foster, among other things, justice, empowerment, dignity, and social well-being. Regrettably, mental health law research, policy, and practice has substantially failed to advance its original goals. Indeed, while we have come to learn a great deal about such matters as jury selection, eyewitness testimony, competency to stand trial, psychopathy, and the like, we know very little about the cultural, political, economic, social, and philosophical forces that inform such concerns. As a consequence, while our technical sophistication on these (and related) law-psychology issues has increased, the connections between this important knowledge and citizen justice, social change, law's legitimacy, consumer empowerment, and the like, have been neglected or, worst, ignored.

Admittedly, some attempts have been made to draw attention to the failings of the law-psychology-crime movement to live up to its initial objectives. Typically, however, these works identify the shortcomings of the field, call for limited or incremental improvements, or acknowledge the need for widespread change without proposing a systematic strategy for reform. In those isolated instances where radical psycholegal scholars have proposed different (or new) approaches to humanizing the law, their efforts have been largely speculative or have been based on selected insights from one or two critical philosophical frames of reference (e.g., chaos theory, anarchism, political economy analysis, postmodernism), without something more. As a result, while this radical agenda for transformation appears most promising, it has yet to be understood fully and to be embraced completely within the academy. Most recently, I have explored the epistemological assumptions of a number of intellectual prisms (e.g., feminism, Marxism, postmodernism) within or linked to radical psychology, arguing that their individual and collective insights represent a blueprint for wholesale change at the law-psychology-crime divide (Arrigo, 2002a). In this article, I defined my approach as *critical psychological jurisprudence*; a strategy that investigated contemporary culture's appreciation for law and mental health in various civil and criminal contexts. Here, too, I note that my overall strategy was mostly metatheoretical, focusing on underexamined models that could be the basis for future theoretical, empirical, and policy inquiries.

Psychological Jurisprudence: Critical Explorations in Law, Crime, and Society charts a new and necessary direction in forensic psychological research and practice. Mindful of the cultural and social forces that manufacture and sustain psycholegal decision-making, this anthology critically investigates how the radical agenda could meaningfully return the law-psychology-crime movement back to its original purpose of promoting citizen justice and social well-being. By focusing on selected, although key, controversies (e.g., predicting dangerousness, adolescent identity) and exploring each on the basis of at least one critical theoretical frame of reference (e.g., anarchism, general/family systems theory), we learn something more or something other about whether (and for whom) justice is advanced by prevailing forensic psychological policies and practices. In this context, then, critical psychological jurisprudence gets underneath, behind, over, around, and through issues or controversies, exposing the cultural, political, economic, social, and philosophical forces that generate and/or sustain them in the mental health law arena. Moreover, critical psychological jurisprudence, through its reliance on radical thought, explains where and how alternative strategies of sense making (e.g., feminist jurisprudence, psychoanalysis) produce fuller, more complete expressions of dignity, autonomy, empowerment, and so on regarding these (and similar) psycholegal matters.

PSYCHOLOGICAL JURISPRUDENCE: SOME PRELIMINARY COMMENTS

The critical agenda in psychological jurisprudence is still in its infancy. Selected articles and book chapters are now appearing. Interestingly, however, full-length monographs and edited texts have yet to be developed. Recent book-length projects consistent with the theme of radical psychological jurisprudence include the works of Williams & Arrigo (2001) and Arrigo (2002b). The former project examined how the insights of chaos theory and nonlinear dynamics could re-frame many pressing civil mental health law controversies in ways more consistent with citizen justice, psychological humanism, and social well-being. The latter project relied on the insights of various radical frames of reference to fashion an argument regarding those conscious and unconscious forces that reduce difference (i.e., mental illness) to sameness (i.e., mental wellness) wherein medicine sanitizes and law legitimizes punishment for psychiatric citizens. Neither of these books specifically examined the domain of psychological jurisprudence. In addition, these works did not consider how the critical agenda could reveal the cultural and social forces underscoring decision making at the crossroads of law and psychology, liberating and, ultimately, transforming these practices in the process.

Psychological Jurisprudence: Critical Explorations in Law, Crime, and Society endeavors to fill this gap in the literature. Building on the developing insights of the radical agenda and its wholesale commitment to meaningfully recasting many of the debates in forensic psychology, this edited volume lays out what direction psycholegal research can and must take if justice and humanism are to be realized in theory, research, and policy. As an original, timely, and provocative contribution to the social science and medicine literature, this book has crossover appeal for the related fields of criminology, law, psychology, sociology, and public policy. As a scholarly text, *Psychological Jurisprudence* is written for upper-division undergraduate and lower-division graduate students. It is conceptually animated, mindful of its appeal for a broad audience of academicians, mental health practitioners, social activists, and policy analysts. At the same time, the book is practical, grounded in the everyday dilemmas found within civil and criminal mental health law. The volume can be used as a supplemental text in such courses as law and psychology, sociology of crime, law and society, cultural studies, law and medicine, criminal behavior, law and social control, and social problems.

As a stimulating and insightful contribution to the field of crime and justice studies, *Psychological Jurisprudence: Critical Explorations in Law, Crime, and Society* provides a comprehensive assessment of this emerging approach to interpreting forensic psychology, investigates several thorny and complex controversies at the law-psychology-crime divide, and explains how greater prospects for justice and humanism are attainable through a sustained engagement with critical inquiry. Reaching beyond disciplinary specific boundaries, established and new scholars from law, psychology, sociology, and criminal justice rely on the insights of cultural and literary criticism, psychoanalysis, philosophy, feminist studies, and more to inform their analyses.

ORANIZATION OF THE BOOK

Psychological Jurisprudence: Critical Explorations in Law, Crime, and Society consists of eight chapters. Chapter 1 broadly documents what the domain of psychological jurisprudence conceptually represents. Chapters 2 through 7 investigate various civil and criminal mental health law controversies informed by radical psycholegal thought. Chapter 8 reviews and assesses the preceding application chapters, mindful of how the social change agenda in psychological jurisprudence can be advanced through future work in theory, research, and policy. In what follows, a more specific description for each chapter is provided.

Chapter 1 identifies the limits and shortcomings of existing psycholegal research, decision-making, and practice, especially in relation to advancing the interests of social well-being, citizen justice, and humanism. Bruce A. Arrigo considers how these ideals can be achieved by exploring the utility of five cutting-edge approaches by which to engage in law-psychology-crime research. These perspectives include the contributions of: (1) political economy; (2) feminist jurisprudence; (3) anarchist thought; (4) postmodernism; and (5) chaos theory. The epistemological assumptions of these five frames of reference are also examined as a basis for explaining where and how the critical agenda advances the aims of justice in ways that conventional forensic psychological research does not.

Chapter 2 reviews the limits of prevailing mainstream approaches to interpreting mental illness, forecasting dangerousness, and mandating civil commitment. Christopher R. Williams questions whether law's legitimacy in such matters is compatible with the humanistic values of psychology. In addition, he considers how the anarchist commitment to epistemic uncertainty, change and difference, creativity and becoming, and self-governance represent an entirely new direction for defining psychiatric disorder and for interpreting the role of the mental health sciences in people's lives.

Chapter 3 investigates the crime of parricide, understood as a psychoanalytic offense. Rather than focusing inward, as classic Freudian psychoanalysis suggests, Phillip C. Shon focuses outward, intimating that the dynamics of gender, race, and class inform the social construction of parricide. In this context, the author argues that what gets defined as crime and who gets labeled a criminal is not a function of an immutable, independent law of nature but is always a function of power. Thus, economics, law, and politics, rather than psychology (psychiatry), are more appropriately linked to and further explain our understanding of crime, including parricide.

Chapter 4 examines the pretrial drama of the Theodore Kaczynski case (i.e., the unabomber). Michael P. Arena and Bruce A. Arrigo argue that the insights of postmodernism, specifically constitutive thought, help us understand the way in which media agencies, law enforcement organizations, and the court system informed and misinformed one another about the unabomber case, creating an aura of injustice prior to the actual trial. The authors demonstrate how this injustice, fueled in part by political motives, produced an outcome that denied Kaczynski his right to self-representation.

Chapter 5 investigates the manner in which juvenile forensic psychology fails to promote the best interests of children, particularly during the critical period of adolescent identity development. Relying on the interpretive tools of general systems theory (e.g., entropy vs. negentropy, closed vs. open systems, homeostasis, adaptation), Jeffrey L. Helms and Bruce A. Arrigo demonstrate how psycholegal decision brokers fail to provide truly "objective and scientific" judgments about youths. The authors examine how Bowenian family systems theory and practice represent a more just and humane lens by which to interpret and respond to adolescent identity development.

Chapter 6 addresses the phenomenon of penal punitiveness developed by a number of prominent penologists and other social scientists as a response to crime and its control. Véronique Voruz takes exception to this doctrine, drawing attention to how the discourse of science, the unspoken but felt presence of anxiety, and our commitment to containment or segregative practices are debilitating reactions borne out of late modernity's own sense of political, economic, social, and cultural insecurity. She concludes by exploring the role that critical criminology has played in sustaining the discourse of crime control and, regrettably, furthering the theoretical basis by which the scientific rationality of penal punitiveness is legitimized.

Chapter 7 considers the phenomenon of "responsibilization." As linked to offender rehabilitation practices, this concept implies that individuals should take responsibility for their criminal wrongdoing and, as such, should be held accountable under the law. Embracing this philosophy is understood to be the path to effective, meaningful rehabilitation. Drawing on ethnographic data, Shadd Maruna argues that scant research substantiates this claim. Moreover, he asserts that there is considerable evidence demonstrating that responsibilization is counterproductive to the rehabilitation of individuals in the prison system. He concludes by exploring how personal autobiography and self-reflection in correctional settings, consistent with the logic of restorative justice, might reduce stigma, encourage recovery, and lower recidivism rates.

Chapter 8 reviews and assesses the application chapters of this volume, mindful of how the authors explored the limits of mainstream forensic psychological and criminological theory, research, and practice. In addition, the chapter assesses how the law-psychology-crime divide could be more consistent with the values of humanism and justice. Bruce A. Arrigo considers major points of convergence within the application chapters, commenting on what work is needed in theory, research, and policy (including education), if the law-psychology-crime movement is to get back to its future of advancing the aims of consumer empowerment, autonomy, dignity, and the like.

Psychological Jurisprudence: Critical Explorations in Law, Crime, and Society moves several of the enduring debates in forensic psychology and criminology forward, and is sensitive to how reform, humanism, and justice are central, rather than peripheral, features of the knowledge process. Admittedly, this volume cannot establish on its own the sort of wholesale change envisioned by the architects of the law-psychology-crime movement established decades ago. Indeed, while certainly a worthwhile enterprise, this task would be much more formidable than what can be reasonably accomplished within the confines of a book. However, the winds of change begin with critical reflection and this anthology cultivates, indeed nurtures, this very possibility. As such, I invite you to consider the potential this book embodies. Without such a purpose, I fear the law-psychology-crime movement will forever remain an artifact of mainstream thought and logic: well-intentioned in what it seeks to explain but limited in how it understands human and social phenomena. From my perspective, much more is needed and the critical agenda has an important role to play in the process, especially if citizen well-being, collective good, and human justice in society are to be achieved.

REFERENCES

Arrigo, B. A. (2002a). "The Critical Perspective in Psychological Jurisprudence: Theoretical Advances and Epistemological Assumptions." *International Journal of Law and Psychiatry* 25(2), 151–172.

———. (2002b). *Punishing the Mentally Ill: A Critical Analysis of Law and Psychiatry.* Albany, NY: Sate University of New York Press.

Williams, C. R. & Arrigo, B. A. (2001). *Law, Psychology and Justice: Chaos Theory and the New (Dis)order.* Albany, NY: State University of New York Press.

Chapter 1

The Critical Perspective in Law-Psychology Research

New Directions in Citizen Justice and Radical Social Change

Bruce A. Arrigo

OVERVIEW

The law-psychology movement emerged in the 1960s with a steadfast commitment to humanizing the law and legal decision making, guided by psychological values and insights. Many observers note that the movement has mostly failed to meet its objectives, unable to produce social change in any radical or otherwise substantial way. One explanation for these disappointing results is that no systematic and thorough attempt has been made to explain what the radical agenda embodies, especially in relation to identifying its core assumptions. Relying on several insights as developed within critical (criminological) theory and as appropriated by radical law-psychology scholars, this chapter describes five, cutting-edge approaches to contemporary psycholegal inquiry. These include the perspectives of: (1) political economy; (2) feminist jurisprudence; (3) anarchism; (4) postmodernism; and (5) chaology. Individually, these orientations provide a clearer portrait of what radical scholarship in the academy has come to represent. Collectively, these approaches suggest a new and much needed direction in law-psychology research, especially in relation to advancing the aims of justice in the legal sphere.

This chapter is adapted from the author's previously published article: Bruce A. Arrigo, 2003. "Psychology and the Law: The Critical Agenda for Ciizen Justice and Radical Social Change." *Justice Quarterly* 20(2), 399–444. Reprinted with permission of the Academy of Criminal Justice Sciences.

INTRODUCTION

The law-psychology movement emerged in the late 1960s, and was institutionalized with the 1968 founding of the American Psychology-Law Society (AP-LS). The expressed purpose of the movement and organization was to restore the place of justice in psycholegal matters (Fox, 1999; Arrigo, 2001), and to "transform a prevailing 'judicial common sense' that had been used to keep the disenfranchised down so long" (Haney, 1993, p. 375). Unfortunately, most observers note that the law-psychology field has been largely remiss in its ability to produce radical social change (e.g., Fox, 1993a, 1991; Melton, 1992, 1990; Roesch, 1995; Ogloff, 2000). Accordingly, the place of justice in directing psycholegal affairs has become so diverted and ineffectual (Fox, 1997) that legal psychologists (e.g., clinicians, researchers, policy analysts) routinely practice with "blinders on when they look at the law and the legal system" (Melton, 1991, p. 1).

One explanation for the lack of meaningful, sustainable change in the law-psychology arena can be traced to the movement's inability to articulate a comprehensive and uniform theoretical statement about the vision of social transformation and citizen justice proponents seek to establish. Indeed, as Ogloff (1994) observes, "the vast majority of [extant] research . . . only provides a description of what happens in the law, rather than providing any explanation of why or how the phenomenon exists. [Legal psychologists have] failed to employ or develop theories to explain the phenomena they study (p. 4; Small, 1993). Thus, while values such as "dignity," "person-hood," "human welfare," "autonomy," "compassion," "self-determination," and "equality" are wedded to the radical agenda (e.g., Tapp & Levine, 1977; Finkel, 1995; Prilleltensky & Fox, 1997), regrettably their meanings remain obscured, misunderstood, or ignored notwithstanding the applied research sympathetic to the radical critique (e.g., Dallaire, McCubbin, Morin, & Cohen, 2000; Arrigo & Williams, 1999a; 1999b; McCubbin & Weisstub, 1998). Indeed, although these studies considerably advance our understanding of the social, political, and economic landscape of alienation and oppression to which mental health consumers are all too frequently subjected, we learn little about the conceptual justifications on which their otherwise noteworthy and compelling analyses are based.

Moreover, when efforts to establish a broad-gauged theoretical approach to transformative and empowering decision making in the law-psychology field are rigorously espoused, they lack sufficient conceptual clarity (Cohen, 1991; Ogloff, 1992), succumb to disciplinary subspecialization (Fox, 1993b; Arrigo & Williams, 1999a), or describe justice in its absence (Shklar, 1990; Simon, 1995; Cohen, 1989). These initiatives, while certainly promising in their own right, produce discouraging results. For example, the diffusion of perspectives leaves some to conclude that it may not be possible to reach consensus on what justice is or about how to eradicate its abuses (Fox, 1999; Simon, 1995). In addition, failed attempts at crafting a macro-theoretical position concerning emancipatory practices in the psycholegal arena suggest that the task is not only daunting but perhaps unrealizable. As a consequence, several scholars lament the discipline's inability to make real the call for radical social transformation. As Haney (1993) observes, "I believe we are beginning to lose a sense of shared purpose in psychology and law. I speak about a sense of the waning of collective effort, a loss of common goals, and an abandoning of a sense of mission-the mission of legal change" (pp. 378–379).

Mindful of the liberatory promise that spawned the AP-LS and cognizant of the movement's shortcomings to date, this chapter examines what radical law-psychology inquiry signifies by describing the epistemological assumptions of several critical[1] (criminological) theories underpinning this critique (for some preliminary comments along these lines see, Arrigo, 2002). The relationship between radical law-psychology scholarship and critical (criminological) inquiry is significant. As this chapter discloses, much of the radical application work engaged in by researchers thus far draws heavily from various strains of critical theory and/or critical criminology (for a discussion of the similarities and differences between these two domains of conceptual exegeses see, Arrigo, 1999). Thus, turning to critical (criminological) theory as a basis to explain the assumptions of radical law-psychology scholarship and as a starting point to rethink how the law-psychology movement can realize its call for systematic and widespread change, seems only logical.

In addition, the emphasis on epistemological assumptions is deliberate. Not only does the focus on critical (criminological) inquiry reveal the knowledge claims at the center of the radical agenda giving meaning to the psychological values identified above, it discloses something more about the nature of "justice" law-psychology proponents seek to establish. Thus, the emphasis on presuppositions directs our attention to where and "how the law can be revised, when necessary, to better reflect the reality of human behavior" (Ogloff, 2000, p. 472). As such, when examining presuppositions not only do we learn something more about critical (criminological) theory's relationship to law and psychology, we begin to discern how meaningful prospects for justice can be attained through future (and redirected) psycholegal theory, research, and policy.

Accordingly, this chapter enumerates five leading approaches for engaging in radical or critical law-psychology research. These include the perspectives of: (1) political economy; (2) feminist jurisprudence; (3) anarchism; (4) postmodernism; and (5) chaology.[2] Each of these orientations tells us something quite distinctive about how to decenter psychology and displace the legal status quo, such that radical and wide-ranging alterations in the law-psychology sphere can occur. Several application chapters delineated within this anthology rely on the conceptual insights of these theories to establish a compelling and thought-provoking basis for a sustained psycholegal critique. Although the application chapters include additional theoretical perspectives not examined here (e.g., (neo)Freudian theory), and although this chapter presents some conceptual exegeses not utilized elsewhere in this book (e.g., feminist jurisprudence), readers should note that these circumstances merely demonstrate the breadth of theoretical scholarship thus far undertaken in the interest of advancing radical reform at the crossroads of law and psychology.

Admittedly, mainstream liberal or progressive researchers began this process of reform. Indeed, efforts to humanize the law through principles of procedural justice (Thibaut & Laurens, 1975; Sydeman et al., 1997) therapeutic jurisprudence (Wexler & Winick, 1996; Winick, 1997) and common sense justice (Finkel, 1995) while certainly disparaging of the prevailing status quo, do not seek change by radically reconfiguring the operation of the psychiatric and legal systems (e.g., Sarason, 1982; Smith, 1990). As Haney (1980) noted, "[p]sychologists have been slow to decide whether they want to stand outside the [legal] system to study, critique, and change it, or to embrace and be employed by it" (p. 152). Thus, for example, proponents of therapeutic jurisprudence who insist that these sort of interventions "can at least potentially lead to legal change in line with their own and society's strongly held normative values" (Winick, 1997, p. 200) legitimize, knowingly or not, the very structures of hegemony that need wholesale dismantling (Arrigo, 1997a). Indeed, eliminating oppression, exploitation and marginalization entails "structural rather than individual solutions" (Haney, 1991, p. 190), and these injustices can only be eradicated through "radically-inspired social and political changes" (Albee, 1982, p. 1044).

Collectively, then, the critical (criminological) theories previously identified and their corresponding assumptions advance the progressive agenda of reform by embodying a new, different, and necessary direction for doing law-psychology research. Given this novel approach, and following the collection of application chapters demonstrating the usefulness of the critical agenda in psychological jurisprudence, this anthology therefore concludes by discussing the implications and lessons of this paradigm for future theoretical, applied, and policy investigations in the field. Consistent with the call for fundamental and widespread change articulated in chapter 1, the concluding chapter concretely highlights the potential contributions of the radical critique for citizen justice and legal reform.

Preliminarily, I accept as given the position articulated by Fox (1993a):

[O]nly fundamental structural transformation can effectively counter trends toward hierarchy, isolation, inequality, and so forth; reduce racism, sexism, homophobia, and other forms of oppression;

and bring about a humane, egalitarian, just society consistent with psychological and societal well-being. (p. 234)

This very sentiment was explicitly conveyed in Roesch's (1995) AP-LS presidential address: As he explained:

> changes in the justice system will never be sufficient to create a just society, nor will within system changes by themselves ever have much of an impact on individuals who come into conflict with the law. The problems inherent in our justice system cannot be resolved simply by addressing problems within that system. We can make changes that will make the system more fair or more effective in dealing with individuals within the system, but, in the long term, I believe that this will not be enough because it will not change the fundamental inequalities in our society at large. (p. 329)

Thus, what has yet to be assessed systematically and extensively is how critical (criminological) conceptual analysis can help effectuate the outcomes envisioned by Fox and Roesch. Indeed, as Ogloff (2000) observed, in support of such theorizing and in search of such change: "[o]nly by applying [sophisticated] theory to the law in an attempt to explain causal relationships between [it] and human behavior will [researchers and analysts] be able to advocate for valid legal reforms, and to finally have a meaningful impact on the law" (p. 473). In addition, however, it remains to be seen what prospects for justice at the law-psychology divide will amount to, given the theoretical assumptions of these various radical formulations. I contend that both of these matters (i.e., the significance of critical inquiry and the focus on justice) return the AP-LS to its original purpose, offering guidance as to how the mission of meaningful, sustainable reform can be achieved.

CRITICAL PERSPECTIVES IN LAW AND PSYCHOLOGY

In this section five approaches for doing radical psycholegal research, informed by critical (criminolgical) inquiry are discussed.[3] Both the theory and its application in the pertinent literature are described. The presentation of each critical lens and its employment in the relevant applied research is not exhaustive. Rather, of particular interest are the distinct epistemological assumptions lodged within each perspective. The incorporation of applied scholarship into the overall conceptual analysis serves three functions. First, it helps ground the otherwise dense philosophical material. Second, the illustrations legitimize the utility of the theoretical perspective in question, especially as a sustainable basis by which to engage in thought-provoking and critical law-psychology analysis. Third, reference to the application studies draws attention to protean areas of noteworthy scholarship ripe for future theoretical explorations, empirical investigations, and policy formulations.

Political Economy

The political economy perspective is rooted in the philosophy of Marx (e.g., 1974/1867; 1984/1859) and neo-Marxian revisionists (Pashukanis, 1978; Althusser, 1971). Although Marx did not develop a detailed theory of law or of judicial decision making, much of his work has been appropriated as a worthwhile backdrop for describing "a unique perspective on law" (Milovanovic, 1994, p. 61) and the society of which it is a part. More pointedly, Marxist jurisprudence "manifest[s] the legitimizing functions of law as a contributor to ideological distortion and as a solidifier of the political status quo . . . , unmasking . . . law's . . . participation in domination and oppression" (Belliotti, 1995, p. 3).

The assumptions of Marx's theory are generally of two sorts: those that relate to his views on economics (i.e, the material nature of society); and those that relate to his views on human nature (i.e., the psychological state of our existence) (Lynch & Stretesky, 1999).[4] The joint effect of these presuppositions represents an elaborate system of thought; one with profound implications for understanding a crucial, though underexamined, focus of law-psychology research and prospects for justice at its crossroads. For purposes of this theoretical excursion, the specific assumptions to which I briefly draw attention include Marx's views on class, alienation, exploitation, and false consciousness.

Marx's assumptions about material society
In stark contrast to Hegel's (1977/1807) idealism and theory of history as thought (popular among both philosophical and political circles at the time), Marx articulated a position of general social development based on real class relationships. He called this his "materialist conception of history" (Marx, 1984/1859, p. 19), and it was to form the basis of his economic theory. Marx (1984/1859) succinctly described his position as follows:

> In the social production of their existence, people inevitably enter into definite relations, which are independent of their will, namely relations of production appropriate to a given stage in the development of their material forces of production. The totality of these relations of production constitutes the economic structure of society,

the real foundations, on which arises a legal and political superstructure and to which correspond definite forms of social consciousness. The mode of production of material life conditions the general process of social, political and intellectual life. It is not the consciousness of people that determines their existence, but their social existence that determines their consciousness. (pp. 20–21)

What is significant about this statement is how Marx anchored social relationships in class. Consequently, it is the material force of class that fundamentally defines how people relate to one another and informs the manner in which conflicts between people of different social standings unfold. This logic has been adopted by critics of psycholegal practices, especially in their assessment of power disparities between clients and psychiatry (McCubbin & Cohen, 1996), the body debilitating and mind altering side effects of tardive dyskinesia (Cohen & McCubbin, 1990), the treatment-control regimen at the root of civil commitment determinations (Dallaire, McCubbin, Morin, & Cohen, 2000), and the ethic of proxy decision making for incompetent mentally ill patients (McCubbin & Weisstub, 1998). In instances such as these, "the interests of clients diverge from the interests of other actors involved in the mental health system . . . [and] the personal and political power of clients to advance their interests is small compared to the power wielded by other actors" (McCubbin & Cohen, 1996, p. 1). According to Marx, what lurks behind these situations of differential or unequal power is class position, making it "one of the most important organizational features of society and a construct that would have to be addressed in any study related to human society" (Lynch & Stretesky, 1999, p. 18).

Marx defined class based on an individual's (or group's) relationship to the mode and means of production. The former refers to the kind of economic system around which a given society is organized (e.g., slavery, feudal, mercantile, capitalist, communist). This economic organization makes it possible for a society to produce and distribute commodities. The latter refers to how production occurs in a society (e.g., manual labor, machine-based, technological). Thus, how people (or groups) relate to the means of production determines their class position (Marx, 1984/1959). In other words, for example, a critical investigation of the real power psychiatric patients possess to influence the course of their hospital care and treatment and to direct the involvement of the justice and mental health systems providing it, requires careful scrutiny of the role of class and one's relation to the mode and means of producing contemporary psycholegal services and interventions. Indeed, "a more complete political economy analysis . . . would identify the interests, powers, and activities of all important actors . . . including other health professions, families, public and private institutions, and drug companies" (McCubbin & Cohen, 1996, p. 1).

For purposes of this assessment of psychology and law, political economy, and Marxist assumptions, what is significant is how class position indicates the amount of monetary and material power an individual (or group) possesses. More important, however, I note that "economic power has always translated into political power, and the group that controls or owns the means of production also controls the rules and often the rulers (if they are not the rulers themselves!)" (Lynch & Stretesky, 1999, p. 19; see also Jost, 1995; Haney, 1997). Quinney (1974), sympathetic to the radical agenda, vehemently expressed this sentiment in his critique of law and the legal order. As he observed:

> [the] state is organized to serve the interests of the dominant economic class, the capitalistic ruling class. . . . [L]aw is an instrument of the state and ruling class to maintain and perpetuate the existing social and economic order. . . . [C]ontrol in capitalist society is accomplished through a variety of institutions and agencies established and administered by a governmental elite, representing ruling class interests . . . , [where] the subordinate classes remain oppressed by whatever means necessary, especially through coercion and violence of the legal system. (p. 16)

It follows, then, that those who exercise political and economic power in the mental health and justice systems establish the form, frequency, and duration of citizen justice and social well-being found within the psycholegal domain. Although Marx's economic theory is useful for explaining how people live (i.e., class position) and the manner in which work is organized in a given society (i.e., mode and means of production), it remains to be seen whether his materialist conception of history is useful for prosocial development. In order to assess this matter adequately it is necessary to review his assumptions about human nature.

Marx's assumptions about human nature

Perhaps the most revealing suppositions underlying Marxist thought are those involving his position on human nature (e.g., Marx, 1964/1844). Marx believed that people were creative, social beings, produced, in part, by their physical and interpersonal environment. For Marx, a distinguishing feature of human sociability and creativity was productivity, especially personal labor. Indeed, "[h]uman fulfillment is intimately connected with the imaginative, unshackled use of productive capacities. Labor is a distinctively human activity and possesses central normative significance" (Belliotti, 1995, p. 4). According to Marx, not only does work allow one to engage in creative self-expression, it establishes a basis for meaningful social interaction (Elster, 1986; Schmitt, 1987). Thus, free, innovative "human labor [i]s the median between individuals and the material world in which they live" (Lynch & Stretesky, 1999, p. 20), ensuring that people "realize unalienated being" (Belliotti, 1995, p. 4).

In capitalistic societies, however, human labor is problematic because it produces both estrangement and exploitation (e.g., Beirne & Quinney, 1982). Mindful of the previous comments on Marx's historical materialism, the labor that one produces (and all the creative, intangible forces of productivity associated with it) are regulated by those who make the rules about working. These rules are codified, legitimized, and enforced by the legal apparatus which "works like a blind, insensate machine . . . [doing] the bidding of those who hands are on the controls" (Friedman, 1973, p. 14). According to Marx (1974/1867), the economic conditions wherein labor is sold in the marketplace is inherently alienating because it denies people "a significant activity that makes [them] human" (Lynch & Stretesky, 1999, p. 21). As Bellioti (1995) observes,

> In sum, capitalist social and economic institutions prevent the actualization of [one's] potential and thereby disconnects workers from [themselves] because they stifle workers' voice, creativity, and imagination; transform labor power itself into a commodity; . . . and fail to mediate the social aspect of labor by cooperation and solidarity. . . . In this fashion, . . . capitalism nurtures workers' desperation for material possessions, not their sense of creative expression. (p. 4)

Some law-psychology researchers have drawn critical attention to various practices and policies that produce and/or minimize alienation for individuals employed in the psychiatric and justice systems. For example, Arrigo (1993a), relying in part on a Marxist-based framework, demonstrates historically how the value of paternalism in mental health law is a commodity that sustains the alienation and victimization of psychiatric patients. Nelson, Lord, & Ochocka (2001), incorporating the narratives of psychiatric consumers/survivors, explain how expressions of empowerment are retrievable in community mental health settings. McCubbin & Cohen (1999), drawing on the analytical perspective of general systems theory, describe a value-based approach to reforming the mental health system wherein patients are acknowledged as "policy *agents* rather than as policy *objects*" (p. 67). These and similar studies expose the manner in which marginalizing forces (e.g., cost and fiscal factors in deinstitutionalization, the disease model of psychiatry, the interiorization of power), embedded in the political economy of the medical and legal system, significantly impede prospects for citizen justice and social well-being at the law-psychology divide.

Related to Marx's position on alienation is his theory of exploitation. Left to their own devices, people would work as much as they needed in order to meet their basic human needs. In a capitalist system, however, workers must sell their labor in order to survive. One's labor becomes a commodity that has value set, not by the worker or seller, but by the capitalist or the buyer (Lynch & Stretesky, 1999). What is significant in this exchange is that the buyer is able to extract surplus value from one's work (i.e., the added labor beyond what the worker needs to subsist for which the laborer is not compensated), giving rise to exploitation. As Belliotti (1995) explains,

> [E]xploitation occurs when one class, the proletariat, produces a surplus whose use is controlled by another class, the capitalists. . . . [T]his kind of exploitation occurs absent the use of explicit duress, physical threat, or other non-economic forces. It is through the capitalists' vastly superior economic bargaining power over workers, their ownership of the means of production, and the lack of real alternatives for workers that exploitation flourishes in a capitalist regime. (pp. 4–5)

Thus, surplus value is the source of profit for the capitalist or the group controlling the means of production, and it is a commodity for which the laborer toils, experiencing victimization in the face of inadequate compensation.

Exploitation is endemic to the overlapping and interdependent operation of the medical and legal systems (e.g, Isaac & Armat, 1990; Prilleltensky & Gonick, 1996; U'Ren, 1997). For example, critics have challenged the surplus power mental health decision brokers appropriate from psychiatric patients, devaluing and exploiting them in the process (Prilleltensky & Nelson, 2002), have described the contradictions, crises, and changes in the psychiatric consumer empowerment movement in the United States (McLean, 1995), and have chronicled the abusive and marginalizing mental-health-care policies from the asylum period to the community treatment era (Grob, 1991). While these and related law-psychology investigations rely somewhat tangentially on political economy assumptions for systematic theoretical support and guidance, it is clear that they draw on Marxist thought because the latter "makes explicit connections to sociological and psychological phenomena . . . providing a philosophical basis for the . . . study of . . . oppression and domination" (Jost, 1995, pp. 399–400; see also, Newnes, Holmes, & Dunn, 1999).

The final epistemological assumption relevant to this critical foray of psychological jurisprudence is Marx's position on false consciousness. False consciousness or "fabrications of justice" (Cohen, 1989, p. 33) refers to a practice wherein subjugated or disenfranchised groups, knowingly or not, "adopt the dominant prevailing ideology and perceptual prism [even though] these dominant ideas do not truly correspond to the experience of the oppressed" (Belliotti, 1995, p. 9). Marx recognized that false consciousness was integral to the operation and maintenance of the capitalist status quo. It functionally legitimated the monopoly of power capitalists wielded against workers by intimating that existing economic disparities (e.g., haves versus have nots) were the result of "natural, appropriate, and inevitable labor dynamics" (Schmitt, 1987, p. 54). In this process of reality construction, the interests of the ruling classes are held out as general human interests, synonymous with the needs of subordinate collectives (Lynch & Stretesky, 1999). Indeed, the material force of such reality construction fosters the interiorization of powerlessness (Prilleltensky & Gonick, 1996) to which oppressed citizens are (unconsciously) subjected. Over time, however, the depth and magnitude of these ideological distortions can (and do) erode as members of or advocates for the subjugated masses experience the injustices administered in the service of the prevailing political and economic order.

Critics have long been vocal in their assessment of how psychology and law jointly operate, adversely affect people, and produce ideological distortions. For example, Fox (1999) suggests that one important access point for the study of psychology and law is the focus on injustice which "makes false consciousness easier to find" (p. 12; see also Finkel, 1998). Relatedly, in his assessment of morals, politics, and the status quo in psychology, Prilleltensky (1994) observes that "unless individuals become reasonably aware of the ideological deception of which they are victims, it is unlikely that they will be able to engage in any process of social change" (p. 189). And, in his critique of common sense justice, capital punishment, and ideological distortions, Haney (1997) notes that "popular views of legal issues and principles and law-related social realities are sometimes highly dependent on messages and lessons that are communicated from legal sources (and their proxies in the media) that serve as agents of socialization" (p. 305). These are sources that disseminate "false or inaccurate beliefs that are contrary to one's own social interests and which thereby contribute to the maintenance of the disadvantaged position of the self or the group" (Jost, 1995, p. 400).

Feminist Jurisprudence and Sociolegal Inquiry

Feminist legal criticism distinguishes itself from studies on gender and the law. Rather than examining the behavior of women "within the legal system" or "the role [that] gender plays in different [legal] phenomena" (Frazier & Hunt, 1998, pp. 1, 7), feminist jurisprudence exposes the taken-for-granted ideology embedded within the very construction of law (Smith, 1995). Pivotal to this critical analysis is the conviction that conventional and progressive legal theory (including the wisdom of the Critical Legal Studies Movement), inadequately account for the lived experience of women.

The feminist prescription for radical reform emerged in the late 1980s (e.g., MacKinnon, 1987, 1989; Menkel-Meadow, 1988; Rhode, 1989).

Although mainstream liberal feminists successfully challenged the ideology inherent in patriarchy that subordinated women (e.g., Brownmiller, 1975; Dworkin, 1981), critical scholars drew attention to the ideology inherent in the law, finding it even more problematic for the condition of women in society. Exploring this dilemma, Goldfarb (1992) noted that "[m]any feminists have identified patriarchy as an ideology more threatening to their lives than legal ideology, and have directed efforts at undermining the former even through the use of the latter" (p. 704; see also Walby, 1990). In this scenario, the dominant ideology of the law is legitimized, and, according to radical feminist legal critics, it is *this* perspective that insidiously dismisses women's ways of knowing, feminine ways of being. MacKinnon (1989) makes this point sharply:

> Liberal legalism is thus a medium for making male dominance both invisible and legitimate by adopting the male point of view in law at the same times as it enforces that view of society. . . . Through legal mediation, male dominance is made to seem a feature of life, not a one-sided construct imposed by force for the advantage of a dominant group. To the degree that it succeeds ontologically, male dominance does not look epistemological: control over being produces control over consciousness. . . . Dominance reified becomes difference. Coercion legitimated becomes consent. In the liberal state, the rule of law—neutral, abstract, elevated, pervasive—both institutionalizes the power of men over women and institutionalizes power in its male form. (pp. 237–238)

With this focus on the marginalizing and oppressive force of legal logic and, by extension, judicial decisions, practices, and institutions, it is not surprising that this brand of legal criticism is "heavily influenced by feminist work in philosophy, psychoanalysis, semiotics, history, anthropology, postmodernism, literary criticism, and political theory" (Milovanovic, 1994, p. 105). Indeed, by focusing on the ideology inherent in the law (i.e., the legitimized power of the male-dominated status quo), radical feminist theory challenges certain mainstream legal assumptions about prospects for gender equality and sexual difference in society (Frug, 1992). These presuppositions include a critique of knowledge, identity, and the legal method. It is to these matters that I now briefly turn.

The critique of knowledge
The statement, "the personal is empirical" (McDermott, 1992, p. 237), characterizes the liberal feminist approach to knowledge. Women's experiences can be retrieved, recorded, and counted; they are statistical variables that can be used, among other things, to convey clearly and compellingly "the magni-

tude and implications of any gender difference[s]" (Frazier & Hunt, 1998, p. 8; see also Eagly, 1995) found in a given data set. However, as Arrigo (1995a) cautions in his assessment of mainstream legal thought, the *empirical is personal;* it is "the site of power and therefore [it] may also advance the subordination of those who experience differently" (p. 461). Thus, for example, radical scholars of feminist jurisprudence question the values embedded within the logic of quantitative law and social science inquiry (Bartlett & Kennedy, 1991). Some have argued that it is so phallocentric (male-dominated) that "any issue brought before the court that substantially deviates from this body of knowledge is less likely to attain a hearing and a favorable resolution" (Milovanovic, 1994, p. 105). Interestingly, this position squarely challenges the logic of many psycholegal scholars who assert that explanatory rationales concerning the law should be based on "the values that make up conventional knowledge of the community of scientific psychology" (Wiener, Watts, & Stolle, 1993, p. 93).

The presence of masculine imagery and logic steeped in legal texts, doctrines and institutions is not to be dismissed (Smart, 1989; MacKinnon, 1987; Smith, 1995). Expressions such as burdens of *proof,* a demand for *factual evidence, actual* legal intent, *expert* testimony, and *causes* of crime are values steeped in masculine reasoning and sensibility (Arrigo, 1992, 1995a). This approach to legal decision making "celebrates the logical, rational, sequential, and, by its proponents' own deductive reasoning, therefore reliable and ethical form of judgements" (Arrigo, 1995b, p. 89). These claims to sense making are veiled statements about power (Smart, 1989), conveying circumscribed truths that dismiss or neglect other ways of experiencing and knowing, including the perspective of women. As Bottomley (1987) concludes, the question is not whether the law

> oppresses women's styles of existence and conversely privileges those of men, but whether the very construction. . . . of legal discourse [and the] representation of the discourse in the academy ... [are] the product[s] of patriarchal relations at at the root of society. (p. 48)

The critique of identity

Radical proponents of feminist jurisprudence acknowledge that working within the legal apparatus can produce some positive change (e.g., Williams, 1987; Cook, 1990; Crenshaw, 1988). However, juridical categories reinforce the "legitimacy of the legal apparatus, the rule of law ideology, and, in the end, the rule of men" (Milovanovic, 1994, p. 106). This condition has led some feminist legal critics to consider whether women are formally equal to men under the law, wherein they receive identical rights. However, the issue of identical rights is itself problematic for women. "Equality doctrine requires comparisons, and the standard for comparison tends strongly to reflect societal norms. Thus, equality for women has come to mean equality with men—usually white, middle class men" (Bartlett & Kennedy, 1991, p. 5; see also Naffine, 1990). Smith (1995) succinctly captures this dynamic. As she explains:

> [the question is] whether women, being different, should argue for equal rights or for special rights. Equal rights (i.e., identical rights) . . . disadvantage women sometimes (e.g., as to pregnancy benefits) . . . and special rights accommodate women's special needs and circumstances. [However], only equal (i.e., identical) rights should be claimed because any special needs or differences acknowledged by women are always used to limit women in the long run, and special rights will be viewed as special favors that accommodate women's deficiencies. The problem is that if that is the way the issue is formulated, then women lose either way because the (unstated) norm is male. After all, who is it that women are different from? Whose rights (if equality is the standard) should women's rights be equal to? And if women's rights should sometimes be different from men's, why is it women's rights that are characterized as special? Why not formulate rights in terms of women's needs and characterize men's rights as special? One way makes as much sense as the other. The question is, who is the norm? (p. 281, n 16)

The problem identified above is intensified when race is factored into the equation (Harris, 1991; Crenshaw, 1988). In other words, for example, does a Latina woman use the standard of white women for reasonableness in arguing her battered women's syndrome defense in a case where she is accused of murder (e.g., Bartlett, 1991; Russell, 1998)? Would it matter if the Latina woman was a third-generation Brazilian-American, fully acclimated to the social norms of life in the United States? Questions such as these draw attention to one of the most contentious issues facing radical feminist legal theory today. In short, the concern is that of essentialism and the "underlying basis of the legal subject" (Milovanovic, 1994, p. 107). Is there something to which we can turn that constitutes an "essential 'woman' beneath the realities of differences between women" (Harris, 1991 p. 242; see also MacKinnon, 1991, pp. 81–91)? Or would it be more consistent with feminine ways of experiencing to acknowledge the multiplicity of a woman's existence, implying, then, that "differences [between them] are always relational rather than inherent" (Harris, 1991, p. 250; Collins, 1990).

This latter approach, popular among several critical feminist legal scholars, produces knowledge that is "situated, contingent, and partial" (Bartlett,

1991, p. 389). In this model, identity is a function of epistemological stand-points (e.g., Currie, 1993). Describing the subject in law entails locating "where and how women and minorities with their differential statuses in society continue to experience exclusion in . . . legal practices" (Arrigo, 1995a, p. 455), and then privileging these statuses because they "give [us] access to oppression that others cannot have" (Bartlett, 1991, p. 385).

The critique of the legal method

The radical feminist critique of knowledge and identity in legal thought gives way to a sustained assault of the juridical reasoning process (e.g., MacKinnon, 1982; Dahl, 1987; Arrigo, 1992, 1995b). "Law's truth outweighs other truths . . . [and] the principal culprit in this realization is the legal method" (Arrigo, 1995b, pp. 92–93). It is at this juncture that we can begin to discern the manner in which studies in psychology and law have thus far contributed to the advancement of the critical agenda. Moreover, I note that this particular line of inquiry forms a pivotal basis for future radical scholarship at the inter-section of gender, justice, law, and society. The contours of the legal method include boundary definition (e.g., scope of what's admissible), defining rele-vance, and case analysis (MacKinnon, 1991). However, missing from this tightly scripted masculine construction is feminine consciousness (e.g., Coombe, 1989, 1992); that is, "the often silenced voice, the voice of the excluded" (Milovanovic, 1994, p. 108). In order to retrieve the voice of and way of knowing for woman in legal analysis, it is necessary to look "beneath the surface of the law to identify the gender implications of rules and assumptions underlying them and insisting upon applications of rules that do not perpetuate women's subordination" (Bartlett, 1991, pp. 373–374).

Critical application studies in psycholegal scholarship embracing radical feminist theory have drawn on the insights of Gilligan (1982) and Gilligan, Lyons, & Hanmer (1990) to articulate a radical vision of gendered justice (Fraser, 1997). Selected works describe how the law can embody the unique concrete experiences of woman in juridical reasoning (Arrigo, 1992), in the articulation of sexual violence, including rape (Arrigo, 1993b) and their psy-chiatric labeling (Stefan, 1994), and in the development of psychological the-ories of equality (Squire, 1989). In addition, researchers, persuaded by the work of MacKinnon (1983, 1989), have appropriated the psychological values of consciousness-raising, narrativity, and interpersonal truth (e.g., Mossman, 1986; Littleton, 1987; Lahey, 1985; Smart, 1995) to establish a feminist legal method. As Arrigo (1995b) observes, these investigations reframe our under-standing of woman in juridical thought and, consequently, in legal practice. Indeed, the model of feminist (psycholegal) thought envisioned here calls for the reconstitution of human social interaction and the communities that we all inhabit.

[A] rediscovery of ritual, not law, constituted by neighbors, not judges, informs this "village" aesthetic as personally meaningful. The metaphors of experience and storytelling displace the language of rules and facts. A communal gathering of residents preempts the calculated courtroom trial. The concernful search for "authentic" justice replaces the mental exercise of legal manipulation. (Arrigo, 1995b, p. 91)

Anarchism

Approaches to anarchist thought vary considerably (e.g., Marshall, 1992). Interestingly, however, the perspective that has generated the most attention and controversy is the mutual aid strain of criticism as developed by Peter Kropotkin (e.g., 1902, 1912). What makes this orientation so provocative are its "scathing and sophisticated attacks against the state and its apparatus of legal control" (Ferrell, 1999, p. 94). This critique is not merely a condemnation of institutionalized authority through destructive political efforts for the sake of negation or chaos alone. Instead, the anarchist assault on legal and state-sanctioned regulation is merely "a transitional phase in which the old [is] destroyed so that the new might emerge, [leading to] a better social order" (Schatz, 1972, p. xii). In this regard, anarchism is a positive doctrine (Williams & Arrigo, 2001), defying the status quo and resisting calcified social arrangements wherein the "concern for humanity [displaces] a respect for authority" (Ferrell, 1999, p. 94).

The method by which this new, more humane order materializes is significant not merely for studies of anarchist thought in general but for understanding the perspective's assumptions in relation to advancing a critically-informed psycholegal theory in particular. As Kropotkin (1912) explained,

[an anarchist] society is one in which all the mutual relations of its members are regulated, not be laws, not by authorities, whether self-imposed or elected, but by *mutual agreement* between the members of that society. . . . [Those relations are] not petrified by law, doctrine, or superstition, but [are] continually developing and read-just[ing], in accordance with the ever-growing requirements of free life . . . a continual evolution—such as we see in Nature. (emphasis added) (p. 68)

To be clear, the anarchist focus on mutual agreement substantially displaces society's reliance on manufactured law and legal decision making, dramatically reorienting our frame of reference concerning the human condition and interpersonal conduct. In short, anarchists value fluid and evolving social relations where identities "are never finished products but always projects under construction within a broader process of inventing and reinventing ourselves and others" (Ferrell, 1999, p. 96). Indeed, proponents of the theory maintain that anarchism is "a way of life and organic growth, of natural order within society, and of peace between individuals" (Woodcock, 1992, p. 19). According to the theory's advocates, the anarchist approach therefore fosters a more just and liberatory society than those based on coerced, mandated, or otherwise artificially induced compliance (e.g., Sonn, 1992; Morland, 1997).

Based on the foregoing comments, it is easy to see how the anarchist agenda has "much to say about the social psychology of law, social organization, and the centralized state" (Fox, 1993b, p. 98). In order to understand the perspective and its utility for radical law-psychology inquiry, it is necessary to review the theory's underlying epistemological assumptions. As a general proposition, these assumptions represent a loose and evolving assemblage of the theory's acknowledged convections These suppositions include the belief that reason and truth are forever uncertain, that change, ambiguity, and difference are to be celebrated, and that mutual aid and shared responsibility are integral to the social fabric of our existences. Comprehending these matters dramatically reframes the law and human behavior relationship, suggesting an entirely different set of psycholegal questions to explore in theory, research, and policy.

The uncertainty of reason and truth

Anarchists reject the notion that any one person, institution, or system "should embody and enforce final knowledge, certainty, or truth" (Ferrell, 1999, p. 95). The finality of reason and logic produces closure to possibilities, ensures the delegitimation of alternative perspectives for knowing and experiencing reality, and impedes prospects for meaningful reform (Ferrell, 1997). The law's complicity in this process is profound. As Fox (1993b) contends, the "law prevents social change through a variety of substantive, procedural, and ideological techniques in addition to the use of coercion" (p. 106). Indeed, the law functions to codify certain truth claims by dismissing other points of view, declaring them to be unfounded, lacking scientific rigor, or outside the scope of reasonably accepted practices (Morland, 1997; Ferrell, 1997; Sonn, 1992). This juridical tendency (i.e., bias) reduces the capacity for people to chart the course of their own affairs, "forcing complex human interactions into an artificial legal framework, creating unhealthy dependency on legal authorities" (Fox, 1993a, p. 238).

To combat this proclivity toward legal ossification and sedimented reasoning, anarchists endeavor to "create situations in which a variety of viewpoints can coexist" (Ferrell, 1999, p. 95). The key to unlocking the potential of these multiple vantage points in ongoing human affairs and civic life is *epistemic uncertainty* (Williams & Arrigo, 2001). Epistemic uncertainty defies the wisdom implied in law-focused solutions that seek to control, regulate, and "routinize social relations" (Kinsie, 1979, p. 6; Morland, 1997). Epistemic uncertainty means that people (as opposed to government) directly confront the social and human problems impacting the communities in which they live, without reliance on statutory guidelines or state-mandated directives (e.g., Marshall, 1992; Sonn, 1992). The logic of uncertain truth and reason, assumed in the anarchist critique, recognizes that "solutions to problems emerge as the problems themselves emerge" (Ferrell, 1999, p. 99). Consequently, the authority of law with its cataloging of rules and regulations is anathema to and disastrous for the pursuit of citizen justice and social change. As Kropotkin (1992/1885) proclaimed:

> when there is ignorance in the heart of a society and disorder in people's minds, laws become numerous. [People] expect everything from legislation and, each new law being a further miscalculation of reality, they are led to demand incessantly what should emerge from themselves. . . . [A] new law is considered a remedy for all ills. (p. 145)

By privileging rules, regulation, and control, law, then, becomes the panacea for all social maladies (i.e., disorder), "plac[ing] outside of oneself the importance of everyday decisions . . . construct[ing] the automatic [self]" (Bankowski, 1983, p. 281). Indeed, following the anarchist critique, the displacement of fixed notions of truth, knowledge, reason, and justice, entails a necessary and dramatic reconfiguration of the individual and of society (Fox, 1993b). The reconfiguration of the individual involves assessing the value of ambiguity in human conduct. The reconstitution of society requires investigating the psychological sense of community. Both assumptions inform the anarchist agenda and are suggestive for advancing the aims of radical social change at the law-psychology divide.

The celebration of change, ambiguity, and difference
The Russian anarchist Bakunin (1974) extolled the virtues of change, believing that individual freedom and, thus, civic consciousness, were lodged within its liberating grip. As he observed: "Let us put our trust in the eternal spirit which destroys and annihilates because it is the . . . creative source of life. The passion for destruction is a creative passion, too" (p. 58). Anarchists recognize that this "creative passion" produces life-affirming opportunities. The value of change rests in "its unlimited capacity to [establish] new vistas of meaning in work, leisure, religious preoccupation, political action, or other expressions of human social interaction" (Arrigo, 2000a, p. 20). In the philosophy of anarchism, the seamless thread of change is wedded to ambiguity and difference.

Ambiguity or unpredictability "constitute fertile ground for new ideas and identities and, at their best, overwhelm any attempts to achieve final solutions or final authority" (Ferrell, 1999, p. 96). Difference represents a state of existence that "allows people to be who and how they are in their communities, freed from the normalizing and external constraints of regulatory and disciplinary regimes (e.g., the mental health system, the criminal justice apparatus)" (Arrigo, 2000a, p. 12).

Mindful of how the anarchist assumptions of change, ambiguity, and difference underscore individual identity, some law-psychology researchers have drawn attention to the theory's critical potential for large-scale reform. For example, Fox (1993a) explained how the mainstream emphasis on procedural justice and law's legitimacy assumes "that the rule of law is always superior to nonlaw [and how it] assumes that the procedurally correct application of general principles is best even when it brings patently unfair results in particular cases" (p. 237). Not only does this logic foster the felt experience of injustice for the sake of law's omnipotence, it dismisses the uniqueness of individual identities, with all their ambiguities, inconsistencies, anomalies, and differences. As Fox (1993a) therefore urged, espousing the virtues of the anarchist cry for radical change,

> [i]n seeking a liberating identity instead, psycholegal scholars should reexamine their assumption that law is sufficiently redeemable and should concentrate on replacing law with nonlegal solutions to human problems. . . . Instead of searching the law for values congruent with our own, we should find our values in our psychological theory, political ideology, and personal and organizational ethics. *Law is simply irrelevant to conceptions of what is psychologically desirable.* (emphasis added) (p. 239)

Anarchism's investment in a person's right to exist freely, and its disavowal of the legal apparatus for guidance in the process, stems from the conviction that law's "distinctive trait [is] immobility, a tendency to crystallize what should be modified and developed day by day" (Kropotkin, 1975/1886, p. 30). For anarchists, however, individual autonomy cannot be realized and celebrated without a sense of community that makes liberating identities possible. The manner in which this psychological sense of place unfolds represents the third and final epistemological assumption embedded in the anarchist perspective.

The centrality of mutual aid and shared responsibility
Anarchists accept people as they are. This is not the same as tolerating "people whom others might see as weird or offbeat, as outside the usual frameworks of propriety, or whose ideas or identities challenge our own sense

of who we are; instead, [anarchists] revel in the strange unpredictability of it all" (Ferrell, 1999, p. 97). The different identities borne of anarchism increase prospects for mutual awareness, and it is this mutuality that makes community not only possible but sustainable (Arrigo, 2000a). Indeed, in anarchist communities people are "more free to be themselves, and at the same time, [are] more directly responsible for themselves and others, than they are in situations regulated by external authority" (Ferrell, 1999, p. 97; Marshall, 1992). Thus, the psychological sense of community anarchists envision is one that is based on mutual aid and shared responsibility (Kropotkin, 1902, 1912).

Mutual aid implies localism, regionalism, or decentralization wherein people participate actively and directly in crafting the identity of their neighborhood or locale (Tifft & Sullivan, 1980; Sonn, 1992; Morland, 1997). As an anarchist assumption, mutual aid "grants the best chance of survival to those who best support each other in the struggle for life" (Kropotkin, 1902, p. 115). It follows, then, that shared responsibility entails the recognition that meaningfully living in a community is an intricate tapestry of vital social relations; one that is "woven tightly enough to care for others but loosely enough to preserve [individual] differences" (Ferrell, 1999, p. 97; Sonn, 1992; Morland, 1997).

Proponents of the anarchist perspective recognize that the legal system cannot ensure the optimal quality of individual life and social well-being intrinsic to this radical agenda (e.g., Godwin, 1971/1798; Goldman, 1969; Bankowski, 1983; Sonn, 1992). Moreover, critical psychological researchers, supportive of the anarchist critique, have demonstrated how legal principles or state-mandated practices limit prospects for social justice and thwart basic human needs and values (e.g., Sarason, 1982; Fox, 1991; see also Prilleltensky, 1994, 1999 for related political psychological commentary). For example, Fox (1993b) examined three areas "where legal doctrine seems especially ambivalent from an anarchist perspective" (p. 102). These included the law versus equity distinction, jury nullification, and the Ninth Amendment to the United States Constitution. What makes each of these phenomena ambivalent is the extent to which they more or less function to neutralize law's dominance in the lives of people, as citizens balance their need to exist autonomously and freely against a psychological sense of community. Indeed, on occasion equal treatment among citizens requires an appeal outside the law; at times citizen justice necessitates jury decision making not restricted by courtroom instructions or mandates; and in some instances rights claiming cannot be immediately ascertainable through the Constitution.

The dismantling of state-sponsored authority implied in each of the above cited legal doctrines demonstrates how "trends toward legalism, centralization, hierarchy, and authority are dangerous to human beings who would be better off in a vastly different society" (Fox, 1993b, p. 106). The anarchist assumption of mutual aid and shared responsibility, so integral to the communal nature of our existences, renounces the law's dominance over people (Tifft & Sullivan, 1980; Morland, 1997). Indeed, as Fox (1993b) concluded in his assessment of law and psychology and the anarchist perspective, "looking to the law for justice is looking in the wrong place, because even when short-term victories may be obtained . . . in the long run the trend is in the other direction. . . . [L]aw is not healthy for people" (p. 106).

Postmodernism

The formal origins of postmodern[5] thought can be traced to political and intellectual developments in France, during the 1960s (Arrigo, Milovanovic, & Schehr, 2000).[6] As it pertains to the law, postmodernism represents a considerable assault on the construction, imagery, and logic of conventional juridical reasoning (e.g., Milovanovic, 1992; Arrigo, 1993c, 1996a; Henry & Milovanovic, 1996; Cornell, 1993). In brief, postmodern legal scholars endeavor to demonstrate how the ideology embedded in the law is a function of language (i.e., words, phrases, statutes, cases), conveying a multitude of hidden assumptions and implicit values that produce violence in speech and thought (Sarat & Kearns, 1992; Butler, 1997) and harm in social consequence (e.g., Conley & O'Barr, 1998; Sarat & Kearns, 1996; Sarat & Felstiner, 1995). The violence and harm perpetrated by language principally occurs when only certain meanings, consistent with the values of the discourse in use, are unconsciously "selected out" and are esteemed as truth, knowledge, or fact, dismissing in the process an array of different interpretations, and the discourse used to talk about them, because these alternative coordinates of meaning are not compatible with the prevailing ideology (e.g., Rosenau, 1992).

The postmodern assault, and its diverse intellectual strains of criticism (see, Arrigo, 1995a), flourished in the decade of the 1990s (Best & Kellner, 1997). Most recently, postmodernism has taken on a decidedly psychoanalytic edge (e.g., Caudill, 1997; Schroeder, 1998; Goodrich, 1997; Arrigo, 2000b). One of the principal architects of applying psychoanalysis to language has been Jacques Lacan (e.g., 1977) and, as Milovanovic (1994) observes, he is "the key figure in the fundamental reorientation to postmodernist thought" (p. 156).[7] In order to appreciate the "linguistic turn" in law, Lacanian psychoanalysis, and the relevance of these ideas for law and psychology, some commentary on assumptions is warranted. For purposes of this inquiry, the most significant of these presuppositions is the critique of subjectivity and discourse.

The critique of subjectivity and discourse
Lacan was a Freudian revisionist (Julien, 1994; Fink, 1995), interested in the inner workings of the unconscious and the manner in which subjectivity (i.e,

identity, agency) and language (i.e., speech, words) were inextricably connected (Bracher, 1993; Bowie, 1991). In other words, for Lacan (1977), the two could not be separated. Underscoring this inherent relationship was desire. "Desire is the core of psychoanalysis. . . . [It is] at the heart of our strivings, despairs, passions, beliefs, and fears" (Arrigo, 1997a, p. 34). Desire is what mobilizes the psychic apparatus, rendering the individual "essentially a desiring subject" (Milovanovic, 1994, p. 159). Thus, the person who speaks always communicates (someone's) desire and every expression of language is itself the manifestation of (someone's) subjectivity (e.g., Evans, 1996; Lee, 1990; Bowie, 1991).

The fundamental problem with the inherent link between discourse and subjectivity, however, is one of decoding whose desiring voice is embodied in the words, phrases, or expressions used to convey the subject's meaning and what, if anything, is lost in the process. In other words, if the language we employ to communicate our thoughts is always saturated with hidden values and implicit assumptions, then discourse itself functions as a "stand-in" for the speaker's genuine identity (Bracher, 1993; Malone & Freidlander, 2000). Indeed, following Lacan (1977), not only does our unconscious selection of language convey particularized meanings at the expense of equally worthwhile alternatives, but the discourse we choose often speaks for us (i.e., in our place), concealing a more complete sense of the speaker's humanity and the humanity of others (e.g., Lee, 1990; Fink, 1995). Lacan (1977) referred to this experience as "the subject's lack in discourse" (p. 47).

Several scholars have drawn attention to the critical potential of Lacanian psychoanalysis to facilitate our understanding of the dynamics of speech and its capacity to obscure the subject's being while conveying circumscribed meaning. For example, Williams (1998) demonstrated how civil commitment determinations abrogated the identity of the petitioner, producing outcomes that first "linguistically and then socially marginalized the juridic subject" (p. 180). Shon (2000) explained how police officers embraced "cop talk" (p. 171; see also, Manning, 1988); a mode of communication that denied them access to better opportunities for reconciling peacefully their interactions with citizen-suspects. Stacey (1996) examined how the gendered and raced dimensions of juridical language deprived Aboriginal women in South Australia their legal identities, wherein "the orthodox, modernist legal narrative [could] not transcribe, [did] not have the words to write of, women, race, and identity outside the [prevailing] discourse of law" (p. 287). And Voruz (2000) explored the psychotic's relationship to legal responsibility, arguing that Lacanian psychoanalysis reveals how one's mind is on trial and, thus, how the psychotic's "grammar should be summoned to the courtroom" (p. 148). As such, she concluded that the law must "be mobilized to respond—not in a way that categorically forgives or condemns . . . but in a way that derealizes the offense while humanizing the criminal" (Arrigo, 2000b, p. 130).

Each of the above examples discloses something about the psychoanalytic force of language in the legal sphere. As Klare (1982) notes, "legal language shapes our beliefs about the experience and capacities of the human species, our conceptions of justice, freedom and fulfillment, and our visions of the future (p. 1358; see also Henry & Milovanovic, 1996). Moreover, the language of law functions as "a form of power that also creates a particular kind of world [where] actors impose [political and social] ideologies or persuade others to take them on as "voluntary" (Harrington & Yngvesson, 1990, p. 143). According to Lacan (1977), the interactive and intrapsychic effects of subjectivity and discourse are responsible for the imposition and maintenance of this ideology. Their unconscious mobilization "thwarts opportunities for better understanding one's felt-longing (i.e., desire) and for more completely comprehending one's intrinsic being" (Williams, 1998, p. 184; see also Fink, 1995). Indeed, so profound is the latent but felt presence of circumscribed desire that Lacan (1977) described its articulation as fundamentally "irretrievable and inarticulable" (p. 302).

The relationship between subjectivity and discourse is especially noteworthy in the domain of psychology and law. Echoing the feminist critique of ideology embedded in legal imagery, doctrines, and logic, Lacanian psychoanalysis questions the extent to which taken-for-granted psycholegal discourse merely reflects certain assumptions about the individuals and agencies constituting the mental health system, justice system, or both (e.g., Schroeder, 2000; Milovanovic, 1996; Shon, 2000; Arrigo, 1994). These are presuppositions that unconsciously value (and privilege) certain ways of talking about, experiencing, and interpreting people and their behavior, dramatically impacting legal decision making (Goodrich, 1997). The point is that "language structures thought in ways that are not neutral, in ways that both conceal the individual's being and reveal systemic meaning, always and already embodying, and, thus, announcing a circumscribed discourse that *speaks for* the . . . desiring subject" (Arrigo, 2000c, p. 129; Williams & Arrigo, 2000; Caudill, 1997; Williams, 1998).

Given the cloaked nature of language, critical psycholegal scholars suggest that future investigators would do well to assess how only certain forms of desire are manufactured in the law-psychology arena (Arrigo, 1996b), how only certain types of knowledge are therefore produced (Arrigo, 1996c), and how other articulations, although dismissed or repudiated, could yield a fuller sense of justice than the ones presently realized (e.g., Arrigo & Schehr, 1998; Arrigo, 1997b). In these explorations, the question is one of coming to terms with whether the discourse of prevailing psycholegal theory, research, and policy is spoken in such a way that it can advance the aims of pro-social change, citizen well-being, and humanism. Arrigo (1997a) pointedly summarizes this dynamic and the deep-seated problems inherent in psychiatric and legal language. As he warns:

all participants (e.g., judges, witnesses, psychiatrists, defendants, hospital administrators) appearing before a medico-legal tribunal are interpellated through (i.e., inserted within and situate themselves) a specialized code; namely, those linguistic parameters defining psychiatric justice. . . . [A]ny attempt to communicate . . . desire from outside this signifying sphere, any offering of an alternative speech code, is objected to, declared non-justiciable, and cleansed (i.e., re-languaged) and made compatible with those coordinates advancing the grammar of "*lawspeak*." . . . Thus, the voice of and way of knowing for . . . all those participating in the medico-legal process at its systemic intersection are first and foremost linguistically silenced. Put another way . . . , before any determination is made regarding [forensic] issues, . . . punishment manifests itself in the form of covert linguistic oppression. (pp. 36–37)

Chaology

The field of chaos theory emerged in the natural sciences, initially in the domain of physics and mathematics (Gleick, 1987). Chaology, nonlinear dynamical systems theory, or general systems theory more broadly (Morin, 1990), empirically questions the researcher's ability to forecast accurately the behavior of complex systems (Briggs & Peat, 1989). Systems (including people) are thought to be complex if they behave in ways that are unpredictable, discontinuous, unstable, or anomalous (Johnson, 1996; Barton, 1994).

One of the chief architects of chaos theory was Albert Einstein (1956, 1961). His work in quantum physics/mechanics demonstrated how understanding the changing character of the natural world was dependent on the one observing it at any given moment. The "subjective" dimension of this relationship made absolute and accurate predictability regarding the behavior of phenomena unattainable and forever in flux (Dupre, 1993). Indeed, Einstein's theorems, postulated as laws of physics, led him to conclude that identifying precisely cause-effect sequences and applying this logic to the world and events in it was beyond mathematical, positivistic reason, given the intervening presence of relativity (Stewart, 1989; Gleick, 1987).

On a more general societal level, Einstein's experiments and conclusions were also of considerable consequence. If the observer always influences the object of inquiry, then the "most basic elements of reality . . . can not be isolated, precisely identified or predicted, or 'grasped' as they really are" (Best & Kellner, 1997, p. 214). This position stands in stark contrast to the modern scientific community's conviction that systems are "constituted by a continuous chain of causally related events" (Williams & Arrigo, 2002a, p. 30; Goerner,

1994). The presence of relativity, indeterminacy and chance that Einstein and other investigators witnessed in the behavior of complex physical systems meant that any accurate description of phenomena in the cosmos was just not possible. Indeed, "the level of uncertainty in the sub-atomic world prevents exact understanding and . . . the predictions it makes involve only probabilities, statistical regularities, and not certainties" (Best & Kellner, 1997, p. 214).

Although principles of chaos were initially employed to study occurrences such as planetary motion, the behavior of sub-atomic particles, and other physical phenomena (e.g., Prigogine & Stengers, 1984; Stewart, 1989), subsequent researchers appropriated the tools of nonlinear dynamical systems theory, finding them relevant for investigations in the social sciences as well (e.g. , Milovanovic, 1997; Butz, 1997; Cohert & Stewart, 1994; Pepinsky, 1991). These studies indicate the utility of chaos theory for explaining the complex, seemingly inexplicable, behavior of systems in the life world. Much like the other critical perspectives identified in this article, chaos theory is based on a number of assumptions about human interaction and social conduct. For purposes of my investigation of psychology and law, two presuppositions are most relevant. These include the order within chaos critique and the order out of chaos critique.

The order within chaos critique

Chaos theory is not the study of complete or utter confusion (Stewart, 1989). The disorder that chaos theory identifies examines the underlying stability within apparently disorganized, chaotic systems (Butz, 1997). This investigative orientation is often termed *order within chaos* (e.g., Gleick, 1987; Briggs & Peat, 1989).

The assumption that order lurks within supposed randomness entails the operation of several chaos theory principles; however, the most significant of these concepts is the attractor. Attactors "are patterns of stability that a system settles into over time" (Goerner, 1994, p. 39). Attractors function in the way that their name suggests. They "exert a 'magnetic' appeal for a system, seemingly pulling the system toward it" (Briggs & Peat, 1989, p. 36). It is this attraction or pull that produces order and stability in an otherwise disorderly, complex system.

A pendulum is an example of an attractor. While in motion, if the pendulum is not propelled by any other external stimuli it will eventually come to rest. The position directly underneath the pendulum when it stops is called a "(point) attractor" (Van Eenwyk, 1991, p. 6). "The single point attractor governs the behavior of the pendulum (i.e., system) by 'magnetically' pulling the pendulum toward itself. Thus, all movement (i.e, behavior) is attracted to a 'single' point" (Williams & Arrigo, 2002a, p. 83).

Attractors can also encourage systems to settle into seemingly nonfixed, disorganized patterns. Behavior governed by this magnetic pull is called strange or "butterfly" attraction (Kellert, 1994). The dynamics of the strange attractor is such that the activity of the system never traces the same path twice. In other words, plotting the pattern out over time reveals order within apparent randomness (Prigogine & Stengers, 1984; Barton, 1994; Abraham, Abraham, & Shaw, 1990). The butterfly attractor is "the epitome of contradiction, never repeating, yet always resembling, itself: infinitely recognizable, never predictable" (Van Eenwyk, 1991, p. 7).

To illustrate this butterfly effect, imagine a magnet at the bottom of a bowl which pulls a marble back and forth across the bowl in various directions rather than at the bottom of the bowl as in the fixed or point attractor. The marble would be pulled "all over the bowl in a complicated, apparently random pattern" (Butz, 1997, p. 13). Chaologists argue that despite this seeming disarray, a design or motif will, over time, emerge. Indeed, the movement of the marble would be confined to certain behavioral parameters. For example, the marble could not bounce "up and down" while moving in the bowl, nor could it leap out of the bowl, nor could it circulate through the bowl. Thus, "even though unpredictable and (locally) disorderly, the behavior . . . still occurs *within* the global confines that the (strange) attractor places upon the system. . . . [T]hough seemingly random, unpredictable, irregular, and out-of-control (i.e, chaotic), with increasing repetition, the system reveals its boundaries; that is, its pattern emerges" (Williams & Arrigo, 2002a, p. 85).

Critical psycholegal scholars have examined the manner in which the system of law behaves as a point (and potentially a strange) attractor. For example, Brion (1993) explained how community hysteria associated with false reportings of child sexual abuse are endorsed by "legal processes and institutions . . . functioning in various ways to initiate and maintain social hysteria" (Caudill, 1997, p. 99; see also, Gardner, 1992). The legal apparatus relies on its own, limited system of communication (i.e., legalese) to ascertain the facts, filters these facts through the narrow prism of a court or other legal tribunal, and restricts the focus of the dispute (i.e., what happened, was there harm), declaring these judgments to be final and the source of truth and justice (Brion, 1993).

Relatedly, Arrigo and Schehr (1998) examined the victim offender mediation process in juvenile cases, arguing that the restoration dialogue fails to produce optimal prospects for justice. As they noted:

> Th[e] choreography [of speech] is especially problematic for juveniles. They are made to conform to procedural and organizational strictures which *already* represent certain values about how to interact with others (i.e,. their victims). Although not spoken, these rules are unconsciously organized to produce limited outcomes consistent with the . . . coordinates of meaning representing the discourse of

victim offender reconciliation. . . . [T]he flow of communication is pre-configured. It is designed to result in definable, self-referential outcomes. These outcomes are to be consistent with the language of restoration and reconciliation as ensured, as much as is possible, by the mediator who, by definition, only speaks to clarify, moderate, reconcile. (p. 647)

In instances such as these, the magnetic pull of the formal and informal justice system harnesses individual behavior, restricting it to routinized patterns of interaction, wherein legal identities become fixed, settled, predictable. Lost in the process are opportunities for sense-making and understanding beyond the confines of that which the legal point attractor imposes on its subjects.

The order out of chaos critique

Nonlinear dynamical systems theory also explores that manner in which order emerges from chaos (Gleick, 1987). This principle is frequently termed *self-organization* (Prigogine & Stengers, 1984). As an integral assumption concerning the behavior of complex, adaptive systems, the thesis of order from chaos directs our attention to the reparative, autopoietic capacities of all organisms, based on empirical verification.

Barton (1994) describes self-organization as "a process by which a structure or pattern emerges in an open system without specifications from the outside environment" (p. 7). In other words, a system may be able "to display an order which is *generated from within*, [largely] independent of influences from without" (Williams & Arrigo, 2002a, pp. 91–92). Researchers have varyingly referred to this phenomenon as "the spontaneous emergence of order" (Davies, 1989, p. 501) and "antichaos" (Kauffman, 1991, p. 79). In brief, the position states that when a system experiences a critical level of disorder, it will "spontaneously self-organize into a new, more complex order" (Butz, 1992, p. 1052). In this context, chaos assumes an important role, enabling a system to transition from a nonadaptive state of order, to one that is conducive to the demands of contemporary life (Goerner, 1994). Indeed, this disorder compels "an orderly but stagnant system . . . into a new, more adaptive order necessary to meet the changing demands of the evolving system in relation to its external and internal environment" (Williams & Arrigo, 2002a, p. 92).

To illustrate this concept of order-from-chaos, consider the behavior of motorists during rush hour traffic.

Driving between rush hour on the thruway, we're only minimally affected by other vehicles. But toward 4 o'clock, traffic becomes heavier and we begin to react and interact with the other drivers. At a certain critical point we begin to be "driven" by the total traffic pattern. The traffic has become a self-organizing system. (Briggs & Peat, 1989, p. 138)

The point is that "out of chaos a new stability forms" (Butz, 1997, p. 14). The critical level of confusion, frustration, uncertainty (i.e., disorder) associated with driving during peak rush hour traffic is *necessary* and *beneficial to* the spontaneous readjustment of our behavior to the system of traffic we now confront.

Radical scholars have examined how the mental health (e.g., Barton, 1994; Butz, 1997; Chamberlain & Butz, 1997), justice (e.g, Brion, 1995; Schehr, 1997) and psycholegal systems (e.g., Arrigo, 1994; Arrigo & Williams, 1999a) function as instruments of social control that impede or deny natural adaptation. For example, Butz (1994) explains how psychopharmacological intervention is antithetical to the logic of self-organization. Psychotropic medication is "the portent of mechanistic linearity with its self-ascribed ability to control and predict human behavior through drug intervention" (Butz, 1994, p. 692). Extending this logic to the matter of treatment refusal, Williams and Arrigo (2002b) note that "pushing through" chaos (Chamberlain, 1994, p. 48) to restore order relegates people to the status of machines that occasionally need fixing. And, in their discussion of civil commitment, Arrigo & Williams (1999a) explain how involuntary hospitalization decisions essentially operate to police public hygiene (Foucault, 1965, 1977). Confinement most often prohibits people from naturally adjusting to the changing conditions of their environment, in their own way and on their own terms. This artificial remedy is potentially counterproductive "especially since the individual is not given the chance to adapt to his or her circumstances as part of one's continual evolutionary process" (Williams & Arrigo, 2002a, p. 228).

Each of the above cited instances dismisses the human potential for self-healing, for redemption, and for personal growth, favoring instead forced interventions that control behavior in ways consistent with prevailing standards of acceptable comportment. Proponents of chaos theory and the notion of order-from-chaos observe, however, that this strategy of containment, regulation, and compliance is extremely dangerous, producing deleterious consequences. Indeed, Barton (1994) summarizes these dangers in his assessment of drug treatment rather than self-organization as the preferred method of efficacious intervention. As he perceptively cautions:

If one [administers] a psychopharmacological agent and it does stop chaotic patterns, have we not also wiped out the seeds of a more adaptive psychological order—an order that may have taken days, weeks, months, or even years to develop in the complex electrochemical organization of the brain? (Barton, 1994, p. 695)

Thus, as critical psycholegal scholars sympathetic to the perspective of chaos theory note, justice demands that all forms of medical care be reevaluated, especially when treatment masquerades as cure (Szasz, 1977), preventing citizens from enjoying their self-actualized autonomy, dignity, and humanity (Williams & Arrigo, 2002b).

CONCLUSION

This chapter provided something of a developing portrait regarding the composition of the radical law-psychology agenda and what it has come to signify in theory and in research. By focusing on the perspective's underlying critical (criminological) foundation and the epistemological assumptions pertaining to it, we learned something more about what justice signifies and how it is attainable through radical psychology's contribution to humanizing, and therefore reforming, the law. Ultimately, although the ideas described herein represented a considerable departure from mainstream liberal efforts at reform, they suggested a new and vital direction by which this vision of transformation could be achieved.

As the next section of this book provocatively discloses, several important strides are now being made that appropriate the insights of radical law-psychology inquiry and that apply them to relevant and topical areas of scholarly and practical interest. As such, these explorations in law, crime, and society represent the next wave of critical research, drawing attention to where and how justice can be realized in the field of psychological jurisprudence. To be sure, this application work is as important as it is timely. Indeed, as an assemblage of conceptually anchored, though practical, forays into the problems posed by existing psycholegal decision making and logic, we understand that greater prospects for citizen justice and social change are possible. However, the first step toward reform entails the articulation of specific law-psychology controversies informed by critical exegeses.

NOTES

1. The critical paradigm in psychological jurisprudence is linked, in part, to the development of critical theory per se. As Arrigo (1999a) explains, the latter "represents a very broad and rich intellectual tradition in the history of Eurocentric thought traced to the Frankfurt Institute for Social Research in Germany and notable scholarly collectives in France. . . . Critical theory is concerned with . . . *the crisis in how we define justice, freedom, equality, and happiness based on subjective rather than objective distinctions*" (emphasis added) (pp. 3–4). Although there is something of an association between the radical law-psychology agenda and critical theory, the two are not synonymous. Indeed, most approaches presented in this article do not directly stem from

the critical theory tradition. Thus, while there is some reliance on the prism of critical theory to advance the overall thesis, other aspects of it are derived from explanatory rationales identified as part of the larger perspective encompassing the radical critique in justice studies more generally (Arrigo, 1999b, 2000a).

2. These five orientations were deliberately chosen. They extend the work of first (e.g., Szsaz, 1963; 1987; Ennis, 1972) and second (e.g., Breggin 1991, 1997; Coplan, 1995) wave radical scholars. In addition, they represent the most cutting-edge orientations found in the psycholegal field, receiving growing attention and respectability in the academy today. I recognize that it is something of an oversimplification to suggest that any one of these five perspectives exists in practice entirely independent of the others; however, each is sufficiently well-developed in the literature that it is useful to present them as somewhat autonomous theories. Moreover, to the extent that other perspectives could have been included in this chapter (e.g., narrative jurisprudence, critical race theory), readers are cautioned that the foregoing analysis is more suggestive of what the radical law-psychology agenda encompasses and what its overall assumptions are than a definitive exposition concerning either or both of these matters.

3. The presentation of the five perspectives represents something of a metatheoretical typology. This organizational template is useful to the extent that it consolidates and categorizes much of the critical law-psychology literature. I am mindful that radical scholars do not easily or necessarily fall into any one conceptual prism. Indeed, several researchers cited in this chapter and throughout this book appropriate the insights of different critical perspectives to advance their ideas. Thus, my intent is merely to suggest a representative blueprint, incomplete though it may be, regarding the development of radical law-psychology scholarship in the academy.

4. Most recently, these assumptions have been linked to the Critical Legal Studies (CLS) Movement and its critique of law as politics (e.g., Unger, 1986, 1987), and to the philosophy of legal deconstructionism and its critique of law as ideology (Cornell, Rosenfeld, & Carlson, 1992; Caputo, 1997). The ideas entertained in these works are more sophisticated applications or reconfigurations of selected Marxist principles beyond the scope of the present article.

5. There are many types of postmodernism: some emphasize deconstructionism; others incorporate the insights of semiotics and post-structuralism; and still others rely on hermeneutics and related interpretive modes of discourse analyses (e.g., Dews, 1987; Rosenau, 1992; Best & Kellner, 1997). It follows, then, that the domain of postmodern law is at least equally vast, encompassing these and related strains of thought. For an accessible overview of these matters in the legal arena see, Arrigo (1995a).

6. Arrigo, Milovanovic, & Schehr (2000) succinctly describe these developments as follows: "rapid economic modernization in the wake of World War II; new forms of mass culture, technology, consumerism, and urbanization that concealed psychological alienation and social oppression; the conceptual demise of Marxism, existentialism, and phenomenolgy, and the intellectual birth of structuralism and post-structuralism; and several new theories about writing and discourse as developed by philosophers, psychoanalysts, and linguists of the infamous *Tel Quel* group" (p. 192, n. 1).

7. The more commonly identified postmodern social theorists include such luminaries as Foucault, Irigaray, Derrida, Baudrillard, Kristeva, Barthes, Deleuze, and Guattari. However, each of these prominent thinkers was known to have attended Lacan's seminars, delivered in Paris, France, and to have incorporated or to have refined many of his elaborate conceptualizations into their respective theoretical work (Arrigo, Milovanovic, & Schehr, 2000). Accordingly, "given the compelling insights of Lacan, and their effects on most of the key figures in the early development of postmodernist thought, it is hard to see how any material claiming to be "postmodern" could in fact be complete without coming to terms with his work" (Milovanovic, 1994, p. 156).

REFERENCES

Abraham, R., Abraham, R., & Shaw, C. (1990). *A Visual Introduction to Dynamical Systems Theory for Psychology*. Santa Cruz, CA: Aerial.

Albee, G. W. (1982). "Preventing Psychopathology and Promoting Human Potential." *American Psychologist* 37, 1043–1050.

Althusser, L. (1971). *Lenin and Philosophy and Other Essays*. New York: New Left Books.

Arrigo, B. A. (1992). "Deconstructing Jurisprudence: An Experiential Feminist Critique." *Journal of Human Justice* 4, 13–29.

———. (1993a). "Civil Commitment, Semiotics, and Discourse on Difference: A Historical Critique of the Sign of Paternalism." In R. Kevelson (ed.) *Flux, Complexity, and Illusion in Law* (pp. 7–32). New York: P. Lang.

———. (1993b). "An Experientially-Informed Feminist Jurisprudence: Rape and the Move toward Praxis." *Humanity & Society* 17, 28–47.

———. (1993c). *Madness, Language, and the Law*. Albany, NY: Harrow and Heston.

———. (1994). "Legal Discourse and the Disordered Criminal Defendant: Contributions from Psychoanalytic Semiotics and Chaos Theory." *Legal Studies Forum* 18, 93–112.

———. (1995a). "The Peripheral Core of Law and Criminology: On Postmodern Social Theory and Conceptual Integration." *Justice Quarterly* 12, 447–472.

———. (1995b). "Rethinking the Language of Law, Justice, and Community: Postmodern Feminist Jurisprudence." In D. Caudill & S. Gold (eds.) *Radical Philosophy of Law: Contemporary Challenges to Mainstream Legal Theory and Practice* (pp. 88–107). Atlantic Heights, NJ: Humanities Press.

———. (1996a). *The Contours of Psychiatric Justice: A Postmodern Critique of Mental Illness, Criminal Insanity, and the Law*. New York/London: Garland.

———. (1996b). "Desire in the Psychiatric Courtroom: On Lacan and the Dialectics of Linguistic Oppression." *Current Perspectives in Social Theory* 16, 159–187.

———. (1996c). "The Behavior of Law and Psychiatry: Rethinking Knowledge Construction and the Guilty but Mentally Ill Verdict." *Criminal Justice and Behavior* 23, 572–592.

———. (1997a). "Transcarceration: Notes on a Psychoanalytically-Informed Theory of Social Practice in the Criminal Justice and Mental Health Systems." *Crime, Law, and Social Change: An International Journal* 27(1), 31–48.

———. (1997b). "Insanity Defense Reform and the Sign of Abolition: Revisiting Montana's Experience." *International Journal for the Semiotics of Law* 29, 191–211.

———. (ed). (1999a). *Social Justice/Criminal Justice: The Maturation of Critical Theory in Law, Crime, and Deviance*. Belmont, CA: West/Wadsworth.

———. (1999b). "Some Preliminary Observations on Social Justice and Critical Criminology." In B. A. Arrigo (ed.), *Social Justice/Criminal Justice: The Maturation of Critical Theory in Law, Crime, and Deviance* (pp. 1–12). Belmont, CA: Wadsworth.

———. (2000a). "Social Justice and Critical Criminology: On Integrating Knowledge." *Contemporary Justice Review* 3(1), 7–37.

———. (ed.). (2000b). *Law, Society, and Lacan*. Special Issue of the *International Journal for the Semiotics of Law* 13, 127–250. The Netherlands: Kluwer Academic Press.

———. (2000c). "Law and Social Inquiry: Commentary on a Psychoanalytic Semiotics of Law." *International Journal for the Semiotics of Law* 13, 127–132.

———. (2002). "The Critical Perspective in Psychological Jurisprudence: Theoretical Advances and Epistemological Assumptions." *International Journal of Law and Psychiatry* 25(2), 151–172.

——— & Schehr, R. C. (1998). "Restoring Justice for Juveniles: A Critical Analysis of Victim-Offender Mediation." *Justice Quarterly* 15, 629–666.

——— & Williams, C. R. (1999a). "Chaos Theory and the Social Control Thesis. A Post-Foucauldian Analysis of Mental Illness and Involuntary Civil Confinement." *Social Justice* 26(1), 177–207.

———. (1999b). "Law, Ideology, and Critical Inquiry: The Case of Treatment Refusal for Incompetent Prisoners Awaiting Execution." *New England Journal on Criminal and Civil Confinement* 25(2), 367–412.

———, Milovanovic, D., & Schehr, R. (2000). "The French Connection: Implications for Law, Crime, and Social Justice." *Humanity & Society* 24, 162–203.

Bakunin, M. (1974). *Michael Bakunin: Selected Writings*. New York: Grove.

Bartlett, K. & Kennedy, R. (1991). "Introduction." In K. Bartlett & R. Kennedy (eds.). *Feminist Legal Theory* (pp. 1–11). Oxford: Westview Press.

Barton, S. (1994). "Chaos, Self-Organization, and Psychology." *American Psychologist* 49, 5–14.

Bankowski, Z. (1983). "Anarchism, Marxism, and the Critique of Law." In D. Sugerman (ed.) *Legality, Ideology, and the State* (pp. 267–292). New York: Academic Press.

Beirne, P. & Quinney, R. (1982). *Marxism and Law*. New York: John Wiley.

Belliotti, R. A. (1995). "The Legacy of Marxist Jurisprudence." In D. Caudill & S. Gold (eds.) *Radical Philosophy of Law: Contemporary Challenges to Mainstream Legal Theory and Practice* (pp. 3–32). Atlantic Heights, NJ: Humanities Press.

Bersoff, D. N., Goodman-Delahunty, J., Grisso, J. T., Hans, V. P., Poythress, N. G., & Roesch, R. G. (1997). "Training in Law and Psychology: Models from the Villanova Conference." *American Psychologist* 52, 1301–1310.

Best, S. & Kellner, D. (1997). *Postmodern Theory: Critical Interrogations*. New York: Guilford.

Bottomley, A. (1987). "Feminism in Law Schools." In S. McLaughlin (ed.). *Women and the Law*. London: University College of London Press.

Bowie, M. (1991). *Lacan*. Cambridge, Mass: Harvard University Press.

Bracher, M. (1993). *Lacan, Discourse, and Social Change: A Psychoanalytic Cultural Criticism*. Ithaca, NY: Cornell University Press.

Breggin, P. R. (1991). *Toxic Psychiatry* New York: St. Martin's Press.

———. (1997). *Brain Dis-abling Treatments in Psychiatry: Drugs, Electroshock and the Role of the FDA*. New York: Springer.

Briggs, J. & Peat, F. D. (1989). *Turbulent Mirror*. New York: Harper and Row.

Brion, D. (1993). "The Hidden Persistence of Witchcraft." *Law & Critique*, 4, 227–245.

———. (1995). "The Chaotic Indeterminacy of Tort Law: Between Formalism and Nihilism." In D. Caudill (ed.) *Radical Philosophy of Law: Contemporary Challenges to Mainstream Legal Theory and Practice* (pp. 179–199). Atlantic Heights, NJ: Humanities Press.

Brownmiller, S. (1975). *Against Our Will: Men, Woman, and Rape*. New York: Bantam.

Butler, J. (1997). *Excitable Speech*. New York: Routledge.

———. (1999). *Subjects of Desire*. New York: Columbia University Press.

Butz, M. (1992). "The Fractal Nature of the Development of the Self." *Psychological Reports* 71, 1043–1063.

———. (1994). "Psychopharmacology: Psychology's *Jurassic Park*." *Psychotherapy* 31, 692–698.

———. (1997). *Chaos and Complexity: Implications for Psychological Theory and Practice*. Bristol, PA: Taylor & Francis.

Caplan, P. (1995). *They Say You're Crazy: How the World's Most Powerful Psychiatrists Decide Who's Normal*. New York: Addison-Wesley.

Caputo, J. (ed.). (1997). *Deconstruction in a Nutshell: A Conversation with Jaques Derrida*. New York: Fordham University Press.

Caudill, D. (1996). (ed.). *The Wake of Psychoanalytic Jurisprudence*. Special Issue of *Legal Studies Forum* 20, 188–343. Boston: American Legal Studies Association and Northeastern University Press.

———. (1997). *Lacan and the Subject of Law: Toward a Psychoanalytic Critical Legal Theory*. Atlantic Heights, NJ: Humanities Press.

Chamberlain, L. L. (1994). "Future Adventures in Psychology's *Jurassic Park*: The Issue of Psychopharmacology." *Psychotherapy Bulletin* 29, 47–50.

——— & Butz, M. (1997). *Clinical Chaos: A Therapist's Guide to Nonlinear Dynamics and Therapeutic Change*. Washington, DC: Taylor & Francis.

Cohen, R. L. (1989). "Fabrications of Justice." *Social Justice Research* 3, 31–46.

Cohen, D. (1991). "Membership, Intergroup Relations, and Justice." In R. Vermunt & H. Steensma (eds.), *Social Justice in Human Relations* (vol. 1, pp. 239–258). New York: Plenum.

——— & McCubbin, M. (1990). "The Political Economy of Tardive Dyskinesia: Asymmetries in Power and Responsibility." *Journal of Mind and Behavior* 11(3/4), 465–488.

Cohen, J. & Stewart, I. (1994). *The Collapse of Chaos: Discovering Simplicity in a Complex World*. New York: Penguin.

Collin, P. H. (1990). *Black Feminist Thought: Knowledge, Consciousness, and the Politics of Empowerment*. Hammersmith: Harper Collins Academic.

Conley, J. M & O'Barr, W. M. (1998). *Just Words: Law, Language, and Power*. Chicago: University of Chicago Press.

Cook, A. (1990). "Beyond Critical Legal Studies: The Reconstructive Theory of Dr. Martin Luther King Jr." *Harvard Law Review* 103, 985–1019.

Coombe, R. (1989) "Room for Maneuver: Towards a Theory of Practice in Critical Legal Studies." *Law and Social Inquiry* 14, 69–112.

———. (1992). "Publicity Rights and Political Aspiration: Mass Culture, Gender Identity, and Democracy." *New England Law Review* 26, 1221–1280.

Cornell, D. (1993). *Transformations: Recollective Imagination and Sexual Difference*. New York: Routledge.

———, Rosenfeld, M., & Carlson, D. (eds.). (1992). *Deconstruction and the Possibility of Justice*. New York: Routledge.

Crenshaw, R. (1988). "Race, Reform, and Retrenchment: Transformation and Legitimation in Antidiscrimination." *Harvard Law Review* 101, 1356–1387.

Currie, D. (1993). "Unhiding the Hidden: Race, Class, and Gender in the Construction of Knowledge. *Humanity & Society* 17, 3–27.

Dahl, S. (1987). *Women's Law*. Oslo: Norwegian University Press.

Dallaire, B, McCubbin, M., Morin, P., & Cohen, D. (2000). "Civil Commitment Due to Mental Illness and Dangerousness: The Union of Law and Psychiatry Within a Treatment-Control System. *Sociology of Health and Illness* 22(5), 679–699.

Davies, P. (1989). *The New Physics*. New York: Cambridge University Press.

Dupre, J. (1993). *The Disorder of Things: Metaphysical Foundations in the Disunity of Things*. Cambridge, MA: Harvard University Press.

Dworkin, A. (1981). *Pornography*. London: Women's Press.

Eagly, A. H. (1995). "The Science and Politics of Comparing Women and Men." *American Psychologist* 50, 145–158.

Einstein, A. (1956). *The Meaning of Relativity*. Princeton, NJ: Princeton University Press.

————. (1961). *Relativity: The Special and General Theory*. (R. Lawson, trans.). New York: Crown.

Elster, J. (1986). *An Introduction to Karl Marx*. Cambridge: Cambridge University Press.

Ennis, B. (1972). *Prisoners of Psychiatry: Mental Patients, Psychiatry, and the Law*. New York: Harcourt Brace Jovanovich.

Evans, D. (1996). *An Introductory Dictionary of Lacanian Psychoanalysis*. New York: Routledge.

Ferrell, J. (1997). "Against the Law: Anarchist Criminology." In B. MacLean & D. Milovanovic (eds.) *Thinking Critically about Crime* (pp. 146–154). Vancouver, CA: Collective Press.

————. (1999). "Anarchist Criminology and Social Justice." In B. Arrigo (ed.) *Social Justice/Criminal Justice: The Maturation of Critical Theory in Law, Crime, and Deviance* (pp. 93–108). Belmont, CA: West/Wadsworth.

Fink, B. (1995). *The Lacanian Subject: Between Language and Jouissance*. Princeton: Princeton University Press.

Finkel, N. J. (1995). *Commonsense Justice: Jurors' Notions of the Law*. Cambridge, MA: Harvard University Press.

————. (1998 March). "But It's Not Fair! Commonsense Notions of Fairness." Paper presented at the meeting of the American Psychology-Law Society, Redondo Beach, CA.

Foucault, M. (1965). *Madness and Civilization: A History of Insanity in the Age of Reason*. New York: Vintage.

————. (1977). *Discipline and Punish*. New York: Pantheon.

Fox, D. R. (1991). "Social Science's Limited Role in Resolving Psycholegal Social Problems." *Journal of Offender Rehabilitation* 17, 117–124.

————. (1993a). "Psychological Jurisprudence and Radical Social Change." *American Psychologist* 48(3), 234–241.

————. (1993b). "The Autonomy-Community Balance and the Equity-Law Distinction: Anarchy's Task for Psychological Jurisprudence." *Behavioral Sciences and the Law* 11, 97–109.

————. (1993c). "Where's the Proof that the Law's a Good Thing?" *Law and Human Behavior* 17, 257–258.

———. (1997). "Psychology and Law: Justice Diverted." In *Critical Psychology: An Introduction*. D. R. Fox & I. Prilleltensky (eds.), (pp. 217–232). London: Sage.

———. (1999). "Psycholegal Scholarship's Contribution to False Consciousness about Injustice." *Law and Human Behavior* 23, 9–30.

——— & I. Prilleltensky (eds.). (1997). *Critical Psychology: An Introduction*. London: Sage.

Fraser, N. (1997). *Justice Interruptus: Critical Reflections on the "Postsocialist" Condition*. New York: Routledge.

Frazier, P. A. & Hunt, J. S. (1998). "Research on Gender and Law: Where Are We Going, Where Have We Been?" *Law and Human Behavior* 22, 1–16.

Friedman, L. A. (1973). *A History of American Law*. New York: Simon and Schuster.

Frug, M. J. (1992). "Sexual Equality and Sexual Difference in American Law." *New England Law Review* 26, 665–682.

Gardner, A. (1992). *True and False Accusation of Child Sexual Abuse*. Creskill, NJ: Creative Therapeutics.

Gilligan, C. (1982). *In a Different Voice*. London: Harvard University Press.

———, Lyons, N. P., & Hanmer, T. J. *Making Connections*. Cambridge: Harvard University Press.

Gleick, J. (1987). *Chaos: Making a New Science*. New York: Penguin Books.

Godwin, W. (1971/1798). *Enquiry Concerning Political Justice*. London: Oxford University Press.

Goerner, S. (1994). *Chaos and the Evolving Ecological Universe*. Langhorne, PA: Gordon and Breach Science Publishers.

Goldfarb, P. (1992). "From the Worlds of 'Others': Minority and Feminist Responses to Critical Legal Studies." *New England Law Review* 26, 683–710.

Godwin, E. (1969). *Anarchism and Other Essays*. New York: Dover.

Goodrich, P. (1997). *Law and the Unconscious: A Legendre Reader*. New York: St. Martin's Press.

Grob, G. (1991). *From Asylum to Community: Mental Health Policy in Modern America*. Princeton: Princeton University Press.

Grisso, T., Sales, B. D., & Bayless, S. (1982). "Law-Related Courses and Programs in Graduate Psychology Departments." *American Psychologist* 37, 267–278.

Haney, C. (1980). "Psychological and Legal Change: On the Limits of a Factual Jurisprudence." *Law and Human Behavior* 4, 147–200.

———. (1991). "The Fourteenth Amendment and Symbolic Legality: Let Them Eat Due Process." *Law and Human Behavior* 15, 183–204.

———. (1993). "Psychology and Legal Change: The Impact of a Decade." *Law and Human Behavior* 17, 371–398.

———. (1997). "Commonsense Justice and Capital Punishment: Problematizing the 'Will of the People.'" *Psychology, Public Policy, and the Law* 3, 303–337.

Harrington, C. & Yngvesson, B. (1990). "Interpretive Sociolegal Research." *Law and Social Inquiry* 15, 135–148.

Harris, A. (1991). "Race and Essentialism in Feminist Legal Theory." In K. Bartlett & R. Kennedy (eds.) *Feminist Legal Theory* (pp. 235–262). Oxford: Westview Press.

Hegel, F. (1977/1807). *Hegel's Phenomenolgy of Spirit* A. V. Miller (trans.). Oxford: Oxford University Press.

Henry, S. & Milovanovic, D. (1996). *Constitutive Criminology: Beyond Postmodernism.* London: Sage.

Horgan, J. (1996). *The End of Science: Facing the Limits of Knowledge in the Twilight of the Scientific Age.* Menlo, Park, CA: Addison-Wesley.

Isaac, R. J. & Armat, V. C. (1990). *Madness in the Streets: How Psychiatry and the Law Abandoned the Mentally Ill.* New York: The Free Press.

Jost, J. T. (1995). "Negative Illusions: Conceptual Clarification and Psychological Evidence Concerning False Consciousness." *Political Psychology* 16, 397–424.

Julien, P. (1994). *Jacques Lacan's Return to Freud.* (D. Simiu trans.). New York: New York University Press.

Kagehiro, D. K. & Laufer, W. S. (1992). "Preface." In D. K. Kagehiro & W. S. Laufer (eds.), *Handbook of Psychology and Law* (pp. xi–xiii). New York: Springer-Verlag.

Kauffman, S. A. (1991). "Antichaos and Adaptation." *Scientific American* 265, 78–84.

Kellert, S. (1994). *In the Wake of Chaos.* Chicago, Illinois: University of Chicago Press.

Kelman, M. (1998). *A Guide to Critical Legal Studies.* Cambridge, MA: Harvard University Press.

Klare, K. (1982). "Labor Law and the Liberal Political Imagination." *Socialist Review* 61, 45–71.

Kropotkin, P. (1902). *Mutual Aid.* Boston, MA: Extending Horizons Books.

———. (1912). *Modern Science and Anarchism.* London: Unwin.

———. (1975/1886). *The Essential Kropotkin* (E. Capouya & K. Tompkins, eds.). New York: Liveright.

Lacan, J. (1977). *Ecrits: A Selection.* (A. Sheridan trans.). New York: Norton.

Lahey, K. (1985). ". . . Until Women Themselves Have Told All That They Have to Tell. . . ." *Osgoode Hall Law Journal* 23, 519–541.

Littleton, C. (1987). "In Search of a Feminist Jurisprudence." *Harvard Women's Law Journal* 10, 1–8.

Lynch, M. & Stretesky, P. (1999). "Marxism and Social Justice." In B. Arrigo (ed.) *Social Justice/Criminal Justice: The Maturation of Critical Theory in Law, Crime, and Deviance* (pp. 13–29). Belmont, CA: West/Wadsworth.

MacKinnon, C. (1983). "Feminism, Marxism, Method, and the State: Toward Feminist Jurisprudence." *Signs* 8, 635–658.

———. (1987). *Feminism Unmodified: Discourse on Life and Law*. London: Harvard University Press.

———. (1989). *Towards a Feminist Theory of the State*. Cambridge, MA: Harvard University Press.

———. (1991). "Difference and Dominance: On Sexual Discrimination." In K. Bartlett & R. Kennedy (eds.) *Feminist Legal Theory* (pp. 81–94). Oxford: Westview Press.

Malone, K. & Friedlander, S. (2000). *The Subject of Lacan: A Lacanian Reader for Psychologists*. Albany, New York: SUNY Press.

Manning, P. (1988). *Symbolic Communication: Signifying Calls the Police Response*. Cambridge, MA: MIT Press.

Marshall, P. (1992). *Demanding the Impossible: A History of Anarchism*. London: Harper-Collins.

Marx, K. (1974/1867). *Capital. Vol. 1*. New York: International.

———. (1984/1859). *Contribution to the Critique of Political Economy*. New York: International.

McCubbin, M. & Cohen, D. (1996). "Extremely Unbalanced: Interest Divergence and Power Disparities between Clients and Psychiatry." *International Journal of Law and Psychiatry* 19(1), 1–25.

——— & Cohen, D. (1999). "A Systemic and Value-Base Approach to Strategic Reform of the Mental Health System." *Health Care Analysis* 7, 57–77.

——— & Weisstub, D. N. (1998). "Toward a Pure Best Interests Model of Proxy Decision Making for Incompetent Psychiatric Patients." *International Journal of Law and Psychiatry* 21(1), 1–30.

McDermott, M. J. (1992). "The Personal is Empirical: Research Methods and Criminal Justice Education." *Journal of Criminal Justice Education* 3, 237–249.

McLean, A. (1995). "Empowerment and the Psychiatric Consumer/Ex-patient Movement in the United States: Contradictions, Crisis and Change. *Social Science & Medicine* 40, 1053–1071.

Melton, G. B. (1988). "The Significance of Law in the Everyday Life of Children and Families." *Georgia Law Review* 22, 851–895.

———. (1990). "Realism in Psychology and Humanism in Law: Psychological Studies at Nebraska." *Nebraska Law Review* 69, 251–277.

———. (1991). "President's column." *American Psychology-Law Society News* (Summer), 1–3.

———. (1992). "The Law is a God Thing (Psychology Is, Too): Human Rights in Psychological Jurisprudence." *Law and Human Behavior* 16, 381–398.

Menkel-Meadow, S. (1988). "Feminist Legal Theory, Critical Legal Studies, and Legal Education or 'The Fem-Crits' Go to Law School." *Journal of Legal Education* 36, 61–79.

Milovanovic, D. (1992). *Postmodern Law and Disorder: Psychoanalytic Semiotics, Chaos, and Juridic Exegeses*. Liverpool, UK: Deborah Charles.

———. (1994). *A Primer in the Sociology of Law*. Albany, NY: Harrow & Heston.

———. (1996). "Rebellious Lawyering." *Legal Studies Forum* 20, 295–322.

———. (1997). *Chaos, Criminology, and Social Justice*. Westport, CT: Praeger.

Morin, E. (1990). *Introduction a la pensee complexe*. Paris: ESF Editeur.

Morland, D. (1997). *Demanding the Impossible: Human Nature and Politics in Nineteenth Century Social Anarchism*. Washington: Cassell.

Mossman, M. J. (1986). "Feminism and the Legal Method: The Difference It Makes." *Australian Journal of Law and Society* 3, 30–52.

Naffine, N. (1990). *Law and the Sexes: Explorations in Feminist Jurisprudence*. Sydney: Allen and Unwin.

Newnes, C., Holmes, G., & Dunn, C. (1999). *This Is Madness: A Critical Look at Psychiatry and the Future of Mental Health Services*. Llangarron, UK: PCCS.

Ogloff, J. R. P. (ed.). (1992). *Law and Psychology: The Broadening of the Discipline*. Durham, NC: Carolina Academic Press.

———. (1999). "*Law and Human Behavior*: Reflecting Back and Looking Forward." *Law and Human Behavior* 23(1), 1–8.

———. (2000). "Presidential Address to the American Psychology and Law Society. Two Steps Forward and One Step Backward: The Law and Psychology Movement(s) in the Twentieth Century." *Law and Human Behavior* 24(4), 457–483.

Pashukanis, E. (1978). *Law and Marxism: A General Theory*. London: Ink Links.

Pepinsky, H. (1991). *The Geometry of Violence*. Bloomington, IN: Indiana University Press.

Perlin, M. (1999). *Mental Disability Law*. Durham, NC: Carolina Academic Press.

Prilleltensky, I. (1994). *The Moral and Politics of Psychology: Psychological Discourse and the Status Quo*. Albany, NY: State University of New York Press.

———. (1997). "Values, Assumptions, and Practices: Assessing the Moral Implications of Psychological Discourse and Action." *American Psychologist* 52, 517–535.

———. (1999, June). "Contesting Surplus Power-Fullness: Towards Professional Depowerment in Helping Relationships." XXIV International Congress on Law and Mental Health, Toronto, Canada.

——— & Gonick, L. (1996). "Polities Change, Oppression Remains: On the Psychology and Politics of Oppression." *Political Psychology* 17, 127–148.

——— & Gonick, L. (2002). *Doing Psychology Critically: Making a Difference in Diverse Settings*. New York: Macmillan Press.

———— & Nelson, G. (1997). "Community Psychology: Reclaiming Social Justice." In D. Fox & I. Prilleltensky (eds.), *Critical Psychology: An Introduction* (pp. 166–184). London: Sage.

Prigogine, I. & Stengers, I. (1984). *Order Out of Chaos.* New York: Bantam Books.

Quinney, R. (1974). *Critique of Legal Order.* Boston: Little, Brown & Co.

Rhode, D. (1991). "Feminist Critical Theories." In K Bartlett & R. Kennedy (eds.) *Feminist Legal Theory* (pp. 333–350). Oxford: Westview Press.

Roesch, R. (1995) "Creating Change in the Legal System: Contributions from Community Psychology." *Law and Human Behavior* 19, 325–343.

Russell, K. (1998). *The Color of Crime.* NY: New York University Press.

Saks, M. (1986). "The Law Does Not Live by Eyewitness Testimony Alone." *Law and Human Behavior* 10, 279–280.

Sarason, S. B. (1982). "Community Psychology and the Anarchist Insight." In S. B. Sarason, *Psychology and Social Action: Selected Papers* (pp. 135–149). New York: Praeger.

Sarat, A. & Kearns, T. (1992). *Law's Violence.* Ann Arbor, Michigan: Michigan University Press.

————. (1996). *The Rhetoric of Law.* Ann Arbor, Michigan: Michigan University Press.

———— & Felstiner, W. (1995). *Divorce Lawyers and Their Clients: Power and Meaning in the Legal Process.* New York: Oxford University Press.

Schmitt, R. (1987). *Introduction to Marx and Engels: A Critical Reconstruction.* Boulder: Westview Press.

Schehr, R. C. (1997). "Surfing the Chaotic: A Non-Linear Articulation of Social Movement Theory." In D. Milovanovic (ed.) *Chaos, Criminology, and Social Justice* (pp. 157–178). Westport, CT: Praeger.

Schroeder, J. L. (2000). "The Hysterical Attorney: The Legal Advocate within Lacanian Discourse Theory." *International Journal for the Semiotics of Law* 13, 181–213.

————. (1998). *The Vestal and the Fasces: Hegel, Lacan, Property, and the Feminine.* Berkeley, CA: University of California Press.

Shklar, J. N. (1990). *The Faces of Injustice.* New Haven, CT: Yale University Press.

Shon, P. (2000). "'He You C'me Here!' Subjectivization, Resistance, and the Interpellative Violence of Self-Generated Police Citizen Encounters." *International Journal for the Semiotics of Law* 13, 159–179.

Simon, T. W. (1995). "A Theory of Social Injustice." In D. Caudill & S. J. Gould (eds.). *Radical Philosphy of Law: Contemporary Challenges to Mainstream Legal Theory and Practice* (pp. 54–72). Atlantic Heights, NJ: Humanities Press.

Small, M. A. (1993). "Legal Psychology and Therapeutic Jurisprudence." *Saint Louis University Law Journal* 37, 675–700.

Smart, C. (1989). *Feminism and the Power of Law.* New York: Routledge.

————. (1995). *Law, Crime, and Sexuality: Essays in Sexuality*. Newbury Park, CA: Sage.

Smith, P. (1995). "Feminist Legal Critics: The Reluctant Radicals." In D. Caudill & S. Gold *Radical Philosophy of Law: Contemporary Challenges to Mainstream Legal Theory* (pp. 73–87). Atlantic Heights, NJ: Humanities Press.

Sonn, R. (1992). *Anarchism*. New York: Twayne.

Stacey, H. (1996). "Lacan's Split Subjects: Raced and Gendered Transformations." *Legal Studies Forum* 20, 277–293.

Stefan, S. (1994). "The Protection Racket: Rape Trauma Syndrome, Psychiatric Labeling, and Law." *Northwestern University Law Review* 88, 1271–1313.

Stewart, I. (1989). *Does God Play Dice?: The Mathematics of Chaos*. Cambridge: Blackwell.

Sydeman, S., Cascardi, M., Poythress, N. G., & Ritterband, L. M. (1997). "Procedural Justice in the Context of Civil Commitment: A Critique of Tyler's Analysis." *Psychology, Public Policy, and Law* 3, 1, 207–221.

Szasz, T. (1963). *Law, Liberty, and Psychiatry: An Inquiry into the Social Uses of Mental Health Practices*. New York: Collier Books

————. (1977) *Psychiatric Slavery: When Confinement and Coercion Masquerade as Cure*. New York: The Free Press.

————. (1987). *Insanity: The Idea and Its Consequences*. New York: John Wiley & Sons.

Tapp, J. L. & Levine, F. J. (eds.). (1977). *Law, Justice, and the Individual in Society: Psychological and Legal Issues*. New York: Holt, Rinehart.

Thibaut, J., & Walker, L. (1975). *Procedural Justice: A Psychological Analysis*.

Tifft, L. & Sullivan, D. (1980). *The Struggle to Be Human: Crime, Criminology, and Anarchism*. Orkney, U.K.: Cienfuegos.

Unger, R. M. (1986). *The Critical Legal Studies Movement*. Cambridge, MA: Harvard University Press.

————. (1987). *False Necessity*. New York: Cambridge University Press.

U'Ren, R. (1997). "Psychiatry and Capitalism." *Journal of Mind and Behavior* 18, 1–11.

Van Eenwyk, J. (1991). "Archetypes: The Strange Attractors of the Psyche." *Journal of Analytical Psychology* 36, 1–25.

Voruz, V. (2000). "Psychosis and the Law: Legal Responsibility and the Law of Symbolization." *International Journal for the Semiotics of Law* 13, 133–158.

Walby, S. (1990). *Theorizing Patriarchy*. Cambridge, MA: Blackwell.

Wiener, R. L. & Hunt, L. E. (1999). "An Interdisciplinary Approach to Understanding Social Sexual Conduct at Work." *Psychology, Public Policy, and Law*, 5, 565–595.

Wiener, R., Watts, B. A., & Stolle, D. P. (1993). "Psychological Jurisprudence and the Information Processing Paradigm." *Behavioral Sciences and the Law* 111, 79–96.

Wexler, D. B. (1990). "Training in Law and Behavioral Sciences: Issues from a Legal Educator's Perspective." *Behavioral Sciences and the Law* 8, 197–204.

——— & Winick, B. (1996). *Law in a Therapeutic Key*. Washington, DC: American Psychological Association.

Williams, C. R. (1998). "The Abrogation of Subjectivity in the Psychiatric Courtroom: Toward a Psychoanalytic Semiotic Analysis." *International Journal for the Semiotics of Law* 11, 181–192.

——— & Arrigo, B. A. (2000). "The Philosophy of the Fift and the Psychology of Advocacy: Critical Reflections on Forensic Mental Health Intervention." *International Journal for the Semiotics of Law* 13, 215–242.

———. (2001). "Anarchaos and Order: On the Emergence of Social Justice." *Theoretical Criminology* 5,2, 223–252.

———. (2002a). *Law, Psychology, and Justice: Chaos Theory and the New (Dis)order*. Albany, NY: SUNY Press.

———. (2002b). "Law, Psychology, and the "New Sciences": Rethinking Mental Illness and Dangerousness." *International Journal of Offender Therapy and Comparative Criminology* 46, 6–29.

Williams, R. (1987). "Taking Rights Aggressively: The Perils and Promise of Critical Legal Theory for People of Color." *Law and Inequality* 5, 103–118.

Wilkinson, S. (1997). "Feminist Psychology." In D. Fox & I. Prilleltensky (eds.), *Critical Psychology: An Introduction* (pp. 247–264). London: Sage.

Winick, B. J. (1997). "The Jurisprudence of Therapeutic Jurisprudence." *Psychology, Public Policy and the Law* 3, 184–206.

Woodcock, G. (1992). *Anarchism and Anarchists*. Ontario: Quarry Press.

Chapter 2

Anarchic Insurgencies

The Mythos of Authority and the Violence of Mental Health

Christopher R. Williams

Overview

This chapter critically examines the mental health sciences, emphasizing the philosophical and practical limits of clinical treatment and state control. I argue that institutional or system-maintaining efforts at defining health and illness, predicting dangerousness, and authorizing civil commitment and involuntary treatment are problematic on both scientific and political grounds. To substantiate this claim, I explore how ontological realism, epistemological objectivism, and theoretical positivism give rise to a mythos of certainty, prediction, and control, which simultaneously indoctrinates mental health practitioners as "experts" and legitimates their interventions into human welfare. In addition, I investigate this mythos based on the insights of constructionism. Specifically, I question the scientific foundations of the mental health sciences informed by several key themes and principles of anarchist theory (e.g., rejection of authority; challenge to epistemic certainty; promotion of self-governance; and emphasis on creativity, change, ambiguity, and becoming). I demonstrate how anarchism concerns itself with displacing coercive authority (i.e., the system of mental health law) in the interest of transforming justice. It regards authoritarian institutions and the persons representing such institutions as impeding more natural forms of order wherein persons are free to become fully human. As I argue, the possibilities for human self-realization and self-determination are negated by the authoritarian structuring of human life undertaken by the mental health sciences, resulting in methods of state control that are employed to enforce such structures (e.g., civil commitment, involuntary treatment). Anarchism's aversion to state sanctioned intervention problematizes efforts to control (i.e., treat) mental disease and disorder.

43

INTRODUCTION

Epistemological anarchist and antiscience mentor Paul Feyerabend (1993, p. 9) once remarked that political philosophy is "excellent medicine" for epistemology and the philosophy of science. Feyerabend was, of course, employing an illness metaphor in his interrogation of scientific sensibilities and calling for an "anything goes" (hence, anarchistic) methodology in our efforts to understand the world. Yet there is, no doubt, an unintended irony in this metaphor which emerges as a telling image of the mental health sciences, their analytical endeavors into human thought, feeling, and behavior, and the often practical interruptions of human welfare that follow. In fact, while the mental health sciences purport to treat what is defined as diseased, the foundations on which their practices are based are, themselves, dis-eased. Indeed, while the mental health sciences profess to treat disorder, the edifice on which their practices are constructed are themselves dis-orderly (Williams & Arrigo, 2001a,b, 2002).

The problem with scientific endeavors into human experience is that they are vulnerable on both political and scientific grounds. Scientifically, explanations of the natural world issuing from the modern paradigm have been subject to penetrating and provocative criticisms on a number of fronts (e.g., Crotty, 1998; Baert, 1998; Best & Kellner, 1997). Given the fundamental differences between the human world and the natural world, one might imagine that explanations of human experience arising from the mental health sciences are no less prone—and perhaps even more so—to many of these same objections. Following Feyerabend, if the "ills" of science necessitate an anarchistic episteme, then the ills of psychology and psychiatry necessitate an anarchic understanding of mental health.

Metaphorically speaking, we can understand the underlying ills of the mental health sciences at their philosophical and theoretical foundations. On a political level, we can regard that which issues forth from such foundations (i.e., the practices of psychology and psychiatry) as their symptoms. These symptoms are of fundamental concern to sociopolitical reconstructions of mental health practices. In addition, the clinical undertakings of psychology and psychiatry exemplify points in psycholegal space ripe for transformations of justice. However, these critical or progressive inroads often exist at subterranean points that define and support—mostly erroneously—the practices they seek to challenge, renounce, and transform.

I note that the clinical endeavors of the mental health sciences continue to exist as legitimated social functions; that is, they operate to treat illness and disorder in a paternalistic vein and to identify the "dangerous" social element, thereby serving a social control or "police" function (Foucault, 1978; 1988; Arrigo and Williams, 1999). More specifically, the realization of these functions comes in the form of civil commitment, expert testimony, violence prediction, and a variety of imposed treatments (e.g., psychotherapy, drug therapy).

Each of these realizations or practices within the mental health sciences exists as part of a larger, cooperative endeavor that legitimizes them by way of the law (e.g., Fox, 1997). Through partnership with the legal order, the psycholegal edifice is a fully sanctioned means by which to intervene in the lives of citizens deemed "in need" of treatment or care. In some cases, intercession occurs at the societal level because it, too, is "in need" of fixing or correcting (e.g., mental health court, drug court). These sorts of interventions are symptoms to the extent that they arise from a deeper, largely unrecognized, illness; that is, an illness affecting or, perhaps, infecting the philosophical foundations that serve as building blocks for theoretical, methodological, and practical (i.e., clinical) mental health science. In the latter case, if disease is defined as a lesion of the body (Szasz, 1997), the clinical undertakings of the mental health sciences must then represent lesions of the social body. Following this logic, clinical fallacies and shortcomings produce significant and, on occasion, devastating physical changes in the social body. For example, those persons defined as deviant, diseased, or dangerous are segregated, expelled, and, in the extreme, terminated on allegedly scientific, though ultimately political and moral, grounds (Szasz, 1970a, 1970b; Williams and Arrigo, 2001a).

Complicating the problematic nature of mental health is the notion of authority. The philosophical foundations of the mental health sciences produce mythic images of certainty, prediction, control, and the possibility of an orderly social world. Upon these images are superimposed mythic images of institutions and individuals with direct access to the means and methods by which to understand, predict, control, and correct. These are the images on which scientific authority is based. This authority justifies coercion notwithstanding one's objection to it, and it is through such invasive practices that injustice is promulgated and perpetuated. These are the points at which the legitimacy of the mental health sciences are plagued by inherent resistance; a recalcitrance that (should) delegitimize their jurisdiction over matters of human welfare and justice. These are the specific points that I seek to expose, explore, and exploit in this chapter.

At its core, what follows is expressly anarchic. Ultimately, anarchism is a critical theory interested in promoting the displacement of coercive authority in light of transforming justice (e.g., Tifft, 1979; Ferrell, 1999). Following anarchist theory, authoritarian institutions, organizations, and persons are to be replaced by voluntary forms of social order wherein persons are free to become fully human (Fromm, 1955; Fox, 1986). Reconstitutions of this sort are, ideally, free from the authoritarian structuring of human life and the coercive methods by which such structures themselves are enforced (Sylvan, 1993).

While there are various strains of anarchist theory ranging from individualist libertarian conceptualizations to communitarian socialist ideals, each shares several core principles. One principle integral to the present critique is the steadfast aversion to state control of the individual (Fox, 1986; Fox, 1993; Williams and Arrigo, 2001b; also see Arrigo in chapter 1 of this text). State control of the individual can be further characterized by the two aforementioned notions of authority and coercion (Clarke, 1978). Thus, much of what follows in this critique will either explicitly or implicitly question the authoritarian structure and coercive techniques embedded in the institution of mental health, legitimized by decisions made in the legal arena. Beyond this, anarchism embodies a number of interrelated principles or themes that will surface in various forms throughout this chapter. Stated briefly, these include the following: a rejection of existing authority; a challenge to epistemic certainty; the promotion of self-governance; and an emphasis on creativity, change, ambiguity, and becoming (Ferrell, 1999). I begin with an exposition of the *affirmative* nature of anarchism, employing the notion of *apophasis*.

APOPHASIS AND ANARCHIC AFFIRMATION

Apophasis is Greek for negation. Its historic usage appears most prominently in Negative Theology or Greek polemics contesting the myths of Olympian gods (Geldard, 2000, p. 23). In addition, anarchism commonly and historically has been regarded as the embodiment of negation. Anarchism is equated with chaos, destruction, and denial for its own sake (e.g., Woodcock, 1992). Unfortunately, public perception of anarchism is informed predominantly by stereotypical judgments stemming from those unfamiliar with the essential principles of anarchist theory and the basic ideals of anarchist social reform (e.g., Williams and Arrigo, 2001b). In both cases (i.e., *apophasis* and anarchism) there is an often unrecognized or misunderstood *primary* motive that is too easily suppressed by purely negative conceptualizations. In fact, the primary motive is affirmative in nature.

While *apophasis* denotatively reflects that which denies or negates, it embodies a potent, though unstated, affirmative connotation. Quite simply, *apophasis* is the process of affirmation through negation. As Geldard (2000) explains, apophatic theology "involved disposing of the myths of the Olympian gods, while affirming a revised vision of the Unknown God, the unreachable, unmanifest but immanent deity" (p. 23). Thus, the apophatic is ultimately affirmative and positive in its motive. Negation is only a means of affirming something that is hidden and, thus, something that can be revealed. Apophasis—the apophatic method—seeks to "penetrate the layers of encrusted myth-making which conceal the bright light of an original truth" (ibid.). With time and perpetuation, myths accumulate, gaining potency and legitimacy and, thus, they methodically suppress or repress whatever possibilities or potentialities await discovery.

To suggest that the spirit of *apophasis* runs throughout anarchism's search for a more human social order is to suggest that humanity and justice require a stripping away, a negation, of that which subjugates the affirmative in life. In the instance of law, psychology, and justice, it is an effort to "de-center organized (and mainstream liberal) psychology and displace the legal status quo, such that wholesale transformation can occur" (Arrigo, 2002, p. 152). The anarchist assault against prevailing social order advances is merely a "transitional phase in which the old [is] destroyed so that the new might emerge" (Shatz, 1972, p. xii). Destroying the old means "stripping away" layers of myth and simultaneously debunking the negative authority that is rooted in those myths. That which emerges from the transitional phase is life-affirming change. Thus, there is a pronounced theme that emerges in each case: that of anarchism, that of *apophasis* and, prospectively, that of justice. In short, each affirms through initial negation.

In the context of mental health, the object of apophatic criticism becomes a collection of myths and practices on which the disciplines of psychology and psychiatry are constituted. As such, the anarchic or apophatic approach embraces a critical spirit of affirmation through negation by which to decenter prevailing notions of mental illness, scientific authority in matters of human experience, and coercive, "curative" practices such as civil confinement and treatment that emerge as manifestations of the mythos of modernity and science. Thus, the apophatic indirectly seeks the affirmation of life through the negation of that which inhibits it. In a word, the apophatic seeks justice.

Anarchism, Apophasis, and Justice

In his essay "On Law and Politics," Arthur Schopenhauer (1970/1851, p. 148) tells us that the search for justice, inasmuch as it is conceptualized in a positive sense, is equivalent to "pursuing a ghost." "For the concept of *justice* is, like that of *freedom*, a *negative* concept: its content is pure negation" (ibid.). Justice, then, is apophatic—it is negation in the interest of affirmation. The positive component, then, is not justice but, rather, *injustice*. For justice is not a thing—it is intangible, with little more than symbolic relevance. Even to speak of the absence of justice is to speak of nothing more than a void—again, intangible and inconsequential for the world of everyday, lived reality. Yet the many forms of *in*justice are very real, very tangible, and very consequential. They are the very realities that prevent the actualization of human self-realization, self-fulfillment, self-determination. Injustice, like the myths of Olympian gods, conceals something deeper and more human; something "unreachable, unmanifest but immanent" (Geldard, 2000, p. 23). It is the injustice that the *apophatic* seeks to negate, yet it is justice which the *apophatic* spirit seeks to affirm.

In his discussion of justice, Schopenhauer's (1970) reference or analogy to freedom is also worth noting. In its prerequisite form, freedom is also negative. Freedom comes in two distinct, yet interrelated, varieties: freedom *from* and freedom *to* something or someone (Fromm, 1941; cf. Berlin, 1991). The former is negative, and it is the negative component of freedom that often escapes attention. Freedom of thought, feeling, speech, and the freedom to grow—to *become* oneself—are misplaced, trivial concerns if one does not have freedom from the bonds that restrain or negate such freedoms. Thus far, we have seen how myths serve as one such negation inasmuch as the freedom to be oneself necessitates freedom from the authority and jurisdiction of myths. I will revisit the concept of myth, as well as other bondages, in a more applied context shortly. However, at this point, it is worth pointing out an operational distinction between liberty, freedom, and human rights. Again, we can turn initially to Schopenhauer.

For Schopenhauer (1970), human rights consist of the freedom to do anything one chooses to do, so long as one's actions do not injure another (p. 148). Interestingly, Schopenhauer defines injustice as injury. We could say, then, that injustice is interference with one's freedom (read human rights) to do whatever one desires, so long as one's freedom does not negate another's freedom. Put another way, there is a fundamental right to be free from injustice, so long as one does not use one's freedom to commit injustices. On this point, the political notion of human rights seems consistent with the principles and ideals constituting the anarchist vision. However, there is an important distinction. The notion of human rights has a storied history in classical liberalism—constituting much of its thematic content (e.g., Lyons, 1979; Waldron, 1993). While anarchism promotes a similar conception of freedom and human agency, the difference is to be found in their contrary perspectives on human nature and consequent conceptualizations of the State (e.g., Wolff, 1996).

In short, liberalism presumes the necessity of the State; that is, of sponsored social control. In theory, persons have the freedom (i.e., right) to realize their own personhood. Unlimited and unrestrained freedom, however, is presumed to lead persons to injure (i.e., commit injustices against) others. Thus, freedom must necessarily be limited in the interests of social order. Freedom, then, becomes reconstituted as myth in that it is subject to constraint (i.e., negation) and control by those granted authority to do so. In contemporary society, privileged authority extends beyond agents of the State to other institutionalized forms. As I will argue in this chapter, one such form includes the mental health sciences and their indoctrinated control agents.

In contrast to liberal political theory, anarchist conceptions of human nature affirm a deeper, more essential, pro-social, and cooperative predisposition (Kropotkin, 1914; 1947). Anarchism recognizes that the antisocial tendencies observed in contemporary social life are the effects of existing under a social order that negates the natural inclinations of human beings. Competition, selfishness, greed, and a host of social problems that follow are mere manifestations of antisocial values that are inevitable given current social conditions (e.g., Bonger, 1969). Displacing authoritative forms of social organization based on coercive techniques and replacing them with voluntary forms of social organization allows people, communities and, ultimately, society the freedom to realize their cooperative tendencies while simultaneously affirming individual experience.

Justice, then, is that which is of principle concern in any genuine anarchist critique. Though Schopenhauer was not an anarchist, he provides us with considerable insight into many of the fundamental principles of justice. Indeed, justice entails negating that which itself negates human liberty, freedom, and the space to become. In this context, "rights" should not be confused with those embedded in the law. This is where a fundamental distinction between anarchic justice and mainstream liberal proposals becomes apparent. Affirming one's rights should not be interpreted as an affirmation of State control by way of reliance on authority for protection of human liberty and welfare. Instead, rights should be read as the collection of affirmative possibilities that exist for human beings in the absence of coercive mechanisms of order maintenance. Thus, rights entail freedom from such state-mandated control and freedom to determine one's own path. Following anarchism, while human rights manifest themselves as legal rights in the Liberal State, they should not be relegated to the status of institutionalized protections and privileges.

Apophasis and Psychological Jurisprudence

Thus far, I have discussed how the apophatic is interested in negation for the purpose of affirmation, how anarchism, while negative *prima facie*, is ultimately affirmative, and how justice—constituted as negative freedom overcoming the threshold of positive freedom—must also be negative in its affirmations. I have also indicated that the pragmatics of freedom entail a collection of human liberties, including those tending to self-realization, self-determination, and, more generally, the liberty to *become*. In this subsection I argue that the pragmatics of freedom as the realization of justice are negated by the practices of the mental health sciences which, in turn, originate from their philosophical and theoretical foundations. Thus, in the interest of promoting the realization of a more just, human existence, the resistance against the practices of mental health must be negative in relation to the foundations of psychological science and, moreover, must be negative in relation to modernist science itself.

Similar to the apophatic, these resistances are against the constructed realities that emerge from the mental health sciences. One should note, though, that there is an uneasy balance formed between construction and creation. Each makes its presence felt throughout the present critique. However, there is a key distinction that we might briefly explore at this point. Critical social studies often speak of the construction of reality and the life-negating or dehumanizing consequences of the habituation and perpetuation of such constructions in human social life. Constructed images of gender, race, ethnicity, human sexuality, and so on, are reified in social institutions and everyday discourse, granting them status as truths and, consequently, allowing them the power to organize our social world (e.g., Thorne, 1982; Jenkins, 1994). Hereinafter, constructed images will fall within the broader categorization of myth.

For our purposes, myths emerge as social and professional constructions and, further, as authoritative impositions that are instituted and perpetuated by existing knowledge/power relations. The latter—in the instance of law and the mental health sciences—provide legitimacy to such myths and propel their circulation. Thus, that which is constructed is negative. Anarchism, however, preserves a privileged location for the creative (e.g., Ferrell, 1999). I will explore the creative in greater detail throughout the present critique. For now, however, we can conceive of creation as an individual act or process of playful self-invention; of imaginative capacity utilized to affirm human life and possibility. The creative is that which exploits ambiguity, disorder, uncertainty, and reconstitutes the unknown as a world of possibility rather than a world unto which constructed order is to be imposed. The creative, then, is read affirmatively—it is self-creation, while the constructed is imposed social/professional invention (i.e., mythos) enshrouded in knowledge/power relations. The creative is an imaginative reality, while the constructed is a reality that is imposed or involuntarily adopted.

Ultimately, then, my exploration is about human liberties and human freedom. This is not so much a plea for human rights as it is an act of defiance against that which imposes or negates what is human. More specifically, however, my position in this chapter is one that advances freedom from the dis-eased foundations that provide justification for current mental health practices (Williams and Arrigo, 2002). As such, the remaining portions of this chapter represent an exploration of the negations or insurgencies necessary for the realization of a more just and more human existence for those labeled mentally ill. Indirectly, these insurgencies symbolize resistances against the legal order in that the latter's recognition of expert knowledge (i.e., authority) allows for the continuation of the negative (i.e., coercive) practices of psychology and psychiatry. The critical explorations that follow, then, are targeted primarily at the philosophical foundations of mental health, and secondarily, but explicitly, at the psycholegal practices of involuntary confinement and involuntary treatment.

THE MYTHOS OF MODERN SCIENCE

I previously noted that the intent of this chapter is to exploit the erroneous assumptions of science and, in particular, those of the mental health sciences that give rise to a host of objectionable clinicolegal practices. To the extent that they have been constructed and perpetuated as truths, these assumptions exist as the *mythos* of mental health science. In the present section, I explore the character of myth, the relationship between science and myth, and the emergence of authority and coercive authoritarian practices from such myths. In short, I argue that positivist science itself appears as a maker of myths; that is, as promoting a constructed doctrine that appears or, rather, is meant to appear in naturalistic form. To the extent that the positivist doctrine is employed pragmatically in an effort to alter the social world (e.g., by instituting efforts to treat, control, and impose order), positivist science not only is a paradigm, but is an ideology. Wrapped in this ideology are constitutive myths of certainty; that of order, control, prediction, and other principles that serve as justifications for injustice. In order to embrace and assimilate itself to the ideology of positivist science, the institution of mental health organizes itself around and is premised on myth and ideology. Moreover, its practitioners stand as ideologues; indoctrinated agents charged with the pragmatic implementation of the mythic principles that constitute the ideology of positivist science. In practice, this translates into impositions on human freedom, liberty, autonomy, and what I have referred to as justice. Contrastingly, the anarchic and apophatic are instruments of deconstruction interested in exposing the myths fostered by positivist science and, further, revealing the practices of the mental health sciences as dependent on such myths for continued legitimacy.

On Myth

By definition, we can think of myth as "a story . . . taken as expressing, and therefore implicitly symbolizing, certain deep-lying aspects of human . . . existence" (Wheelwright, 1974, p. 538). Myth, then, is *metaphorical* narrative (Noth, 1990, p. 374). It is that which employs linguistic (rhetorical) devices to present and perpetuate stories that have symbolic value for its receivers.

Interestingly, myth has always been distinguished from that which is "scientific" or rational. The Greeks distinguished between *mythos* and *logos*, a distinction that found its fullest embodiment in the Enlightenment. During this period, myth or the mythical was equated with falsehood and opposed to "reality." Myth was antithetical to "science" (Noth, 1990, p. 374). Interestingly and significantly, the Enlightenment was not so much an exercise in stripping away mythic images, as creating new ones. Modernity, with its promises of understanding, control, prediction, order, and its faith in science to achieve these promises, can be regarded as the embodiment of a constellation of new myths. As such, modernity, through its assemblage of particularized myths, represents an elaborate story mythologized and aggrandized by the scientific community responsible for its very construction.

In the sense used hereinafter, myth appears less as a historical narrative with value that is primarily symbolic. Rather, when referring to myth I mean that which exists as a surreptitious ideological component of everyday life (Barthes, 1972). Myths have the effect of structuring everyday life by grafting meaning onto the experiences of our everyday life-world. These meanings are often ideological and serve to conceal the phenomenology of everyday life. Myths *naturalize* that which is purely constructed—ideology replaces fact by making ideology appear *as* fact (Barthes, 1972). Further, in terms of the subject/object of the myth, the ideological constructions are saved from critical analysis in that mythic understandings are presented and perpetuated as universal truths (Barthes, 1977, p. 165; Noth, 1990, p. 376).

For Barthes, the goal of critical analysis was to destroy myth by removing its ideological content and revealing the "reality" of the subject/object. Barthes's (1977) notion of "mythoclasm" is, in our terms, an exercise in *apophasis*. The apophatic is about critical removal of that which blinds us to phenomenological reality. It is about removing layers on layers of ideologically motivated connotations that appear as natural, common sense, universal truths. The apophatic is about negating myth on the road to affirming the truly human.

Myths, then, construct a certain reality (Barthes, 1972), a construction that, as we have noted, conceals and obscures whatever unadulterated reality may exist. We can also think of myths as constructing an economy of thought or conceptual reality in which its consumers are saved the additional investment to *think for themselves*. One may be reminded of Nietzsche's polemics, exemplified in such sarcasms as "*O sancta simplicitas!*" (Nietzsche, 1989, p. 35; BGE 24). While the world is not simple, orderly, and certain, human beings desire a world that is simple, orderly, and certain. It is easy enough to construct such a world in the face of discomfort. Myths, then, can be reassuring, protective, and seem affirmative. However, what myths affirm is nothing more than a constructed reality, a constructed knowledge and, thus, a false sense of security against the unknown. While myths may appear affirmative they are, in fact, false affirmations or *negations* themselves. By imposing and confining human beings within their constructed world, they negate the positive, life-affirming freedom to construct one's own reality, knowledge, and life experiences—in short, to realize one's actualized self and one's becoming.

The creation and perpetuation of myth—the myth-making process—"always embellishes," while the apophatic "strips away" (Geldard, 2000, p. 23). Myth-makers "construct attractive landscapes of metaphor and explanation "which, in the hands of the apophatic critic, are to be revealed as falsehoods in the interest of "awaken[ing] a new sensibility" (ibid.). By turning to the apophatic act of negation; that is, by stripping away that which negates, we are, in fact, affirming that which is more human. We are affirming a new sensibility that concerns itself, not with the sanctity of simplicity, but with the affirmation of life. Given the human inclination to search for and bond with the artifice of order and control in the face of disorder and unpredictability, it becomes, in the name of simplicity, too human to place faith in that which claims simple answers and simple means. This is the simplicity of science; a simplicity that needs uncritical mythic belief for its perpetuation. In the instance of psychological science, its most indiscriminate presumption is the ontological status of mental illness. This status is steeped in the modernist commitment to ontological realism.

Ontological Realism and the Mythic Foundations of Modern Science

The foundations of modern science consist of the following philosophical and theoretical assumptions: ontological realism, epistemological objectivism, and theoretical positivism (e.g., Crotty, 1998). In the first case, science must adhere to certain assumptions regarding the nature of reality. Ontologically, modern science subscribes to an immodest version of realism. That is to say, modern science acknowledges that the world consists of "real" things, facts, conditions, etc., and that the existence of those things is independent of human consciousness (Trigg, 2001). Thus, the "things" of the world are objective in that their existence is not dependent on the ability of human beings to recognize them or construct them as realities. Further, science purports that we can make observations and statements about the world that are pure descriptions and, thus, have factual value since statements about truth and falsehood are dichotomous. Modern science affirms the capacity to attain truths about the things of the world and, perhaps more consequentially, advises that we believe the truth claims made about such realities.

To a large extent, the mental health sciences have subscribed to a perspective on human thought, affect, and behavior that is equally based in realist pretense. First and foremost, there exists throughout all practical mental health endeavors an implicit understanding that psychiatric illness is "real" and that its reality is not significantly constructed, disturbed, or altered by human consciousness (i.e., professional observation). Thus, mental disorders are real and they can be observed and understood by mental health scientists. We find these assumptions at their most forceful in psychiatric diagnoses. These diagnoses are intended to convey precision and certainty. They are identified with an air of scientific authority and professional competence. The latter perpetuates and reinforces professional and popular conceptualizations of mental illness as real and, perhaps more important, justifies intervention in the eyes of professionals, citizens, and the State. The image of the mental health "scientist," then, carries with it ontological and epistemological assumptions concerning both the objects of scientific inquiry as well as the ability to know and understand such objects. Thus, we could say that there is a certain *mythos* regarding the mental health scientist. This mythos requires some critical scrutiny.

Various theoretical criticisms have been launched at realist understandings of mental illness, notably from the social constructionist camp (e.g., Scheff, 2000), iconoclasts in existentialism (e.g., Laing, 1967; 1969), civil libertarianism (e.g., Szasz, 1961; 1970), philosophy (e.g., Foucault, 1965; 1977), and, more recently, critical/radical psychology (Fox and Prilleltensky, 1997). These criticisms present considerable evidence challenging popular notions of mental health/illness, modernist science, and/or the practical clinical undertakings informed by both. In short, these efforts indicate that mental illness may be less of an objective reality and, instead, something wholly, or at least partly, dependent upon human consciousness for its existence. Most recently, critiques of this sort have been situated in assays regarding the nature and practice of science itself (e.g., Williams and Arrigo, 2001a; 2001b). Rather than assaulting the social reality of mental illness independent of philosophical and theoretical criticisms, these examinations provide a potent response to the convictions of modern psychological science, drawing from ontology, epistemology, and ethics, as well as sociopolitical commentary. These critical insights inform the next section of this chapter.

Truth *De Jure* Possession: Ontology, Knowledge, and (Legal) Authority

Anarchism defies the legitimacy of authority and the coercive techniques employed by order maintenance institutions and agents in all its forms. Thus, the anarchist critique most directly challenges that which emerges from the presumptions of ontological realism in the mental health sciences. That is to say, while realism constitutes a necessary philosophical condition for current conceptualizations of mental illness, the effects of its assumptions in psychology or psychiatry are problematic. In particular, I refer to the truth-value of claims arising from the mental health sciences. To the extent that such claims are granted status as truths, their representatives or advocates are themselves granted authority and, as such, are endowed with (coercive) power to alter the reality involving those truths. Thus, the problem with ontological realism is fully realized when its philosophical assumptions transcend their hypothetical status and emerge as instituted truths.

In short, the legitimation of scientific assertions involving mental illness and psychological experience, transforms scientific assertions into power/knowledge truths (Foucault, 1965, 1977). However, claims to truth cannot reflect any factual correspondence to reality. By scientific truth, I am referring to that which issues from science, is encoded with factual claims, and is subsequently decoded as having a factual relationship to reality. However, the process of decoding is informed by presumptions of authority and knowledge and, consequently, the hypothetical becomes popularized in scientific and public communities as carrying the value of knowledge. Additionally, presumptions of knowledge are institutionalized in the law and form the basis of decisions in the psycholegal arena. The mental health sciences can be regarded as having *legal* possession of knowledge in the context of mental health issues. This is the point at which science and the law become wedded in the collaborative pursuit of order and control. This is also the juncture at which the anarchist assault becomes keenly relevant as a virulent critique of mental health law practices and decisions.

While I have described the problem of realism and the nature of reality as fundamentally constructed, there is, nevertheless, a pervasive image of science as seeking, at times discovering, and, further, delivering knowledge of reality to a wider audience. Ontological assumptions concerning the realness of objects is the basis for the scientific search for the "truth" of such realities. The search for truths entails epistemological assumptions that reality *can* be known and, further, that there are certain ways (i.e., methods, procedures, techniques) of discovering such truths. For modern science, these ways of knowing are consistent with its episteme and are privileged to the near exclusion of any alternatives. If ontological claims are questioned in light of replacement understandings of knowledge acquisition (e.g., reconstituting reality as a human social construction or, at least, acknowledging that it is mediated by human consciousness), the assertion that there is an objective reality and, hence, an objective *knowable* reality becomes suspect (e.g., Anderson, 1995; Phillips, 2000). As a result, truth claims are revealed as hypotheses, authority based on such truth claims becomes illegitimate, and coercive practices resulting from this knowledge/power relationship foster injustice.

THE MYTHOS OF MENTAL HEALTH

Throughout the history of ideas, ontological realism has met resistance in the form of alternative understandings of reality. Most damaging, perhaps, are resistances that have emerged in the latter part of the twentieth century that have challenged the legitimacy of previously accepted truths concerning the nature of reality and the capacity of science to know that reality (Dupre, 1993). Quantum physics and chaos theory, for example, have both contributed to a revaluation of order, certainty, control, prediction, and the like (e.g., Briggs & Peat, 1989; Porter & Gleick, 1990; Williams & Arrigo, 2001a). In recent history, the most extreme opponent of ontological realism has been that of idealism. Idealism holds that, in short, reality is purely mental in nature (e.g., Trigg, 2001). An objective reality does not exist independent of human consciousness but, rather, a reality exists that is entirely dependent on human minds, conceptual schemes, language, and the like. Without such mediators, nothing is real. Perhaps the most celebrated form of idealism is that promoted by postmodernists, namely, linguistic idealism. From this perspective, reality is entirely a product of our linguistic schemes. Thus, our linguistic and social categories impose a reality onto the things of the world which, otherwise, would not exist as part of our reality.

A more moderate contrary position to realism is a form of constructionism. Constructionism does not deny the existence of an independent reality, but holds that the nature of that possible reality is largely irrelevant to our everyday social functioning (e.g., Crotty, 1998). The social world we inhabit is one we have constructed primarily with our minds. Constructions of reality may have, at some point, issued from an interaction between objective reality and human consciousness, yet such interactions have led to constructions by which we now understand our reality. Thus, while social constructions of reality may have originally reflected an independent reality, such original reflections have long since given way to a world based on mental constructions. We construct reality with concepts and language and, in our everyday lives, these constructions are relevant and socially significant—not those that correspond with an independent reality. The ontological perspective informing what follows is a version of constructionism, with ample attention to the linguistic nature of social constructions. For my purpose, it is the construct(ion) of mental illness that necessitates some critical review and commentary.

Constructions of Illness

The construct of mental illness represents the foundation of all clinical undertakings within the mental health arena. Psychotherapeutic treatment, drug therapy, and civil commitment are each premised on the assumption of a real, certain, and demonstrable ontological presence. To be sure, psychological diagnostics demand categorization based on the presence of identifiable cognitive, affective, and/or behavioral abnormalities (see APA, 1994). These abnormalities are presumed to exist independent of professional recognition (Szasz, 1997). That is to say, a psychotic is psychotic regardless of whether he or she is identified, diagnosed, categorized, and subsequently treated *as* a psychotic. Mental illness, then, is presumed to be an ontologically real physical phenomenon about which the mental health sciences can draw etiological conclusions, resulting in accurate classifications and effective treatments (Scheff, 2000). However, unlike physical illness, psychiatric illness fails to conform to the techniques of scientific measurement. We cannot "see" mental disorder, except in its affective, cognitive, and behavioral manifestations. Notwithstanding advances in physiological psychology, no evidence exists to absolutely support a physical, biological, or physiological basis for mental "illness" (Scheff, 2000). Thus, manifestations must be taken as evidence of underlying illness. As the basis for all clinical undertakings, however, the very construct of mental illness must be subjected to criticism of the apophatic sort; that is, criticism aimed at removing layers of myth. The layers of myth are characterized as scientific constructions or, perhaps, constructions under the name of science.

Positivist science, built on realist ontology, holds that "worldstuff" has an objectively real character. The "new sciences" of quantum physics and chaos theory, however, echo the sentiments of a constructivist ontology (e.g., Zohar & Marshall, 1994). "Worldstuff" is not objectively real but, rather, is constructed through interaction of observer and observed. Heisenberg's (1958) physical universe is one of possibilities—of potential, nothing more. The world beyond potential or, what we commonly regard as the realized world, is not a world that has been *identified* (and, hence, understood) through observation; rather, it is a world that has been *constructed* through observation. In fact, it is a world that, by being observed, has lost its potential and, consequently, lost its potential for realization (e.g., Merleau-Ponty, 1962). That which is unobserved, then, remains potential; that which is observed, in turn, has its potential quashed by the very act of observing.

Heisenberg's (1958) uncertainty principle embodies the physical reality of observer altering that which is observed. Conceptually speaking, we can say that observation performs the key function of concretizing, defining, labeling, and so forth, that which previously existed in an indeterminate, undifferentiated state. Metaphysically, concretizing potential is problematic for orthodox versions of realism, particularly in such domains as the mental health sciences. Objective "reality" can no longer exist in a determined state independent of human consciousness. Rather, it is human consciousness that constructs reality by imposing categorical distinctions unto the previously indeterminate. The resulting image, then, is that of the scientist "actively constructing scientific knowledge rather than passively noting laws that are found in nature" (Crotty, 1998, p. 31). Contrary to Cartesian dualism, nothing can be identified, described, understood, etc., apart from the experiencing subject—as an entity isolated from the effect (read pretensions) of the experiencing subject.

Pretension, then, becomes wedded to observation. As such, constructions of reality issue forth, in part, from the pretensions of the observing subject. Education, training, experience, the prevailing scientific paradigm (Kuhn, 1970), and so on, all act in concert to produce "eyes" primed to recognize or identify certain realities from within a maze of uncertainty (Pfohl, 1994). We can variously describe this phenomenon as the "co-emergence of knower and known" (Macy, 1991; Williams & Arrigo, 2001b). Nothing can be known (i.e., identified, defined, conceptualized) without the concurrent existence of a knower purported to have the ability to recognize or know it. Ability, here, is best read as pretension. To the extent that "ability" is determined by education, training, and *indoctrination*, ability is no more than a constellation of preconeptualizations, paradigmatic categorizations, and the privileged knowledge/power truth claims (Foucault, 1965) that ensue accordingly. The consequent practices stemming from such scientific pretensions become, in turn, legitimated pretexts.

The Language of Myth

> Men have an all but incurable propensity to try to prejudge all the great questions which interest them by stamping their prejudices upon their language.
>
> —Sir James Fitzjames Stephen

Principally, I note that constructed realities are linguistic realities (Sapir, 1921; Whorf, 1956). Language *precedes* constructed reality and, in turn, language becomes a heuristic device that has the effect of imposing definition and certainty unto the uncertain and the potential. Traditional notions of language as denominational—as merely representing or articulating experienced reality—are replaced by notions of language as a formative, structuring system of meanings (Saussure, 1916). The meaning we attach to objects, events, and persons are predefined and limited to our available lexicon. Scientifically speaking, observations and explanations are compelled to be representations of linguistically constructed scientific categorizations. We are, then, constituted by language and our observations are, in turn, predetermined by language.

Language exists, not as an instance, but as a constrictive system (Saussure, 1916). Individual instances of observation, recognition, definition, and so forth are constrained by and subsequently driven by the operative, culturally (professionally) constructed system of language. We can reconceptualize scientific observations as instances preceded by baptismal absorption into the system of scientific language. The "ability" to speak (i.e., observe) in a given instance is dependent on knowledge of the "rules of the game." Learning such rules is an exercise in attaching appropriate meanings to observed objects, events, and/or persons. Linguistic distinctions, then, reflect disciplinary models of reality. Within such disciplines, "speakers" of that language come to think, feel, and act in ways consistent with learned (linguistic) realities.

In the case of the mental health disciplines, we can regard the psychological and psychiatric sciences as a community of shared-language users. Within such a community, there is a professional lexicon learned through training, and a specific education necessary for indoctrination into the professional community and subsequently necessary for effective communication within that collective. The insertion of specialized terminologies into the vocabulary of an individual professional (e.g., the discourse of psychiatry as a medical or disease model), will inevitably shape the way the person perceives reality. In short, these perceptions will be consistent with recognized or dominant interpretations of reality as constructed within that professional community. However, perceptions of reality outside this context (at the level of phenomenology) become difficult if not altogether impossible. Recognition of a reality *precedes* an understanding of that (unique) reality, and the (unique) reality becomes lost in the abyss linguistic reductionism.

The most potent example of linguistic constructionism in the mental health sciences involves diagnoses (e.g., Hare-Mustin & Marecek, 1997). The diagnostic label represents a linguistic category that, while initially constructed in the interest of denomination, rapidly achieves the status of a structuring heuristic device. That is to say, while diagnostic labels were and are created in the interest of supplying some experienced phenomenon a name, they soon become the "eyes" through which subsequent experiences are made sensible. Again, the diagnostic label shapes reality often before such reality is even experienced. This is particularly the case when labels follow persons (i.e., clients/consumers) throughout their tenure in the clinicolegal system. The diagnostic label shapes not only how the system and professionals within the system respond to the client, but also shapes how the consumer imagines and responds to such characterizations (Goffman, 1959; 1963; Scheff, 2000). Both the professional mental health community and persons voluntarily and involuntarily subjected to systemic interventions experience a world of self and other that is mediated by and, consequently, shaped by linguistic constructions.

The American Psychiatric Association's (APA) *Diagnostic and Statistical Manual of Mental Disorders* (*DSM*), now in its fourth edition, represents the epitome of linguistic categorizations (APA, 1994). Currently, there are over 340 diagnostic categories, and this number is sure to increase as the manual is revised for future editions (Hare-Mustin & Marecek, 1997). As categories multiply, so does the extent to which human thought, feeling, and behavior is subject to monitoring and regulation. As regulation increases, possibilities and potentials are proportionately negated.

It is also of interest that the diagnostic categories of the mental health sciences have become more medicalized over the years (e.g., Szasz, 1961; Foucault, 1965; Conrad, 1975). Hare-Mustin & Marecek (1997) suggest that the medical model of mental illness has been prevalent since the conservative shift of the 1980s. That is to say, the political shift of the 1980s coincided with a shift not only in diagnostic mental health but in theorizations of etiology, prognosis, and treatment. Ideologically, it is significant to note that the medical model privileges a conceptualization of mental illness that distracts attention from the social aspects of individual experience and focuses policy on "curing" diseased individuals. It is easier, then, to justify reductions in welfare, increased regulation of difference, and the absence of initiatives aimed at large-scale social change.

The problem with such conceptualizations is that, while brain disease may be a "real" medical (physical) condition, there is no evidence that other forms of psychological "illness" are real in any identifiable physical sense (Szasz, 1997). The medical model relies on an illness *metaphor* in understanding and treating dis-ease rather than any scientific (empirical) evidence of bodily lesion associated with disease (ibid.). Again, the politics of illness becomes an exercise in linguistic constructionism. Thus, we have, it would seem, a mental health system that relies on metaphor to understand its dis-eases; a system that employs metaphor to label its dis-eases; an intricate and elaborate diagnostic manual consisting of over 340 metaphorical images; and a wealth of treatments which are offered as metaphorical "cures" for metaphorical dis-eases. In this context, the politics of mental health are, in many ways, the politics of language or, perhaps, the language of politics.

Linguistic Authority and Constructions of Coercion

Given the previous observations on the language of myth in the discourse of mental illness, we can think, then, of constructions of reality becoming perceived truths and assuming a certain nature only through their embodiment in the linguistic schemes of science and its varied subdisciplines. The time-honored question, What's in a name? is capable of being answered only in a negative sense: the content of a name is purely negative. As labeling theorists have suggested, naming something (read labeling) negates the potential for that something to become something other than what it has been identified as. Thus, naming, diagnosing, categorizing, and so on negates potential (e.g., Scheff, 2000). The potential to become is regained only through outright *defiance* over the constructed identity.

Additionally, and perhaps more important, naming creates the *appearance* of certainty, understanding, "realness" in relation to its object. If some thing has earned a place in the professional lexicon, its character is presumed to be real; that is, there is a presumption that we have some understanding of it, and that we can identify it when it is seen. The existence of mental illness or any of its more specific forms in professional parlance (e.g., schizophrenia, paranoid type, delusional disorder, borderline personality disorder) perpetuates the myth of understanding, objective identification and, to some extent, the legitimization of control efforts. Under these circumstances, the interplay between linguistics, authority, and coercion is clear: that which is constructed and provided a place in language carries with it the presumption that some persons are capable of identifying it (authority) and that such persons are in a unique position to control, contain, treat, alter, and predict it. Thus, statements of authority are dependent upon constructions of an ontological nature. Authority is premised on myth, codified and perpetuated through language.

Anarchist criticism, however, is not directed solely against authority, but also at the violence produced through the actions of authority figures or promoted under the auspices (e.g., knowledge) of authority. With the legitimation of authority comes the legitimation of coercive techniques that are consistent with authoritarian knowledge. If the mental health sciences "know" mental health/illness, they are presumed to be in the best position to know how to effectively treat and control it. The violence enacted through the overlapping effects of knowledge, power, and coercion is the subject of the next section. However, before moving on, let me briefly identify what an anarchist critique of the mental health sciences would profess to resist. Summarily, this would include the following:

1. in the wake of the Enlightenment, science became the dominant measure of what is real and how to go about understanding what is real;

2. the widespread faith in science provided a legitimacy in the eyes of both professional and public milieus and, consequently, the mythos against which science was a reaction gave rise to the mythos of science itself;

3. the mythos of science is constituted by philosophical assumptions including ontological realism and epistemological objectivism, whereby the objects of scientific study are "real" and science is capable of knowing such realities;

4. in the interest of attaining legitimacy, psychology and psychiatry assumed the position of science by adopting the philosophical assumptions, the theoretical convictions, and the methodological standpoints of science in studying both its subjects and its objects;

5. constituting the "sciences" of mental health, psychology and psychiatry must implicitly subscribe to ontological realism (i.e., mental illness is real and independent of human consciousness) and epistemological objectivism (i.e., knowledge claims concerning mental illness stem from objective, value-free observations about which there is widespread professional agreement);

6. resistance to ontological realism has been launched on a number of fronts, most significantly from social constructionist camps wherein the subjects/objects of scientific inquiry may be regarded as less concrete realities than products of human (i.e., professional) consciousness;

7. this notwithstanding, phenomena presumed to be "real" and "knowable" emerge as linguistic realities within professional circles and, subsequently, are codified in professional literature thus securing their status as real, identifiable, knowable and, in many instances, treatable;

8. as "sciences" of mental health, psychology and psychiatry are granted legitimacy by the public at large and by the State (e.g., legal legitimacy);

9. legitimacy provides the mental health sciences with authority status in matters of psychiatric illness and society's response to it; and

10. the authority granted to the mental health sciences—based on presumed scientific and, thus, nonmythic understanding and knowledge of psychiatric health/illness—further legitimates coercive techniques (e.g., involuntary incarceration, involuntary drug treatment) intended to "treat" (read control) mental illness and, thus, promote mental "health."

ANARCHIC INSURGENCIES

In this section I explore the ways in which authority and coercion act to produce violence and injustice through the negation of ambiguity, potential, difference, change, and becoming. More specifically, I address the ways in which the mental health sciences, legitimated by law, function to quash these very experiences through coercive methods of treatment. I first address the notion of authority at the intersection of science, law, and mental health. Subsequently, I examine the notion of mental health treatment as violence and, further, the anarchist notion of defiance in relation to scientific authority. Finally, I address the notion of possibility, potential, and becoming as points of resistance and points of transformation for human beings and civil society.

The Anarchaos of the Self

While the impetus behind modern science has been the search for universal, certain truths and identifiable cause-effect relationships, Western society has unequivocally subscribed to the notion that certain individuals are capable of ascertaining, understanding, and working with these discoveries. Because of their knowledge, education, training, and experience, these individuals can perceive that which is perceivable as they are uniquely qualified. Most important, these persons are often commissioned for guidance and empowered with authority in matters falling within their recognized realm of expertise. Such epistemic authority is *granted*—it "accrues to [a person] simply by being institutionally certified" (Dupre, 1993: 222). Put another way, scientific expertise follows from indoctrination.

Feyerabend (1993) tells us that "normal" science is based on the principle of indoctrination. That is, scientists—as a rite of passage—are granted special status as experts, much like priests in the world of religion. This indoctrination, complete with the conferring of privileges, is not unique to the scientific world (cf. Szasz, 1970). Indeed, one need not look any further than the prominence of diviners or witch hunters in the prescientific world of demonology to find primitive scientists of human behavior. In the premodern world, accusations of witchcraft or demonic activity drew attention from those with alleged special powers or a God-given "second sight" (Pfohl, 1994, p. 24) that allowed demonological experts to determine the presence of evil. Having reached a diagnosis or categorical determination, the "expert testimony" of the diviner became the basis for further measures of social control. While the expertise of diviners rested, quite literally, on nothing more than articles of faith, Feyerabend's (1993) point is that the expert opinions of scientists are no more epistemologically sound than the expert beliefs of psychics, voodoo doctors, and the like. In many ways, science is faith without the mask of theology.

Feyerabend was no psychologist, nor was he concerned with deviance, expert testimony, or social criticism more generally. Feyerabend was, in fact, arguing for the inclusion of less privileged forms of knowledge in the research process. His primary argument, however, translates well into language that is critical of the expertise proclaimed by the mental health sciences. Ultimately, Feyerabend's attack was an assault on the epistemic authority claimed by all forms of science. If science's self-proclaimed expertise is refutable or, at the very least, uncertain, then the knowledge and expertise it espouses through its various social and behavioral scientific outlets (e.g., psychiatry, epidemiology) is equally questionable. Nevertheless, expertise continues to be the basis on which the mental health community makes decisions, establishes programs, and implements policy.

In the mental health community, scientific indoctrination entails the broad authority to diagnose and treat. More specifically, however, the legitimation of the mental health scientist has consequences that reach into the province of human liberty. These specialists are recognized by society and, more important, the law, as uniquely able to perceive the presence of mental illness and the impact of it on the behavior and *future* behavior of an individual. Diagnosis of mental illness and prognostication of violent or otherwise harmful conduct often entails, in practice, the legally justified commitment of persons to psychiatric hospitals, enforced treatment, or both. First and foremost, such practices are interruptions to the freedom of one's body; that is, the right of an individual to be free from physical imprisonment absent any criminal violations deemed punishable. Relatedly, such practices interrupt (and forestall) one's freedom to think as one chooses.

Psychotherapy, in many of its forms, is employed as a means to correct irrational, illogical, and deviant thought processes and affective states (e.g., Beck & Weishaar, 1995). As Rychlak (1981, p. 32) suggests, it is an effort aimed at "readjusting the *disordered* personality" (my emphasis). Most intrusively, forced drug therapy represents an effort to correct thoughts, feelings, and behaviors *physiologically*. Of course, for those deemed mentally ill and dangerous, physical incapacitation, psychotherapy, and drug therapy are often employed *en masse*. In any case, one's freedom to think, feel, and behave as one chooses is supplanted by the interests of the collective social order, and its maintenance falls within the purview of indoctrinated mental health scientists (Foucault, 1977). Thus, challenging the fictions of mental health science means rejecting this purview.

Embracing epistemic uncertainty, the process of becoming, and the individual as self-shaped and self-governed, entails an outright denial and rejection authority (Ferrell, 1999, p. 97). Anarchism's rejection of authority extends into every realm of the social world within which indoctrination operates: from religion, to politics, law, science and, of course, the institution of mental health. In each case, we find familiar examples of indoctrinated experts, privileged forms of knowledge and experience, and a large-scale enforcement of conformity and existential confinement (cf. Fromm, 1955). In each case, anarchism challenges and, in fact, defies such authority in the name of diversity, tolerance, community, and self-determination.

Defiance (read negation) is, as we have noted, always in the interest of affirmation. Take the example of religion. According to anarchists, while priests and others are (historically) regarded as having special knowledge of the divine and, therefore, of life and its proper course, it is to be actively defied. Religion should not be considered merely an analogue to the world of mental health. Indeed, for much of Western civilization definitions of deviance were produced by religious authority (Pfohl, 1994). Additionally, the ability to define deviance as such provided one with the (state sanctioned) power to control it in particular cases. Under these conditions, religion was a primitive agent socially controlling thought, feeling, and behavior.

Of related interest is Szasz's (1970) comparison of the Inquisition and the mental health movement. As he explains, there are important similarities and interrelationships between religious authority and mental health authority (see also Szasz, 1978). Finally, as Skinner (1953, p. 383) noted in his exegeses on behaviorism and psychotherapy, "the therapist may gain a degree of control which is more powerful than that of many religious or governmental agents." If anarchism promotes defiance in the face of falsely privileged forms of religious and governmental control, its defiance of mental health science practices is equally pronounced.

Authority is Violence: Uncertainty and Becoming

Reality, as I have noted, is largely inconsistent with modern realist ontology. The power of language to construct reality—to precede our experience of reality—is a recognition that has spawned a shift away from orthodox (naive) realism and toward linguistic idealism. Somewhere in between we find a workable ontology wherein objects are not real, not created through language, but constructed via interaction under the influence of linguistic categories. Our observations are and must be categorical, and such categorical distinctions represent an interpretive code that privileges a dualist perception of reality. Namely, we are imprisoned in a conceptual world whereby "things" *either* exist *or* do not exist. If an observation or experience falls outside the realm of linguistic reality, we construct a linguistic category for it. Problematically, however, the moment uncertainty is named, it is made certain. The moment reality is defined, its potential is subjugated. The problem with such commonsense ontology is that its categorical distinctions fail to allow for alternative possibilities. Subjected to the logic of the dialectic, we find that "being" and "not-being" are, in fact, two aspects of the same reality. Everything is *both* being *and* not-being. In short, every reality is *becoming* reality and, therefore, every reality is an indeterminate and uncertain reality.

To suggest that reality is uncertain is to deny the very claims instituted by the mental health sciences. Under the auspices of positivism, mental health seeks to identify and define *certain* ontological realities (e.g., the presence of mental illness) and, in turn, to engage in practices aimed at altering those realities in various ways. The authority of the mental health sciences rests on the assumption of both the certain existence of ontological realities and the certain ability of the mental health sciences to identify, define (i.e., diagnose), prognose, and treat those realities that do not conform to pretensions of health. Any valid claims against the ontological status of mental illness, for example, raises serious questions about the practices of the mental health sciences.

The alteration of individual reality, as a social usage of psychological pretensions concerning mental illness, is a process we might call "violence." It is most interesting, however, that such alterations are performed under the rubric of treatment (read compassion, care, *parens patriae* as parental love). It is the responsibility of the State to offer care to those judged in need of treatment. In practice, this means placement in a psychiatric facility or mental health system in which the intervention is legally sanctioned. At this point, we may appreciate R. D. Laing's (1967) provocative love-violence opposition. As he suggests, "love lets the other be . . . violence attempts to constrain the other's freedom, to force him to act in the way we desire" (p. 58). Laing's ironic assault on moral conventions is a thinly veiled rejection of operative pretensions in the mental health sciences; namely, that treatment work in the name of compassion is the farthest from what happens. The practice of compassion (i.e., love), rather than imposed treatment, consists of letting the other become and of appreciating alternative experiential realities. Laing's "violence" is akin to Schopenhauer's (1970) injustice, and Laing's "love" appears as tolerance, peace, and mutual aid in anarchist thought.

Laing's (1967) assault on conventional morality and conventional understandings of love is intended to show that such conventions are, in fact, violent, life-negating impositions. We are taught what and how to experience out of the whole range of potential experiences—such is the form of negation through socialization (cf. Marcuse, 1964, 1966). Potential and subjectivity are precisely what is subject to violent abrogation. Quoting Colby (1925), Laing writes "men do not become what by nature they are meant to be, but what society makes them . . . [experience] . . . is amputated to fit us for our intercourse with the world" (Laing, 1967, p. 65). It is presumed, then, that limiting the range of human experience and, thus, limiting what a person may become, is necessary to assure social order. Laing writes of family, religion, education, and other institutions as purveyors of this form of violence. Yet there will always be those who, through conscious rebellion or intolerance of environmental/social conditions, will step outside the range of dictated experience. These persons we call psychiatrically disordered, and these persons are subjected to processing by the mental health system.

Systems like the mental health apparatus embody certain values and, by way of the power or indoctrinated authority of the actors within that system, impose a circumscribed way of life on its subjects (cf. Tolstoy, 1900; Bookchin, 1982). Without exception, these systems are hostile to life. Nietzsche (1990), in his anti-Christian polemics, ascribes the same role to the

Church (i.e., the moral "system" that the Church preaches): "to attack . . . passions at their roots means to attack life at its roots" (p. 52). Systems attack at the very level that makes people uniquely human. The individuality of human beings; that is, the desire to be an individual, is castigated when potential is shaped and uniqueness supplanted by institutionalized morals. Indeed, systems and institutions oppose human life. It is in such institutionalized morality that "the concepts 'true' and 'false' are necessarily reversed: that which is most harmful to human life is called 'true,' that which enhances, intensifies, affirms, justifies it and causes it to triumph is called 'false'" (Nietzsche, 1990, p. 132; *A*, 9). In other words, we could say that that which is most harmful to human life is called "healthy," and that which enhances, intensifies, affirms, and justifies it and causes it to triumph is called "ill." The triumph of human life necessitates uninhibited free play in a creative endeavor (cf. Wilde, 1948). It requires individual mastery, overcoming of self, artistry, and the development of individual potentials. However, creation of this sort is possible only without the restrictions of previously constructed truths, realities, predefined values and ways of thinking, and the systemic structures that maintain them (cf. Nehemas, 1985, p. 174). All of these are expressions of authority as violence, masquerading as truth and reality.

Defiance

As previously noted, anarchism is actively defiant of authority. Although often regarded as defiance for its own sake, this rebelliousness is grounded in a deeper rejection of claims to epistemic certainty (e.g., Ferrell, 1999). In principle, anarchism denies the notion that epistemic certainty is possible and, further, rejects the conviction that a privileged few have access to such knowledge (cf. Tolstoy, 1990; Fromm, 1947). Anarchism asserts that there is no absolute truth, final interpretation, or certainty in any form. Rather, life in its natural dynamic is characterized by uncertainty, flux, becoming, and multiple perspectives and interpretations (e.g., Williams & Arrigo, 2002). Thus, any claims to epistemic certainty are not only to be challenged but actively and directly renounced. In this regard, anarchism embraces a more experientially and scientifically sound epistemic *uncertainty*.

The relationship between the rejection of authority and the rejection of epistemic certainty, then, is one of challenging privileged viewpoints. Public and professional (e.g., legal) acknowledgment of claims to epistemic certainty introduces omnipotent truth claims into social discourse. Subsequently and correspondingly, it becomes morally acceptable and socially desirable to enforce these truths in the interest of social order (i.e., to ensure, by way of intervention, conformity to predefined ways of thinking, feeling, and being). What is less-than-human in this equation is its negation of that which makes us all too human; namely, difference and diversity. Constructing a social order based on presumptions of epistemic certainty stands in direct contrast to experiential human reality: a unidimensional and homogenous way of being is endorsed based on a univocally constructed portrait of being human (e.g., Marcuse, 1964).

Arguably, Nietzsche was the preeminent critic of existential prescription. While Nietzsche may not have been an anarchist, his polemics are certainly of the apophatic sort. Following Nietzsche, we could say that the objective of any ideology or system of purported truths is "to present a picture of the world and a conception of values which makes a certain type of person possible and which allows [the individual] to prosper and to flourish" (Nehemas, 1985, p. 128). We might add that the adoption and prescription of such values and truths through the recognition of epistemic authority on the institutional level allows *only* a certain type of person to flourish. What results is a particular negation of individuality in the interest of systemic order. Ultimately, such negation inhibits the potential for self-realization—the potential to become—for those deemed "outside the inside" (Williams, 1999). In other words, for those whose ways of being fail or refuse to conform to epistemically authoritarian preconfigurations of social order, they are corrected, confined, or otherwise controlled (Williams & Arrigo 2001a, 2002).

Anarchism, then, represents a potent critique of unidimensional, univocal truths in that it seeks to allow all realities and knowledges equal expression and space to become. In anarchist thought, there exists not only a tolerance of alternatives, but a celebration of variety and diversity (Ferrell, 1999). As such, the theory accepts that there are multiple interpretations of reality and, thus, multiple truths or perspectives on the same. Perhaps most important, anarchism holds that among these discordant expressions of multiplicity, differences can amicably coexist. As no perspective can be regarded as epistemically certain, claims to authoritative truth and certainty resting on privilege are to be rejected as no more than ideologically based pretensions. While it may be the case that some perspectives can be more or less true or certain than others at different times, all are mere interpretations. As interpretations, these perspectives are to be questioned in the interest of social criticism, human justice, and in the furtherance of the subjective nature of our existences. Thus, we can say that "one's own views are the best for oneself without implying that they need be good for anyone else" (Nehemas, 1985, p. 72). In other words, the appreciation of difference means that one's values are not to be imposed on others. This logic obtains to the extent that one's values do not lead one to impede the development and freedom of others. The general spirit of anarchism, then, can be summed up as "a certain odd balance between tolerance of alternatives and intolerance for those who would limit them" (Ferrell, 1999, p. 95).

Becoming Anarchaotic: Human Transformations

Perhaps the most significant theme informing much of anarchist thought is that of becoming. Like Laing, Nietzsche, and others, anarchism dispels the myth that any person or situation can be defined exclusive of the processes by which the person or phenomenon are coconstituted. The prevailing atomistic paradigm, adopted by modern science and contemporary mental health, holds that people are to be regarded as "separate, self-contained, unitary particles or atoms" that act largely in isolation (Slaton, 1991, p. 45). Atomistic conceptions of human being neglect the deeper quantum realities that point to a web of life (Capra, 1996). Nietzsche (1967, p. 337) anticipated this ontological fallacy in rejecting what he saw as the "fictional insertion of the subject." In contrast to mythic notions of the enduring, individual subject, what emerges is a portrait of human being as a process—always interrelated and mutually dependent—of continual creation and re-creation. The mythos of "being" is antithetical to the reality of "becoming."

The notion that all (human) life is in a perpetual state of becoming serves as a foundational theme on which anarchistic principles such as uncertainty, ambiguity, change, defiance of structure and authority are based. Unlike the rigid formulations that constitute the fundamentals of institutionalized science, mental health, and other variations of systemic structure, life and its elements are an emerging process (Ferrell, 1999). Becoming, like life itself, does not aim at a final state. "If the motion of the world aimed at a final state, that state would have been reached" (Nietzsche, 1967, p. 377; *WP*, 708). It becomes merely for the purpose of becoming. It continues simply to continue. It desires only a continuation of desire itself—not a definable object (cf. Schopenhauer's "will," and Nietzsche's "will to power"). Its aim in the dance of life is simply to continue dancing. As Nietzsche (1967) tells us, "[b]ecoming must be explained without recourse to final intentions" (p. 377). Thus, without final intentions, ultimate aims, and omnipotent truths, there is no one way to become, no one "thing" that one should be or become—one must become only what one becomes. Any attempt to identify, define, categorize, and so on is premised on false assumptions of ontological being. Given that this "being" is always only momentary in the process of becoming, it must remain uncertain.

However, one might ask, what is it that mental illness intends to become or, perhaps, *how* can it become without guidance from the system of which it is a part and from which it takes on meaning and significance. In response, we would do well to visit the anarchaotic thesis of self-organization (Williams and Arrigo, 2001b). The anarchaotic points to the life-affirming consequences of the *presence* of dis-order. Much like Laing's (1967) intellectual "journey," chaos theory finds that periods of disorder are functional.

Disorder emerges when the present state of a system is not in perfect equilibrium with its environment. There are, we could say, environmental perturbances that push a previously stable system into far-from-equilibrium conditions. However, these periods are *creative* interruptions; that is, they are periods of becoming. While the knee-jerk reaction to disorder is to draw upon exogenous forces to reinstate orderly relations (e.g., mental health and legal intervention), chaos theory suggests that such an approach is ultimately more harmful than beneficial. What imposed order denies or *negates* is the process of becoming something different—a process referred to as *self*-organization (e.g., Chamberlain, 1994; Butz, 1994; Williams and Arrigo, 2001a, 2001b, 2002).

Self-organization, creation, and becoming are critical vindications of autonomy, self-determination, and treatment refusal. Self-organization is a process (i.e., "journey") wherein a pattern *emerges* without external dictation. The notion of emergence is antithetical to mainstream mental health treatment. Within the latter, we can include most forms of psychotherapy and, most assuredly, drug therapies. Each of these imposed treatment regimens negates the process of becoming; that is, the process of self-organizing or pushing through chaos (Chamberlain, 1994) toward a re-created reality. Self-organization or anarchaotic becoming leaves little room for mental health intervention. This is not to suggest the absolute elimination of all forms of mental health treatment. At most, we could imagine the therapist as a co-explorer, covoyager, coseeker, or mutual facilitator rather than a teacher, guide, or authority (Laing, 1967). The "journey" toward emergence of a new order is a playful, though not always enjoyable, experiment of the self. What anarchism rejects, defies, and seeks to negate is that which demonstrably abrogates the affirmative possibilities of human life. As noted in the introduction, what is to be negated is the authoritarian and the coercive; what is to be affirmed *through* negation, is the potential to become fully human.

REFERENCES

American Psychiatric Association (1994). *Diagnostic and Statistical Manual of Mental Disorders*, 4th ed. Washington, DC: American Psychiatric Association.

Anderson, W. (1995). *The Truth about Truth*. New York: G. P. Putnam's Sons.

Arrigo, B. A. (2002). "The Critical Perspective in Psychological Jurisprudence: Theoretical Advances and Epistemological Assumptions." *International Journal of Law and Psychiatry* 25, 2, 151–172.

——— & Williams, C. R. (1999). "Chaos Theory and the Social Control Thesis: A Post-Foucauldian Analysis of Involuntary Civil Confinement." *Social Justice* 26 (1), 177–207.

Baert, P. (1998). *Social Theory in the Twentieth Century*. NewYork: NYU Press.

Barthes, R. (1972). *Mythologies*. A. Lavers (trans.). New York: Hill and Wang.

———. (1977). *Image—Music—Text*. New York: Hill and Wang.

Beck, A. & Weishaar, M. (1995). "Cognitive Therapy." In R. Corsini & D. Wedding (eds.), *Current Psychotherapies*, 5th ed. Itasca, IL: F. E. Peacock Publishers.

Berger, P. & Luckmann, T. (1966). *The Social Construction of Reality*. New York: Doubleday.

Berlin, I. (1991). "Two Concepts of Liberty." In D. Miller (ed.) *Liberty*. Oxford: Oxford University Press.

Best, S. & Kellner, D. (1997). *The Postmodern Turn*. New York: Guilford.

Bonger, W. (1969). *Criminality and Economic Conditions*. Boston: Little, Brown.

Briggs, J. & Peat, D. (1989). *Turbulent Mirror*. New York: Harper and Row.

Butz, M. (1994). "Psychopharmacology: Psychology's Jurassic Park?" *Psychotherapy* 31 (4), 692–698.

Capra, F. (1996). *The Web of Life*. New York: Anchor Books.

Chamberlain, L. (1994). "Further Advances in Psychology's Jurassic Park: The Issue of Psychopharmacology." *Psychological Bulletin* 29 (3), 47–50.

Clarke, J. (1978). "What is Anarchism?" In J. Pennock and J. Chapman (eds.) *Anarchism*. New York: NYU Press.

Conrad, P. (1975). "The Discovery of Hyperkinesis: Notes on the Medicalization of Deviant Behavior." *Social problems* 23 (1), 12–21.

Dupre, J. (1993). *The Disorder of Things: Metaphysical Foundations of the Disunity of Science*. Cambridge: Harvard University Press.

Ferrell, J. (1999). "Anarchist Criminology and Social Justice." In B. Arrigo (ed.) *Social Justice/Criminal Justice: The Maturation of Critical Theory in Law, Crime, and Deviance*. Belmont, CA: Wadsworth.

Feyerabend, P. (1993). *Against Method*, 3rd ed. New York: Verso.

Foucault, M. (1988). "Confinement, Psychiatry, and Prison." In *Politics, Philosophy, and Culture: Interviews and Other Writings 1977–1984*. New York: Routledge.

———. (1978). "About the Concept of the Dangerous Individual in Nineteenth Century Legal Psychiatry." *International Journal of Law and Psychiatry* 1, 1–18.

———. (1977). *Discipline and Punish*. New York: Pantheon.

———. (1965). *Madness and Civilization*. New York: Vintage.

Fox, D. (1997). "Psychology and Law: Justice Diverted." In D. Fox and I. Prilleltensky (eds.) *Critical Psychology: An Introduction*. Thousand Oaks: Sage.

———. (1993). "The Autonomy-Community Balance and the Equity-Law Distinction: Anarchy's Task for Psychological Jurisprudence." *Behavioral Sciences and the Law* 11, 97–109.

———. (1986). "Four Reasons for Humanistic Psychologists to Advocate Anarchism." *Transformations* 2 (1), 17–23.

——— & Prilleltensky, I. (1997). *Critical Psychology: An Introduction.* Thousand Oaks: Sage.

Fromm, E. (1941). *Escape from Freedom.* New York: Henry Holt & Co.

———. (1955). *The Sane Society.* New York: Henry Holt & Co.

———. (1947). *Man for Himself.* New York: Holt, Rinehart, & Winston, Inc.

Geldard, R. (2000). *Remembering Heraclitus.* Lindisfarne Books.

Goffman, E. (1961). *Asylums: Essays on the Social Situation of the Mental Patients and Other Inmates.* New York: Doubleday.

———. (1963). *Stigma: Notes on the Management of Spoiled Identity.* New York: Simon and Schuster.

Hare-Hustin, R. & Marecek, J. (1997). "Abnormal and Clinical Psychology: The Politics of Madness." In D. Fox and I. Prilleltensky (eds.) *Critical Psychology: An Introduction.* Thousand Oaks: Sage.

Heisenberg, W. (1958). *Physics and Philosophy.* New York: Harper Torchbooks.

Jenkins, R. (1994). "Rethinking Ethnicity: Identity, Categorization, and Power." *Ethnic and Racial Studies* 17, 197–223.

Kropotkin, P. (1914). *Mutual Aid.* New York: Porter Sargent.

———. (1947). *Ethics: Origin and Development.* New York: Tudor.

Kuhn, T. (1970). *The Structure of Scientific Revolutions,* 3rd ed. Chicago: University of Chicago Press.

Laing, R. D. (1969). *The Divided Self.* New York: Pantheon.

———. (1967). *The Politics of Experience.* New York: Ballantine.

Lunn, E. (1973). *Prophet of Community: The Romantic Socialism of Gustav Landauer.* Berkeley, CA: University of California Press.

Lyons, D. (1979). *Rights.* Belmont: University of California Press.

Macy, J. (1991). *Mutual Causality in Buddhism and General Systems Theory: The Dharma of Natural Systems.* New York: SUNY Press.

Marcuse, H. (1966). *Eros and Civilization.* Boston: Beacon Press.

———. (1964). *One-Dimensional Man.* Boston: Beacon Press.

Merleau-Ponty, M. (1962). *Phenomenology of Perception.* C. Smith (trans.). New York: Humanities Press.

Nehemas, A. (1985). *Nietzsche: Life as Literature.* Cambridge, MA: Harvard University Press.

Nietzsche, F. (1967). *The Will to Power.* W. Kauffman & R. J. Hollingdale (trans.). New York: Vintage Books.

———. (1990). *Twilight of the Idols/The Anti-Christ*. R. J. Hollingdale (trans.). New York: Penguin.

———. (1989). *Beyond Good and Evil*. New York: Vintage Books.

Noth, W. (1990). *Handbook of Semiotics*. Bloomington: Indiana University Press.

Pfohl, S. (1994). *Images of Deviance and Social Control: A Sociological History*, 2nd ed. New York: McGraw-Hill.

Phillips, J. (2000). *Contested Knowledge: A Guide to Critical Theory*. New York: Zed Books Ltd.

Porter, E. & Gleick, J. (1990). *Nature's Chaos*. New York: Penguin.

Rychlak, J. (1981). *Introduction to Personality and Psychotherapy: A Theory-Construction Approach*, 2nd ed. Boston: Houghton Mifflin.

Sapir, E. (1921). *Language*. New York: Harcourt.

Saussure, F. (1916). *Course in General Linguistics*. W. Baskin (trans.). New York: McGraw-Hill.

Scheff, T. (2000). *Being Mentally Ill: A Sociological Theory*, 3rd ed. New York: Aldine de Gruyter.

Schopenhauer, A. (1970). *Essays and Aphorisms*. R. J. Hollingdale (trans.). New York: Penguin Books.

Shatz, M. (1972). *The Essential Works of Anarchism*. New York: Quadrangle Books.

Skinner, B. F. (1953). *Science and Human Behavior*. New York: Macmillan.

Slaton, C. (1991). Quantum Theory and Political Theory. In T. Becker (ed.), *Quantum Politics*. New York: Praeger.

Sylvan, R. (1993). "Anarchism." In R. Goodin and P. Pettit (eds.), *A Companion to Political Philosophy*. Cambridge, MA: Blackwell.

Szasz, T. (1961). *The Myth of Mental Illness*. New York: Hoeber-Harper.

———. (1970). *The Manufacture of Madness: A Comparative Study of the Inquisition and Mental Health Movement*. New York: Harper and Row.

———. (1978). *The Myth of Psychotherapy: Mental Healing as Religion, Rhetoric, and Repression*. New York: Doubleday.

———. (1997). *Insanity: The Idea and Its Consequences*. New York: Syracuse University Press.

Thorne, B. (1982). "Feminist Rethinking of the Family: An Overview." In B. Thorne (ed.), *Rethinking the Family*. New York: Longman.

Tifft, L. (1979). "The Coming Redefinitions of Crime: An Anarchist Perspective." *Social Problems* 26 (4), 392–402.

Tolstoy, L. (1990). "The Slavery of Our Time." In *Government Is Violence: Essays on Anarchism and Pacifism*. London: Phoenix Press.

Trigg, R. (2001). *Understanding Social Science,* 2nd ed. Malden, MA: Blackwell.

Waldron, J. (1993). "Rights." In R. Goodin and P. Pettit (eds.) *A Companion to Political Philosophy.* Cambridge, MA: Blackwell.

Wheelwright, P. (1974). Myth. In A. Preminger (ed.) *Princeton Encyclopedia of Poetry and Poetics.* Princeton: Princeton University Press.

Wilde, O. (1948). "The Soul of Man Under Socialism." In *Complete Works of Oscar Wilde.* Glasgow: Harper Collins.

Williams, C. R. (1999). "Inside the Outside and Outside the Inside: Negative Fusion from the Margins of Humanity." *Humanity and Society* 23 (1), 49–67.

———— & Arrigo, B. A. (2001a). *Law, Psychology, and Justice: Chaos Theory and the New (Dis)order.* New York: SUNY Press.

————. (2001b). "Anarchaos and Order: On the Emergence of Social Justice." *Theoretical Criminology* 5 (2), 223–252.

————. (2002). "Law, Psychology, and the 'New Sciences:' Rethinking Mental Illness and Dangerousness." *International Journal of Offender Therapy and Comparative Criminology* 46(1), 6–29.

Wolff, J. (1996). *An Introduction to Political Philosophy.* New York: Oxford University Press.

Woodcock, G. (1992). *Anarchism or Chaos.* Willimantic, CN: Lysander Books.

Zohar, D. & Marshall, I. (1994). *The Quantum Society: Mind, Physics, and a New Social Vision.* New York: William Morrow.

Chapter 3

A Critical Perspective on Freud's Theory of Parricide and Crime in General

Phillip C. H. Shon

OVERVIEW

Parricide is often thought to be a psychoanalytic crime, with motives that can be reduced to psychological variables. Consequently, social structure variables such as class, race, gender, and general rate of violence are thought to be irrelevant in explaining parricide. The psychoanalytic theory of parricide (and crime) is best illustrated in the work of Freud who always turns the analytical lens inward. In this chapter I argue that by doing so, he misses a rudimentary lesson in crime and punishment: what gets defined as a crime and who gets defined as a criminal is not determined by an already existing, immutable, independent law of nature, but is always a function of power. Crime—that is, what gets defined as one—is more appropriately linked to economics, politics, and law than it is to psychology. I argue that Freud has no theory of parricide in particular nor of crime in general. To substantiate the analysis, I explore the relevant psychoanalytic and empirical literature differentiating patricide and matricide.

INTRODUCTION

Parricide is a crime filled with tension on many levels. That tension can be witnessed foremost at the theoretical level: parricide has been—and still is—conceptualized exclusively as a psychodynamic crime (see Freud, 1945, 1914); that is, with motives that are deeply ingrained in the offender's unconscious. Consequently, social structural variables such as general rate of violence, weapon availability, and circumstances surrounding the event are thought to be irrelevant in explaining parricide. Recently, however, criminologists have argued that parricides are no different from ordinary homicides (Shon & Targonski, 2001). In other words, social factors that influence general rates of violence also affect rates of parricide. At the weapon level, parricide is filled with tension because the emotional logic behind patricide and matricide appears to be vastly different: the former bearing a striking resemblance to a crime of reason, the latter looking more like a crime of passion. In this chapter, I argue that Freud's theory of patricide cannot be empirically substantiated.

The psychoanalytic theory of parricide—and crime in general—is best illustrated in the work of Freud. Moreover, since Oedipus Rex and Freud (1914), the dominant research in this area has been conducted by psychiatrists, psychologists, and psychoanalysts who use limited clinical samples. However, in this chapter, by using recent findings from sociological studies of parricides based on the FBI's Supplementary Homicide Reports as data (Shon & Targonski, 2001), I show how Freud's theory of parricide is valid only within the set of assumptions he presupposed prior to any theoretical grounding and empirical validation. Moreover, Freud had to assume a rather simplistic view of crime, the criminal, and law in order for his theory of parricide and crime to work. By doing so, Freud missed a basic lesson in crime and punishment; that is, what gets defined as a crime and who gets defined as a criminal is not determined by an already existing, immutable, and independent law of nature, but is always a function of power. Thus, what gets defined as a crime is more fundamentally linked to social forces such as economics, politics, and law than it is to psychology. Consequently, I argue that Freud has no theory of parricide in particular nor of crime in general.

PRIOR WORK ON PARRICIDE

According to Freud, parricide is not only criminological, but it is also political, legal, and theological (Schoenfeld, 1992). Moreover, the crime is timeless and primal: everyone is guilty of the original murder. The beginning of Freud's (1914) theory of parricide centers on the concept of the Primal Horde and the Primal Father. The Primal Horde can be thought of as a fiction, a Hobbesian "state of nature" where life is "short, nasty, and brutish" and where individuals (men) compete with one another for scarce resources. Those scarce resources are, for Freud, sexual access to women: there is a jealous and violent father who keeps all the women (wives, daughters) for himself and drives away his sons and other males from his harem.

Carpetto (1984) writes that the father's harem represents his most important possession; namely, procreative powers. This is the primary motivation that propels the horde to have murderous wishes: the primal father sets up prohibitions and forbids incestuous sexual activity. "The boy wants to be in his father's place because he admires him and wants to be like him, and also because he wants to put him out of his way" (Freud, 1945, p. 4). Eventually, the ones who were forbidden from the father's lot (brothers, sons) banded together and "slew him," and "devoured their father and put an end to the patriarchal horde" (Freud, 1914, p. 18). After the murder, the Primal Horde falls into a period of rampant promiscuity (Carpetto, 1984) but, more significantly, since the ruler has been murdered, there is no one to keep the peace. Thus, the Primal Horde falls into social disorganization (Freud, 1914). Consequently, the horde realizes the need for another father figure, someone to watch over—govern—them, and enforce the laws. The horde's relationship to the primal father is marked by a severe tension: the father is loved and hated at the same time. He is hated for setting up the prohibitions, and loved because he represents the only means of true freedom available; that is, through the introduction of law. For Freud (1914, 1945), the function of such prohibitions (laws) is to guard against parricide and incest (Schoenfeld, 1992). In other words, the prohibitions maintain order.

For Freud, not only is this horror of incest and patricide at the heart of political theory, but it is also the origin of religion. Freud (1914, 1995) theo-rizes that the taboo against incest and patricide, along with the residual guilt from the original crime, necessitates the ritualistic sacrifice of a totem, a sym-bolic representation of the Primal Father, in animal form, which, in every cul-ture, cannot be killed. Through these ritualistic sacrifices—symbolic murder rather than literal sleighings—a society's taboo on patricide and incest is maintained.

This is the original context from which Freud's theory of parricide evolved. The themes are unmistakably clear: they are sexual, instinctual, and primal. It is from this starting point that Freud builds his theory of the Oedi-pal conflict. Freud's interpretation of *Oedipus Rex* is etched into the intellec-tual and popular history of our time. Maybe Freud understood the conflicting nature of desire and demand, the ego and the superego, and the individual and society; consequently, he had a theory of neurosis and parricide. But can Freud's theories be extended to real people in ordinary life situations, who are mired in the trivial, domestic, and sometimes not so frivolous vicissitudes of life, and not limited just to literary characters in hypothetical places? Would it be valid to infer a theory of crime, homicide in particular, from such a cre-ative theoretical imagination? To begin to answer these questions, I review the work that sociologists, criminologists, psychologists, psychiatrists, and psychoanalysts have advanced since Freud.

Parricides make up a small percentage (2–3%) of homicides in general (Heide, 1992; Weisman & Sharma, 1997). Compared to other types of homi-cides, such as intimate-partner and gang-motivated murders, parricides are rare occurrences. For instance, in Daly and Wilson's (1988) examination of Detroit Police homicide records in 1972, out of the 690 homicides, 11 cases were parricides. In the West of Scotland (1953–1974), Gilles (1976) came across 14 parricides out of a total of 307 murders. In Gudjonsson & Peturs-son's (1982) investigation of homicides in Iceland (1900–1979), there were 2 matricides out of a total of 45 homicides. In a frequently cited article on matricide, Green (1981) found that between 1968 and 1978, parricides accounted for 2–4 percent of all homicides in England (Broadmoor). In another frequently cited source, Sadoff (1971) found that 12 out of 122 homicide offenders who had been admitted to the Ontario Hospital had committed matricide. In Europe, parricides account for 2–5 percent of all homicides; in the United States, about 2 percent of all homicides (Weisman & Sharma, 1997); in Canada, about 6 percent (Millaud, Auclair, & Meunier, 1996).

There appears to be a general consensus in the parricide literature that its occurrence is not correlated with general levels of violence in society. For example, Weisman and Sharma (1997) assert that parricide rates are negatively correlated with the general rate of violent crime and the availability of handguns. Young (1993) also asserts that parricide rates are negatively correlated with the general rate of violent crime. In other words, when general rates of violence (including homicide) increase, parricides decrease or, at best, show little variation. That is because parricide, as a homicide event, is thought to differ in its emotional logic from "ordinary" homicides. This difference in affective and moral logic can be illustrated in the way homicide offenders are classified.

For example, there are two types of violent offenders: the "street criminal" and the "violent family offender" (Young, 1993, p. 171). Street criminals are those who engage in violence in a rational and calculated manner, motivated by instrumental gain. Robbery would be a prototypical example of the street criminal. Violent family offenders are not driven by monetary and material concerns. They are psychologically distressed and marked by rage (see also Katz, 1988). Since Young (1993) finds a negative correlation between parricide rates and general rates of violence, he concludes, "parricide cannot be understood by using general explanations of criminal violence" (p. 172). Thus, the steady rate of parricides and its stable proportionality in relation to general violence indicates that there are other dynamics at work. As such, a separate line of inquiry is often justified (i.e., psychodynamic). However, Marleau & Webanck's (1997) analysis of Canadian homicide data from 1962–1985 indicates a positive correlation between parricide rates and general violence rates. In other words, variables that affect general homicide also affect parricide. This appears to be the exception.

The arguments put forth by renown homicide researchers such as Richard and Carolyn Block would also seem to buttress the claim made by psychoanalysts and psychiatrists; namely, that parricides are psychodynamic, not sociological, crimes. Richard Block (1976) analyzed the Chicago Homicide Data using the "expressive" versus "instrumental homicide syndrome" distinction. He concluded that "familial killings do not increase as rapidly as homicides in general" (p. 2). In his analysis, however, Block did not specify parricide cases per se; rather, victim-offender relationships within the family were merely coded as familial killings (Block, 1976). After examining the data for twenty-five years up to 1989, the Blocks again reiterated a position that supported findings in psychodynamic research: intrafamilial expressive homicides accounted for only 4 percent of homicides in general (C. Block & R. Block, 1991; R. Block & C. Block, 1992).

Harlan's (1950) study of 500 homicide cases in Jefferson County, Alabama demonstrated that close to 10 percent of homicides are "Type I" categories or the killing of a family member. In the three examples he uses to illustrate the nature of family killings, he relies on the case of patricide and fratricide. Since family killings are not restricted to parricides in Harlan's study, we could speculate that instances of parricide would have to be lower than 10 percent. Both Block and Harlan's nonspecific data on familial killings can be reviewed in light of the discussed material on parricide rates. Since the literature on parricide rates across countries indicates that these figures remain consistently low, and since Block and Harlan's data include parricide in their all-encompassing family violence rate, it is reasonable to infer that their parricide rates should resemble the ones reported by Weisman & Sharma (1997) and Millaud et al. (1996), provided parricide cases could be isolated.

Shon & Targonski (2001) recently used data from the FBI's Supplementary Homicide Reports (SHR) to examine the trends in parricides in the United States. Unlike previous studies of parricide which used limited samples from clinical psychiatric reports and works of fiction, they relied on the SHR because it was one of the most reliable, comprehensive, and up to date means available for homicide research. To illustrate, with each instance of homicide, data are collected on the weapon used, the circumstances surrounding the offense, the victim-offender relationship, and the race and sex of both the victim(s) and offender(s).

Of the 439,947 homicides recorded between 1976 and 1998, 7,176 (1.6%) were parricides. Shon & Targonski (2001) selected parricides based on the variable "relationship of victim to offender" being coded as father, mother, stepfather, or stepmother. Using this rich, extensive dataset, they were able to examine parricide on a national basis. Shon & Targonski's (2001) purpose was to evaluate trends over time and see how they compared to the findings and theories based on studies with small samples. They were concerned with several elements of parricide that could be discerned from the SHR, including gender, weapon, age of offenders and victims. Circumstance and race were not examined because of the high amount of missing or ambiguous data.[1] In addition, they did not examine race because, according to the logic of psychoanalysis, parricide is an exclusively psychodynamic crime. Consequently, and in accordance with the assumptions presupposed by psychodynamically oriented researchers, social variables such as race and class would not have been significant for the analysis.

Patricide

Men are generally victims and offenders in violent crimes, including homicides. When gender is further disaggregated, the offenders are usually young, poor, live in depressed areas of the city, and are likely to be members of the minority (Short, 1997; Block, 1976; Harlan, 1950; Hawkins, 1995; West, 1968). Patricide also follows the patterns of general homicides. Whether it is the murder of one's father or mother, the gender of the offender is uniformly distributed: they are almost always likely to be male. Parricide offenders were either all men or nearly all men in prior clinical studies with samples greater than ten (see Campion et al., 1985; Weisman & Sharma, 1997; Sadoff, 1971; Mohr & McNight, 1971), less than ten (Scherl & Mack,1966; Maas, Prakash, Hollender & Regan, 1984), and even among the mentally ill (Millaud et al., 1996).

Shon & Targonski (2001) also found that young males were responsible for a disproportionate number of patricides. Moreover, there was also an uncanny distribution of age in the men who killed. In male offender patricides, the offenders were most likely to be in their adolescence and late adolescence. That is, patricides peaked when the offenders were in their teenage years (14–17). Fathers were at the greatest risk of being killed by their sons when they were in their early forties. When teenagers reached their twentieth birthday, patricides dramatically declined. Shon & Targonski (2001) referred to this near vertical increase in adolescent offender murders as the *"No, dad, what about you?" Syndrome.*

One of the most commonly found factors associated with patricide is family history of violence (Millaud et al., 1996). The pervasiveness of such abuse is well documented in clinical reports (Campion et al., 1985; Maas et al., 1984; Raizen, 1960; Sadoff, 1971; Scherl & Mack, 1966; Tanay, 1975; see also Heide, 1996, 1992). Patricides are the consequences of young males who are the victims of physical, psychological, verbal, and sexual abuse, or who witness these events, but then finally "stand up" to their despotic and abusive fathers. Thus, reminiscent of social misfits in the movie *Breakfast Club*, or lyrics in a *Twisted Sister* song, the adolescent offender, during one of the recurrent abusive episodes, decides "we're not gonna take it anymore" and proclaims his freedom from the father's tyranny, oppression, and reign of terror. The offender's liberation, however, results in the father's demise. The term "we" is used to refer to the offender's perspective. Often the father is not only abusive toward the subject but also to the rest of the family, particularly the subject's mother, the victim's wife. Thus, when offenders kill in those situations, they are proclaiming their own independence and that of others whom they have liberated through their murderous actions.

In terms of weapon usage, patricides are, again, no different from other types of general homicides in that they are committed with firearms. More specifically, fathers are murdered with handguns and shotguns and rifles. This finding may be attributable to the gross discrepancy in physical strength. Young teenage offenders, both male and female, cannot expect to overpower their fathers; hence, firearms would be a rational choice. To summarize male offender patricides I note the following: most boys kill their fathers in an all-out, warlike, *blitzkrieg* manner, during their teenage years, with firearms. Boys rarely kill their fathers after they have passed into adulthood.

MATRICIDE

Males do not kill their mothers as much as they prefer to kill their fathers. When offenders do kill their mothers, they are likely to occur when the offender is in his late teens and the mother in her early forties. However, the peak is not nearly as dramatic as it is for male offender patricides. That is, male offender patricides are marked by sharp upsurges in the offender's adolescence; male offender matricides, however, are a protracted affair. They also peak when the male offender is seventeen, but they are the pinnacle of a closely knit cluster; that is, there is no significant difference in the number of matricides committed by fifteen, sixteen, seventeen, eighteen, and nineteen year olds. Although male offender matricides decline as offenders age, we see this similar type of cluster formation occurring until the offenders reach the age of fifty. Moreover, offenders who are older than fifty are more likely to kill their mothers than their fathers. In other words, male offender matricides are not all-out wars like male offender patricides with a clear point of invasion and retreat. Instead, they are a series of long, drawn-out battles and skirmishes akin to guerilla warfare.

In terms of weapon usage, male offender matricides differ from male offender patricides and general homicides. In Green's (1981) study of matricide by sons, stabbing and battering accounted for 62 percent of the cases; in Millaud et al.'s (1996) study of parricide, both mothers and fathers were killed equally with a knife—58 percent of the cases. If the weapons data were recoded in the latter study with blunt objects and personal weapons included as a contact method, along with knives, then 90 percent of the parricides in their study would have been committed with weapons other than a firearm. Stabbing and beating accounted for 66 percent of parricide cases and 68 percent of attempted parricide cases in Weisman & Sharma's (1997) study. Even in prior clinical research, with limited samples, knives seem to be a common method of murder.

Shon & Targonski (2001) also found that knives were used more in matricides. Their usage actually outnumbered reliance on handguns. Moreover, other contact methods such as blunt objects and personal weapons roughly equaled long-gun usage. There is a plausible explanation for this finding:

generally speaking, mothers are physically weaker than fathers. Consequently, the level of violence required to accomplish the murder is not as lethal. Thus, offenders can use a blunt object or a knife and still reasonably expect to do fatal damage, which is not the case for the killing of fathers.

Clinicians have captured a noteworthy point about matricides, but they have erred in another. In Green's (1981) study, 12 percent of matricides were committed with firearms while only one subject used a firearm in Millaud et al.'s (1996) study. Firearms accounted for 24 percent of successful parricides and 16 percent of attempted parricides in Weisman & Sharma's (1997) forensic analysis of parricides and attempted parricides. However, Shon & Targonski (2001) found that firearms were responsible for the bulk of parricides in the United States; hence, the recent findings by Shon & Targonski (2001) provide empirical evidence that contradicts prior findings. Generally speaking, when killing parents the use of firearms is a primary, not secondary, method of murder, contrary to what prior clinically animated studies would lead us to believe. In addition, while knives are not used as much as firearms overall in parricide cases (they are in instances of matricide), their symbolic significance in relation to the crime warrants an explanation. So, too, does the act of stabbing, especially since it is the preferred means to inflict death by matricide offenders.

Why are knives and the use of other edged or bladed instruments employed in the killing of mothers or maternal surrogates? Nonfirearms utilized in the act of parricide and the manner in which death is caused are pertinent because they reveal the emotional logic of offenders. The parricidal crime scene has been characterized as an "overkill" (Weisman & Sharma, 1997). This description refers to the presence of supererogatory force or vigor that is more (or greater) than what is required to kill. Stabbing one's mother or father 100 times, eviscerating their entrails, or severing the genitals of one's parents after they have been killed, is a bit strange; emptying a twelve-round magazine on a parent, and then reloading another and finishing that off, is, literally, overdoing it. In other words, the killing continues even after the victim is dead. Similarly, beating one's mother to death with a frying pan until gray matter oozes from her head, or asphyxiating her with a plastic shopping bag, then posing her in a lewd and obscene way for investigators to view, is not a "typical" murder. In these "overkill" cases merely murdering one's parents cannot be the primary objective; however, something else is.

The "overkill" of victims is a trademark of lust murderers (Douglas & Olshaker, 1995). Elsewhere (Shon, 1998), I have argued that knives are significant to killers for their role in transcendence. For example, in Indian religions, the human body is seen as a microcosm of the cosmos; each anatomical part is assimilated into folk homologies, thereby providing equivalent images (i.e., universe, house, body) as being capable of making passage to another world possible. In religious texts, two images pervade the notion of transcendence of the human condition: flight and breaking of the roof. In order to pass from one mode of being to another, to bring about a "veritable ontological mutation," this passage is necessary (Eliade, 1957). In my previous research in this area, I argued that postmortem mutilation and evisceration of sexual parts are meaningful to lust killers precisely for such existential and phenomenological reasons: stabbing is not only an expression of rage, but also the beginning of an ontological mutation, an attempt to transcend the profanity of one's existence (Shon, 1998).

However, there may be a practical reason why knives are commonly used in matricides, without getting overly psychoanalytical or metaphysical. To understand the dynamics that unfold in the murder, we need to consider the situational exigencies or circumstances in which parricides occur. Since matricides have a "sexualized" component to them, Shon & Targonski (2001) initially hypothesized that the motive would be sexual; that is, somehow related to a lover's triangles or a lover's disputes. However, that was not the case. Moreover, contrary to popular opinion, parricides committed in the course of another felony (robbery) were quite low and stable. Similar to ordinary homicides, parricides began as arguments about money, property, and other trivial things (see Wolfgang, 1958). But this adds little to our understanding of parricide. Again, the question is why are knives often preferred? Why are victims stabbed 100 times rather than shot once in the head? Knives could be the weapon of choice in matricides because of where the weapon originates. In other words, an argument begins in the kitchen, insulting language is exchanged, one party begins to shove the other, and suddenly one of the parties picks up the kitchen knife that was on the cutting board. If we are able to pinpoint the location of the crime, then a more detailed narrative can be constructed. However, such detailed information is not available to academic researchers using coded homicide data sets. This type of information is available only to detectives and other crime scene technicians. In other words, only those who are there can tell us what they saw. So how then do we account for the choice of weapon?

THE TENSION IN FREUD AND POST-FREUDIAN PSYCHOANALYSIS

Parricide appears to be a crime of passion and a crime of reason. More significantly, it is not an incidental and unwitting crime, as told by Sophocles. Parricides are crimes in which offenders exercise their creativity, skill, and talent. It is creative in that, like other homicides, we see a whole gamut of methods used to kill parents—some very logical, some tinted with elements of unexplainable rage, and some just plain odd. For example, if a fourteen-year-old boy or girl wants to do away with his or her 300-pound, ex-marine,

Desert Storm–veteran father, a blunt object such as a frying pan, kitchen knife, or golf club would be a poor weapon choice. However, a handgun is not a poor choice. It is easy to conceal, carry, point, and shoot. A shotgun, a rifle, or any other type of long-gun, would work just as well. But the point is that the parricide offender has to arrive at that conclusion. This takes forethought, calculation, and the ability to think rationally.

Firearms are either used in an instrumental fashion almost like an assassination attempt, or as the result of chance and luck. For example, in Heide's (1992) description of the Terry Adams case, the teenage offender is shoved into the father's closet after a brief struggle, and he incidentally picks up a long-gun and kills both parents. In addition to firearms, knives, and blunt objects, we see a diverse range of weapons used in parricides. Parents are poisoned, drugged, and blown up with explosives; they are also set on fire, asphyxiated, strangled, drowned, and beaten to death with the offender's own hands and feet. It does not take much expertise to douse a sleeping parent with gasoline and light a match, but rigging the car so that it explodes on ignition requires certain technical skill and expertise.

Overall, weapons used in parricides can be divided into two categories: firearms and nonfirearms. The latter needs a bit more qualification. Firearms can be used from a distance: murder can be successfully executed without coming into direct contact with the victim; however, with knives, blunt objects, hands and feet, strangulation, drowning, and asphyxiation, the offender must have some intimate contact with the victim. Simply put, parricides are far more dynamic and lively than an offender who unwittingly murders his father at the crossroads of some obscure traffic stop. This particular tale of murder looks more like an instance of road rage than anything else.

The discrepancy between the narrative of a fictitious parricide and actual cases is not the only instance of tension. Tension can be seen at the theoretical, circumstantial, and weapon level. At the theoretical level it is filled with tension because the two main theories that seek to explain it hold diametrically opposing presuppositions about parricide and crime in general. Parricide is fraught with tension at the circumstantial level because its situational details do not differ all that much from contexts in which ordinary homicides occur; that is, parricide occurs in the course of general domestic arguments. Finally, it is fraught with tension at the weapon level because the choice of weapon in patricides is consistent with a structured, calculated, and instrumental way in which the murder unfolds, while in matricides it appears impulsive, passionate, and imbued with sheer unbridled rage. How do we reconcile the apparent tension between the psychodynamic aspects of the crime (choice of weapon, manner of death), and the finding that other features of the crime seem to indicate a structural explanation (i.e., rationality in the choice of firearms, circumstances surrounding the offense)?

That apparent tension between theory and data in parricides appears to be substantially less in matricides. In clinical reports, there appears to be a consensus that matricides are committed by male adults who are usually diagnosed with mental illness (see Campion et al., 1985; Green, 1981; Millaud et al., 1996). According to Campion et al. (1985) schizophrenic matricides should be understood as a "reaction to a fantasy of physical or psychological annihilation, a desperate, violent act of self preservation to separate from the mother" (p. 315). The fact of the adult male offender's mental illness and the decision to wean himself from the maternal bond can be illustrated, ironically enough, in a classic Greek tragedy.

Orestes' father is murdered by his mother Clytemenstra and her illicit lover. Orestes is rescued by his sister Electra and sent away to live far from his mother and her paramour. When he returns to his home as a man, he has already made a vow to the gods that he will take vengeance on his father's behalf by killing his seductress mother. When his mother discovers Orestes' intentions, she attempts to change his mind by appealing to his maternal bond: "here often your head lay in sleep, while your soft mouth sucked from me the good milk that gave you life and strength" (in Fingarette, 1963, p. 454).

Put in the terms of Jacques Lacan (1977), a major Freudian revisionist, the mother invokes her function as the thing to reposition Orestes' subjectivity by activating imagoes of the "Real." In a Freudian sense, the Real is the realm of unbridled sexuality, the blissful state of sexual satisfaction (Samuels, 1993), or what Lacan (1977) aptly calls *jouissance* (i.e., that which is beyond or in excess of desire). The Real is the obstacle that each subject must negotiate; it is the source of anxiety in that it is without name or language and remains undifferentiated. Although its presence makes itself known, it exists absent a vocabulary to call its own. In this way, it is alienated from the social convention of language, culture and, hence, all recognition. Inevitably and unmistakably, this leads to the loss of identity and the absence of selfhood. The Real is primordial and without boundaries. Consequently, the threat of disintegration and dissolution are ever present. Simply put, the Real is the loss of reality and the territorial domain of psychosis.

This is the psychological disintegration that Orestes is trying to overcome. By seeking revenge against his mother, Orestes has successfully identified with the father and is on the verge of weaning himself from the tyrannical maternal bond: he is ready to assume his desire and fully integrate himself into the Symbolic—the sphere of culture, language, and symbol. For Lacan (1977), the Symbolic is, in a Durkheimean and Jungian sense, collective (Michelman, 1996); it is the "discourse of the Other" (Dor, 1997). Simply put, when Orestes rejects his mother and identifies with the father, he is assuming the role of a social being, identifying with the law of the father and the father's (i.e., culture's) social order. Hence, he is ready to become a subject, an individual, in his own right, rather than to act as a vassal (i.e., an infant) to his mother's desires.

In Orestes' case, the theme of liberation, freedom, growth, and maturity can be clearly discerned. Not only is Orestes a purifier, he is also a destroyer and a defender of all that is sacred. He has accepted his responsibility without self-deceit and although initially hesitant, he assumes his duty and breaks free from the shackles of his mother. His matricide can be viewed as a rejection of the mother. Indeed, it confirms and validates his proclamation that he has no need of the breast since he has the phallus (Friedman & Gassel, 1951). This Orestesian pattern in matricides is also common in juvenile matricides. Consider the following account:

> When I was 15 she began to act unseemly for a mother. She would disrobe in front of me in the living room. The first time this happened, I said to my father: "what the hell is that woman doing!" My father told her to go to the bedroom if she wanted to disrobe. She answered: "he's my son. I guess I can take my clothes off in front of him if I want to!" Do you know that at the age of 15 she still wanted to bathe me? . . . She would kiss me as a mother shouldn't kiss a son . . . She came to my apartment alone; she made advances of trying to draw me to the couch while kissing me. I repulsed her. (Raizen, 1960, pp. 279–281)

The mother's sexual gestures are overt and when the subject turns to the father, he asserts his paternal authority. Yet, the mother takes a possessive attitude toward her son; she merely sees him as an object of her desire, her lacking the phallus. But this sentiment is not shared by the male subject. The boy's choice of the word *woman* offers a glimpse of the subject's psychic organization. The subject has already established himself as transcendent to the mother. He has identified with the father and asserted the possession of the phallus. The mother, however, does not agree. She attempts to seduce the son, to make him the substance and source of her desire. By doing so, the mother forcefully attempts to take the son from the Symbolic to the Real.

No mentally healthy individual would want to regress to the Real because it is the realm of psychosis (Lee, 1990). By adolescence, the journey from the Real to the Imaginary to the Symbolic already has been completed. When the mother attempts to undermine the subject-hood of the individual, the boy has to resist and guard against the loss of self to the anxiety producing primordial Real. By rejecting the regression into the Real and by taking a stand in defense of subjectivity and selfhood, the matricide conforms with his desire; that is, the desire to be recognized by the Other (Lacan, 1977). In this instance, the Other is not the object of the boy's first love (the typical scenario in Lacanian psychoanalytic sexual identity) but, instead, the realm of the Symbolic is. This is the substitution of one stabilizing master signifier (i.e., one expression of identity fulfillment) with another that is illusory.

In this sense, matricide is heroic because it establishes a new, emancipatory relation between the boy and the world. By rejecting the tyrannical mother, the subject assumes his individuated position as a social being, meaningfully and healthily connected to others. The paradox and irony of matricide stem from the fact that achieving this fully functioning state of identity fulfillment as a human being entails murdering the mother; the very person who recognized the boy as a fully vital subject in the first place. Thus, there is in matricide not only an element of self-preservation against the engulfing maternal bond, but also a defense of an emerging self. This motive is also found in adult matricides where the offenders are mentally ill.

Consider the following vignette.

> Mr. A, a 24 year old white man, was an only child who lived with his mother. He described his mother as "a sadist . . . she kept torturing me, fed me rancid food, stole my clothes." Mr. A had eight hospitalizations in the three years before the matricide; he had recurrent hallucinations, delusions, and disorganized thought. He . . . attempted suicide to escape his mother's "persecution." The matricide occurred when his mother began to scratch Mr. A during an argument. He beat her and strangled her to death with extreme violence in her bedroom. (Campion et al., 1985, p. 314)

According to Samuels (1993), it is the overpresence of the motherly gaze in the intimate exchange between the mother and the infant that serves as the genesis of delusional persecution understood as mental illness. The desire of the subject is constrained by the superego or the Symbolic code, while the instinctual drives toward *jouissance* are dominated by the Real, or the Id (Lacan, 1977). The subject is situated in a valley of conflicting desires; however, unlike the adolescent hero of matricide, these adult subjects have introjected (i.e., internalized) their impulses into their Imaginary (i.e., fantasy constructions).

The Imaginary provides illusory constructions of wholeness and completeness; it is here that the ego begins to develop (Lacan, 1977). The infant has no control of its bodily functions and is completely dependent on others for the satisfaction of its demands. Experiencing the world in this way, the infant-child assumes, falsely, that this is how his or her identity is constituted. In other words, the child takes itself for what it is not (Lacan, 1977). This misplaced identity has serious implications for one's subjectivity. The mentally ill adult male matricide offender, caught between the regressive intentionality of the mother who wishes to objectify the subject as a phallus and the Symbolic Order's exertion of its influence on the adult male, turns against himself. Indeed, rather than killing the mother, he attempts to kill himself, as clinical studies report. Clinical data also seem to support the notion that in schizophrenic matricides, the crime is understood as a "reaction to a fantasy of physical or psychological annihilation; a desperate, violent act of self assertion to separate from the mother" (Campion et al., 1985, p. 315).

The motive in adolescent and adult matricides does not appear to be radically different. The adolescent matricide offender fears regressing into the Real; this fear evokes a defense of subjectivity. The fear in the adult matricide offender lapses into the Imaginary, providing false imagoes of fulfillment. The fact that most offenders in the latter category have attempted suicide and have had delusions indicates that a part of their being has introjected their aggressivity. Thus, as I have asserted elsewhere (Shon, 1999), subjects of adult matricide lead lives of "self deception." "They . . . collude with themselves in deceiving their own desire and . . . pa[y] the ultimate price in subjectivity: they [are] castrated from being and [lead] an inauthentic existence" (Shon, 1999, p. 268). It is only when they assume their desire for their autonomy, individuation, separateness from the (maternal) tyrannical bond and unity with the Symbolic, that they become heroes. It is in this context, then, that adult matricides are a long-delayed defense of subjectivity.

The noteworthy theoretical point regarding matricide is the notion of delayed defense. The recent findings by Shon & Targonski (2001) suggest that the affective logic of matricides is different from patricides. In patricides, adolescent male offenders in their late teen years kill their fathers in a *blitzkrieg*-like manner. In matricides, the male offenders continue killing their mothers well into their middle-age years. Thus, what the clinicians have been asserting all these years does seem to be corroborated by empirical data. The clusterlike formation in the age of men who kill their mothers does resemble a protracted battle. And, as I have argued previously (Shon, 1999), that battle is within the men themselves: mental illness results from accepting illusory maternal imagoes rather than asserting one's freedom from the breast and proclaiming one's phallus. Since the men fight themselves as much as they do their mothers, the clusterlike distribution of age in the men who kill resembles guerrilla warfare rather than a full-blown battle. Thus, when distinguishing the two forms that parricide takes, I note that in patricides male offenders fight one enemy (i.e., the father); however, in matricides male offenders fight two enemies (i.e., the mother and the self).

The tension in psychoanalytic theory (Freudian) on the issue of parricide is more salient in patricides. Recall that for Freud (1945) patricide is the original crime that threatens the social and political order. And the underlying motive is sexual. If Freud's theory is correct, the crime scene and the situational and circumstantial characteristics of the crime should reflect this. The following excerpt taken from a fictional case represents a candidate match for Freud's Oedipal explanation:

> Oskar's dream of possessing Maria comes to a crashing conclusion when he discovers that his father is having coitus with her . . . [Oskar] ferociously climbs on the father's back while the father is having intercourse with Maria. (Marill, 1991, p. 549)

The preceding passage is a scene from the movie, *The Tin Drum*. The main character is Oskar, a sixteen-year-old boy, trapped in the body of a three year old. He has thrown himself down a flight of stairs after witnessing the perversions of the adult world. After his mother passes away, his father hires a maid, Maria. She is also a teenager and develops a fondness for Oskar: she takes care of him, becomes his girlfriend, a quasi-sister, and a maternal figure (Marill, 1991). The cited passage is the discovery that Maria is having sex with his father, too.

This excerpt would be a textbook illustration of male sexual jealousy and Oedipal conflict. Oskar's behavior would not only support Freud's theory, but sociobiological explanations as well (Daly & Wilson, 1988). However, another tension arises when prototypical scenarios of patricide are examined. Consider the following:

> On Sunday afternoon, the victim (male, age 46) was killed in his home by a single shotgun blast at close range. The killer (male, age 15) was the victim's son. All the circumstances were familiar to the investigating police. The victim, employed as a sandblaster, had a criminal record that included two convictions for assault. The home was a scene of recurring violence in which the victim had assaulted his wife and sons, had shot at his wife in the past. On the fatal Sunday, the victim was drunk, berating his wife as a "bitch" and a "whore," and beating her, when their son acted to terminate the long history of abuse. (Daly & Wilson, 1988, p. 98)

The details of the above vignette support several aspects of prior research. The ages of the offender and victim, the weapon used, and the circumstances (dispute) are consistent with Shon & Targonski's (2001) recent findings. Furthermore, the father not only abuses alcohol, but he also physically abuses his family members. However, there is nothing in the details that would lead one to believe that the crime was, even remotely, sexually motivated. To resolve this apparent deficiency, two interpretations are possible. One view rejects the claim that the crime was sexual in nature; the other endorses this claim.

In the first instance, these types of domestic argument-turned-patricide cases could be labeled as nonsexual in nature; however, this characterization undermines Freud's theory of patricide. In order to support Freud's theory of patricide, it is necessary to show that the son's behavior was motivated by sexual jealousy. But again, there is nothing in the situational characteristics of the crime that provides justification for this assumption, unless violence itself is somehow equated with sex.

In the second instance, this scenario could be labeled as sexual in nature. Interestingly, this is precisely the psychoanalytic interpretation that Bunker (1944) formulates in his analysis of matricides in myth and legends. He literally equates violence with sex. Thus, when Hamlet's ghost father commands him to avenge his death, "but never thrust sword through mother's heart," Bunker (1944) reasons that the son, Hamlet, should not engage in sexual intercourse with his mother. Again, if the initial premise concerning the equivalent link between violence and sex is accepted, Bunker's conclusion, as applied to the vignette above, is valid. Intuitively, however, the father's abuse of alcohol and his abuse toward his wife and family would lead us to look away from Freud's theory of patricide in adolescent cases, as supported by prior research.

Discussion and Conclusion: Relieving the Tension in Freud

Freud was not a criminologist, but his psychoanalytic theories of crime can be inferred from his general theory of human behavior (Bohm, 2001). However, there are times when Freud does explicitly talk about the criminal. For example, Freud (1945, p. 1) writes that "[t]wo traits are essential in the criminal: boundless egoism and a strong destructive impulse. Common to both of these, and a necessary condition for their expression, is the absence of love, the lack of an emotional valuation of human objects." Thus, according to Freud, being a criminal means that two traits must be present and another, cunningly slipped in as a medium, must be absent. He precedes each trait with a modifier and the way he uses them (i.e., "boundless" and "strong," respectively), places a near immovable constraint on those features. However, these modifiers are anything but set in stone; they are actually interchangeable. If the two traits (i.e., egoism and impulse) are absent, there would be no need for the medium (i.e., love) to express itself since it would already exist. In other words, the two things absent that are "essential" in the criminal are boundless love and strong emotional attachment to objects.

Freud has to import the two traits (i.e., ego and impulse) from some magical place and then develop his theory or else it will never work. These two assumptions—that we are instinctively driven by a principle of self-interest and possess an inherent capacity to destroy (e.g., rape, rob, murder)—are put in place, a priori. Without these two assumptions, his theory of crime, much less of human nature, cannot make sense. Hence, what appears to be an "essential," inevitable, natural, and "necessary" condition of being human is assumed. This presupposition is inserted arbitrarily and theoretically by Freud as the psychological, mental, and internal processes that subjects undergo when in fact the only thing psychological about his theory are his own machinations on the matter.

By tastefully and selectively borrowing words more commonly reserved for biology and theology to explain criminology, there is a particular view of crime and criminals that Freud must necessarily reject. In short, criminals are not produced in a sociological sense; however, when they are created, they are, in a psychoanalytic sense, formed early in life as a consequence of "repression of the hatred of the father in the Oedipus Complex" (Freud, 1945, p. 4). We see, then, that Freud always turns the analytical lens inward. However, by doing so, he misses a rudimentary lesson in crime and punishment: *What gets defined as a crime and who gets defined as a criminal is not determined by an already existing, immutable, independent law of nature, but is always a function of power.* Indeed, what gets defined as crime is more appropriately linked to economics, politics, law, and social forces than it is to psychology (e.g., Foucault, 1977; Garland, 1993; Henry & Milovanovic, 1991, 1996). This notwithstanding, clinical psychologists, psychiatrists, and psychoanalysts continue to rely on "internal" and "essential" concepts, though they have somewhat relaxed the dogmatic precepts of Freud. This position is best represented by Frederic Wertham, who is often cited and regarded as the authority on parricide since Freud.

Wertham does not borrow Freud's vocabulary of "boundless egoism" and "strong destructive impulse." Instead, he has his own expression: "catathymic." By this he means that the killing of parents is the "result of a building up of unconscious tension due to external situational pressure" (Sadoff, 1971, p. 65). By admitting to the impact of exogenous variables influencing a subject to kill, notwithstanding the essential, instinctual, and unconscious impulses to do so, Wertham and subsequent clinicians open the door to the logical conclusion that external or outward factors help explain crime. Indeed, Wertham's use of the phrase "situational pressure" is another way of implicating the circumstances of the crime. Hence, for example, during a destructive encounter in the kitchen, a verbal dispute ignites, it turns into a heated argument, one participant begins to push the other, one person grabs a knife left on the kitchen table and repeatedly stabs the other. These types of situational pressures are common not only in "catathymic violence," but also in ordinary homicides motivated by domestic arguments.

What is situational may appear to be relevant only to the immediacies of the ensuing event, but it is also influenced by social forces. Nowhere is this more poignantly illustrated than in the choice of weapon. Parricide offenders, most of whom are juveniles, kill with firearms and the crucial link between juveniles and deaths by firearm is their availability (e.g., Blumstein & Cork, 1996; Zimring, 1996). The intimate relationship between adolescent parricide offenders and firearms points to two gross contradictions in Wertham's use of "catathymic," much like the way Freud uses "boundless egoism" and "strong destructive tendencies." In the first place, catathymic violence actually means situational violence but then this would rob psychology of its "internal" bite. In the second place, catathymic really means what it implies: unconscious (i.e., internal) tension. However, in this context, the two words he uses in the very definition (external, situational) would lose their significance and have no place in the sentence as they would be robbed of their meaning. Clearly, Wertham's definition of catathymic is fraught with tension and uncertainty. Much like Freud before him, Wertham may have had a theory of neurosis, but he simply did not have a bona fide theory of crime, including homicide in general and parricide in particular.

Parricide is not a crime committed by fictitious characters in an imaginary place. It is committed by real people, during the course of real happenings, in real life. As a homicide event, it is not one crime but many (Block & Block, 1992). Put differently, homicide is not a unidimensional event; rather, it is a crime with a "constellation of related characteristics" along with "sibling offenses" (Block & Block, 1992, p. 3). Sibling offenses refer to those crimes in which fatal outcomes did not occur. This view presents a unique understanding of the homicide situation since it brings exogenous variables (chance, luck) into the explanation. Thus, the "external" and "situational pressures" that Wertham relies on can be summed up in one sentence: "the loser of the confrontation is the person who dies; the 'winner' becomes the offender" (Block & Block, 1992, p. 4).

The homicide syndrome perspective suggests that there is nothing inert about the interactional properties of homicides; rather, it is a concatenation of events, linked in time, space, and history. Maltz (1998) captures the sequential nature of homicide when he notes that homicide is the fatal outcome of other crimes. For instance, child abuse turned deadly is infanticide, robbery turned lethal is a felony homicide, and domestic abuse turned fatal is the murder of an intimate. This line of reasoning inevitably leads us to ask, What precedes parricide? The literature on this point is quite unequivocal: abuse. But just as all child abuse cases do not become acts of infanticide and just as all cases of robbery do not become acts of felony homicide, all instances of parental abuse do not result in acts of parricide. Admittedly, when delving through clinical reports and life histories of parricide offenders, some of the insights of psychoanalysts seem pertinent and make sense (e.g., the explanation for stabbing especially in cases of matricide). However, when the totality of parricides (i.e., the total number of occurrences, trends over time, context, age, and gender) are matched against the total number of homicides in general and intimate-partner homicides in particular, the former strongly resembles the latter (Shon & Targonski, 2001). Furthermore, the role of firearms in parricide cases suggests that they are linked to the overall pattern of violence in society and not to a struggle between one's ego and superego.

DETERMINISM, PSYCHOANALYSIS, AND PARRICIDE

There is one final interpretation that psychoanalytically oriented researchers could make to undermine sociological accounts of homicides. In short, they could turn an ontological discussion of parricide into a deterministic and volitional one. In other words, similar to Freud (1945), they could argue for the existence of impulses, but contrary to Freud (1945), deny these impulses their inherent and biological basis. Instead, psychoanalysts and other mental health clinicians could introduce the concept of voluntary action (i.e., free will or control). In this conceptual model, they would need to compare parricide offenders with other homicide and violent offenders and test the control of impulses for the respective groups. If parricide offenders tested higher for poor impulse control than other violent offenders, the deterministic/volitional thesis would obtain.

Previous research has conceptualized parricide offenders as individuals lacking self-control (Sadoff, 1971). To test the theory, Corder, Ball, Haizlip, Rollins, & Beaumont's (1976) chose 10 subjects charged with: (1) parricide; (2) murdering a close relative or acquaintance; or (3) murdering a stranger. They then compared the ten cases in each group against one another to assess which group had better impulse control. On each of the measures utilized, more parricide offenders had abusive and maladjusted parents than the other violent offenders assessed in the study. For example, 7 out of 10 subjects reported having been abused by their parent(s), 7 out of 10 subjects reported having parents who abused alcohol or suffered from mental illness, 5 out of the 10 parricide subjects reported having fathers who were abusive toward the subject's mother, 6 out of 10 subjects reported a home marked by social disorganization (i.e., parental marital conflict and neglect), 6 out of 10 subjects reported being overly attached to their mothers. Simply put, the parricide offenders had every reason to become deviant and criminal: they experienced a dysfunctional upbringing, elevated rates of social disorganization, and poor social networks.

However, when the parricide offenders were measured against the subjects in the other two groups, subjects who murdered strangers or close relatives scored higher on the poor impulse control measure. In other words, subjects who killed their parents had better control of their impulses. Thus, based on this study, the deterministic/volitional thesis that clinical researchers could put forth as a psychoanalytic explanation for the crime of parricide did not prevail. Once again, it appears that efforts to look inward at the internal workings of the individual, and then to use this logic as both conceptual and empirical justification to interpret the crime of parricide, is simply inadequate.

The fact that the parricide offenders in the Sadoff (1971) study scored lower on impulse measures than their homicide offending counterparts indicates that, to some degree, the crime was not precipitously committed. Simply stated, parricide offenders just do not kill their fathers in a psychotic, irrational, and irresponsible outburst. However, the use of edged instruments prevalent in instances of matricide, convey impetuous, impulsive, and passionate elements; a rage that is beyond mere reason and calculation. For example, we get a sense of what male offenders in matricides are fighting about if we consult the psychiatric and clinical literature. When matricides occur in the later stage of the male offender's life, he is more likely to be mentally ill (Dutton & Yamini, 1995; Millaud et al., 1996). In addition, male offender matricides are extremely sexualized. The manner in which the victims are murdered, the often lewd positioning of the bodies after their death, and the location of the crime (in the mother's bedroom), make the classification of these offenses sexual in nature, regardless of whether the victim is or is not the offender's mother. Again, the struggle for the matricide offender occurs within the individual, in one's mind, and if the psychologists, psychiatrists, and psychoanalysts are correct, the "cause" of their mental illness is a mother who is overbearing, domineering, sexually seductive, and tyrannical. Thus, in prototypical cases of matricide, the mother is depicted as the devil, a witch, a monster; the male offender, unable to metaphorically (and, in some case, literally) separate himself from the mother's breast, to sever the maternal bond, must sleigh her to experience liberation and individuation.

CONCLUSION

As I have pointed out in this chapter, that weaning process in adult male matricide offenders is a protracted affair, paid in full by years of mental illness within one's psyche. Prior investigators have maintained a similar position, but only using limited samples and works of fiction. In this paper, I also used works of fiction; however, they were supported with empirically verifiable data. Whether persuaded by the psychoanalytic or the empirical literature, it appears that men have trouble tearing themselves away from the maternal breast (i.e., the primal sexual bond).

Contrastingly, men do not have trouble tearing themselves away from their fathers. In fact, data on patricide indicate that they are the offenders' favorite targets. This is because when males kill their fathers they murder in response to physical, psychological, sexual, and domestic violence. Furthermore, the males who kill their fathers are not men at all but are boys. In the tale told by Freud (1945), it is the father's procreative (i.e., sexual) power that incites murderous intentions and actions. However, when this provocative theory is tested against real cases of parricide, his conceptualizations prove woefully inadequate for explaining this criminal behavior. As I argued in this chapter, this is because Freud has no theory of crime in general and no theory of parricide in particular. The little that we can infer from his existing work on the matter mostly relies on a rudimentary view of crime, criminals, the law, and punishment. Psychologist, psychiatrists, and other mental health clinicians influenced by Freud's formulations would do well to considerably rethink their practice work on the matter. Indeed, the theoretical and empirical distinctions on matricide and patricide identified throughout this chapter signal the limits of the psychoanalytic lens and its approach to the crime of parricide.

NOTES

1. Most of the circumstances concerning parricides were coded as being "other arguments," meaning that the murder was not financially or sexually motivated.

REFERENCES

Block, Richard. 1976. "Homicide in Chicago: A Nine Year Study." *Journal of Criminal Law & Criminology* 66(4): 496–510.

Block, Carolyn Rebecca & Richard Block. 1991. "Beginning with Wolfgang: An Agenda for Homicide Research." *Journal of Crime and Justice* XIV, 2, 31–70.

Block, Richard & Carolyn Rebecca Block. 1992. "Homicide Syndromes and Vulnerability: Violence in Chicago Community Areas over 25 Years." *Studies on Crime and Crime Prevention, vol. I, no. 1*, National Council for Crime Prevention.

Blumstein, Alfred & Daniel Cork. 1996. "Linking Gun Availability to Youth Gun Violence." *Law and Contemporary Problems* 59(1): 5–23.

Bohm, Robert. 2001. *A Primer on Crime and Delinquency Theory.* Belmont, CA: Wadsworth

Bunker, Henry Alden. 1944. "Mother-Murder in Myth and Legend: A Psychoanalytic Note." *Psychoanalytic Quarterly* 13:198–207.

Campion, John, Cravens, James M., Rothocl, Alec, Weinstein, Henry C., Covan, Fred, & Murray Alpert. 1985. "A Study of 15 Matricidal Men." *American Journal of Psychiatry* 142, 3, 312–317.

Carpetto, George. 1984. "Machiavelli's *Prince*: Stylistic Ambivalence and the Primal Father." *American Imago* 41(3): 309–322.

Corder, Billie F., Ball, Brenda, Haizlip, Thomas M., Rollins, Robert, & Ralph Beaumont 1976. "Adolescent Parricide: A Comparison with Other Adolescent Murder." *American Journal of Psychiatry* 133 (8): 957–961.

Daly, M. & Wilson, M. 1988. *Homicide.* New York: Aldine De Gruyter.

Dor, Joel. 1997. *Clinical Lacan.* Northvale: Jason Aronson.

Douglas, John & Mark Olshaker. 1995. *Mindhunter.* New York: Scribner Books.

Dutton, Donald G. & Sanaz Yamini. 1995. "Adolescent Parricide: An Integration of Social Cognitive Theory and Clinical Views of Projective-Introjective Cycling." *American Journal of Orthopsychiatry* 65(1): 39–46.

Eliade, Mircea. 1957. *The Sacred and the Profane.* New York: Harcourt Brace.

Fingarette, Herbert. 1963. "Orestes: Paradigmatic Hero and Central Motif of Contemporary Ego Psychology," *Psychoanalytic Review* 50: 437–461.

Foucault, Michel. 1977. *Discipline and Punish.* New York: Pantheon

Friedman, Joel & Sylvia Gassel. 1951. "Orestes: A Psychoanalytic Approach to Criticism," *Psychoanalytic Quarterly* 20: 423–433.

Freud, Sigmund. 1995. *The Basic Writings of Sigmund Freud.* Translated and Edited by A. A. Brill. New York: Modern Library.

———. 1945. "Dostoevsky and Parricide." *The International Journal of Psycho-Analysis* XXVI, 1 and 2, 1–8.

———. 1914. *Totem and Taboo: Resemblances Between the Psychic Lives of Savages and Neurotics.* NY: Vintage Books.

Garland, David. 1990. *Punishment and Modern Society: A Study in Social Theory.* Chicago: University of Chicago Press.

Gillies, Hunter. 1976. "Homicide in the West of Scotland." *British Journal of Psychiatry* 128, 105–127.

Green, Christopher M. 1981. "Matricide by Sons." *Medical Science and Law* 21, 3, 207–214.

Gudjonsson, Gisli H. & Hannes Petursson 1982. "Some Criminological and Psychiatric Aspects of Homicide in Iceland." *Medical Science and Law* 22(2): 91–98.

Harlan, H. 1950. "Five Hundred Homicides." *Journal of Criminal Law & Criminology* 40: 736–752.

Hawkins, Darnell, ed. 1995. *Ethnicity, Race, and Crime: Perspectives Across Time and Place.* Albany, NY: State University of New York Press.

Heide, Kathleen. 1996. "Dangerously Antisocial Kids Who Kill Their Parents: Toward a Better Understanding of the Phenomenon," pp 228–233 in *The Nature of Homicide: Trends and Changes. Proceedings of the 1996 Meeting of the Homicide Research Working Group.* NIJ Research Report.

———. 1992. *Why Kids Kill Parents: Child Abuse and Adolescent Homicide.* Columbus, OH: Ohio State University Press.

Henry, Stuart & Dragan Milovanovic. 1996. *Constitutive Criminology: Beyond Postmodernism.* Thousand Oaks, CA: Sage.

———. 1991. "Constitutive Criminology." *Criminology* 29(2): 293–316.

Katz, Jack. 1988. *Seductions of Crime: Moral and Sensual Attractions of Doing Evil.* New York: Basic Books.

Lacan, Jacques. 1977. *Ecrits: A Selection.* New York: Norton Books.

Lee, Jonathan. 1990. *Jacques Lacan.* Amherst: University of Massachusetts Press.

Maas, Richard L., Prakash, Rudra, Hollender, Marc H., & William M. Regan. 1984. "Double Parricide-Matricide and Patricide: A Comparison with other Schizophrenic Murders." *Psychiatric Quarterly* 56(4): 286–290.

Maltz, Michael D. 1998. "Visualizing Homicide: A Research Note." *Journal of Quantitative Criminology* 15(4): 397–410.

Marill, Irwin H. 1991. "The Tin Drum: A Cinematic Portrayal of an Oedipal Tyrant." *International Review of Psycho-Analysis* 18: 541–553.

Marleau, Jacques & Thierry Webanck. 1997. "Parricide and Violent Crimes: A Canadian Study." *Adolescence* 32(126): 357–358.

Michelman, Stephen. 1996. "Sociology Before Linguistics: Lacan's Debt to Durkheim." In *Disseminating Lacan.* Edited by D. Pettigrew and Francois Raffoul. Albany, NY: SUNY Press.

Millaud, Frédéric, Auclair, Nathalie, & Dominique Meunier. 1996. "Parricide and Mental Illness." *International Journal of Law and Psychiatry* 19(2): 173–182.

Mohr, J. W. and C. K. McKnight. 1971. "Violence as a Function of Age and Relationship with Special Reference to Matricide." *Canadian Psychiatric Association Journal* 16: 29–32.

Raizen, Kenneth H. 1960. "A Case of Matricide-Patricide," *British Journal of Delinquency* 10(4): 277–295.

Sadoff, Robert L. 1971. "Clinical Observations on Parricide." *Psychoanalytic Quarterly* 45: 65–69.

Samuels, Robert. 1993. Between Philosophy and Psychoanalysis: Lacan's Reconstruction of Freud. New York: Routledge.

Scherl, Donald J. & John E. Mack. 1966. "A Study of Adolescent Matricide." *Journal of American Academy of Child Psychiatry* 5: 569–593.

Schoenfeld, C. G. 1992. "The Origins of Law: A Psychoanalytic Interpretation." *The Journal of Psychiatry and Law* Fall, 351–374.

Shon, P. C. H. 1999. "Parricide: Desire, Dedifferentiation, and the Emergence of an Ironic Hero." *Journal for the Psychoanalysis of Culture and Society* 4(2): 265–271.

———. 1998. "The Sacred and the Profane: The Trascendental Significance of Erotophonophilia in the Construction of Subjectivity." *Humanity & Society* 23(1): 10–31.

Shon, Phillip C. H. & Targonski, Joseph. "Trends in U.S. Parricide: 1976–1998." Paper presented at the Annual meeting of the Academy of Criminal Justice Sciences, Washington D.C. April, 2001.

Short, James F. Jr. 1997. *Poverty, Ethnicity, and Violent Crime.* Boulder, CO: Westview Press.

Tanay, Emanuel. 1975. "Reactive Parricide." *Journal of Forensic Science* 21: 76–82.

Weisman, Adam M., & Kaushal K. Sharma (1997). "Forensic Analysis and Psycholegal Implications of Parricide and Attempted Parricide." *Journal of Forensic Science* 42 (6): 1107–1113.

West, D. J. 1968. "A Note on Murders in Manhattan." *Medicine, Science, and the Law* 8: 249–255.

Wolfgang, Marvin. 1958. *Patterns in Criminal Homicide.* Philadelphia, PA: University of Pennsylvania Press.

Young, Thomas J. 1993. "Parricide Rates and Criminal Street Violence in the United States: Is There a Correlation?" *Adolescence* 28(109): 171–172.

Zimring, Frank. 1996. "Kids, Guns, and Homicide: Policy Notes on an Age-Specific Epidemic." *Law and Contemporary Problems* 59(1): 25–37.

Chapter 4

Media Images, Mental Health Law, and Justice

A Constitutive Response to the "Competency" of Theodore Kaczynski

Michael P. Arena and Bruce A. Arrigo

Overview

Constitutive criminology is largely recognized as a postmodern approach to reconceptualizing the way in which society envisions crime. The perspective broadens the definition of crime to include the many forms of harm resulting from the unequal distribution of power. As we demonstrate, this unique approach provides a prism through which one can analyze and understand the Theodore Kaczynski case (aka the Unabomber), and the complex issues it presented to and within the forensic mental health arena. In short, the constitutive framework offers insight into how Mr. Kaczynski, media agencies, and his court appointed defense counsel informed and misinformed one another; resulting in an aura of "injustice." This chapter explores how Kaczynski was linguistically and socially marginalized, was denied an opportunity to utilize a defense strategy of his own choosing, and was thwarted in his efforts to express himself through self-representation. The chapter concludes by assessing the implications of our analysis for future cases of similar high profile status.

Introduction

Theodore John Kaczynski was arrested on April 3, 1996, at his ten-by-twelve-foot mountain cabin in Lincoln, Montana. Kaczynski stood accused of being the notorious Unabomber,[1] the mastermind behind sixteen bomb attacks that killed three people and injured twenty-three others between 1978 and 1995 (Gibbs, Lacayo, Morrow, Smolowe, & Van Biema, 1996; Graysmith, 1997). On June 18, 1996, Kaczynski was indicted on ten counts by a federal grand jury in Sacramento, California. He was charged with four counts of transporting an explosive with intent to kill or injure—18 U.S.C. Section 844 (d); three counts of mailing an explosive device with intent to kill or injure—18 U.S.C. Section 1716; and three counts of using a destructive device in relation to a crime of violence—18 U.S.C. Section 924 (c) (1). Because count eight [18 U.S.C. Section 844 (d)] and nine [18 U.S.C. Section 1716] allegedly took place after the passing of a 1994 crime bill that made such violations a capital crime, Kaczynski would be eligible for the death penalty.

After it became clear that Kaczynski's trial would be held in California, his defense team was assembled. Quin Denvir, the federal public defender from the Eastern District, was appointed lead counsel (Mello, 1999). Denvir quickly added Judy Clarke to the team, the defense attorney responsible for saving Susan Smith from the death penalty (the woman charged with drowning her two sons in South Carolina). Another attorney would soon join the team, Gary Sowards, an expert in mounting mental illness defense strategies. After the jury selection phase commenced in December 1997, U.S. District Judge Garland E. Burrell, Jr., met with Kaczynski and his lawyers to discuss problems revolving around his defense strategy (Finnegan, 1998). Kaczynski claimed that his attorneys had failed to inform him that they intended to mount a "mental defect" defense strategy regardless of his adamant refusal to be depicted as mentally ill. His attorneys, who were staunch opponents of the death penalty, believed that this strategy was his only hope for avoiding capital punishment (Mello, 1999; see also Bardwell & Arrigo, 2002, chapter 8). On January 5, opening statements were delayed when Kaczynski requested the right to fire his lawyers and to hire an attorney who would mount a defense based on his political beliefs not his alleged mental illness.[2] His request was denied. In an act of desperation, Kaczynski attempted suicide by hanging himself while in his jail cell. He explained that he felt frustrated and depressed over the way his case had progressed and that he would rather be put to death than proceed to trial with a defense strategy he did not want (Johnson, 1998). On January 8, 1998, Kaczynski asked if he could *pro se* the case; that is, pursue the path of self-representation. In response to this request, Judge Burrell ordered a psychiatric evaluation to be conducted to determine if Kaczynski was competent to stand trial and if he was up to the task of self-representation. On January 17, 1998, Bureau of Prisons psychiatrist, Sally Johnson, reported that Kaczynski was competent to stand trial, but gave him a provisional diagnosis as being a paranoid schizophrenic. Five days later, overlooking the results of the examination, Judge Burrell rejected Kaczynski's efforts to invoke his Sixth Amendment right to *pro se* the case.

Soon thereafter, Kaczynski pled guilty to the charges, avoiding the "mental defect" defense and the death penalty.

Finnegan (1998) explains that the case raised some fundamental questions about "a defendant's right to participate in his own defense, the role of psychiatry in the courts, and the pathologizing of radical dissent in both the courts and the press" (p. 54). Constitutive criminology provides a unique prism through which one can make sense of the Kaczynski case and the complex issues it presents for the criminal justice system and the forensic mental health arena. Constitutive criminology can be defined as a holistic, integrated theory that is informed by the postmodernist critique (Henry & Milovanovic, 1996). Constitutive criminology stems from a view of legal decision making that maintains "that law should be considered neither as an autonomous nor as a dependent body of rules and that law is codetermined by subjects within historically situated social relations. . . . Rather than assuming that any one factor, alone, is accountable for the development of law, the constitutive approach recognizes co-determination" (Milovanovic, 1994, pp. 172–173). Therefore, constitutive criminology is based on the premise "that crime and its control cannot be separated from the totality of the structural and cultural contexts in which it is produced" (Henry & Milovanovic, 1999, p. 7). From this perspective, crime is (re)conceptualized to be the many forms of harm that are perpetrated against others, particularly those harms resulting from the unequal distribution of power.

The constitutive framework provides insight into the way in which media agencies, the court system, and Ted Kaczynski coproduced a reality that fostered a sense of "injustice." Reality is created, recreated, and preserved through discourse. More specifically, the coproduction of Kaczynski's humanity as a "mad genius," notwithstanding the court appointed forensic psychiatric determination that he was "competent to stand trial," became justification for denying him the right to mount his own legal defense and for denying him the opportunity to express himself through the Constitutional guarantee of self-representation. At the outset, we note that this chapter is not an attempt to absolve Kaczynski of his heinous crimes. There is no doubt that Kaczynski was a malicious, calculating, serial terrorist. However, as citizens of this nation we all deserve our proverbial "day in court." This is something that the Unabomber has yet to receive. We contend that constitutive criminology can help explain why this happened at the level of human agency and social structure, mediated by language. We conclude the chapter by commenting on how the analysis potentially helps in our understanding of future controversial and media manufactured cases. However, in order to appropriately attend to this commentary, we begin with a brief overview of the constitutive criminological framework and explain how the identity of the Unabomber was coproduced by Kaczynski, the media, and the system of mental health law.

CONSTITUTIVE CRIMINOLOGY:
A REVIEW OF BASIC PRINCIPLES

In contrast to the nihilistic and fatalistic nature of "skeptical" postmodernism (e.g., Derrida's deconstructionism; Baudrillard's semiotic and simulated reality), constitutive theory is rooted in the more optimistic and humanistic philosophy of "affirmative" thought (Henry and Milovanovic, 1996). In line with the postmodern critique, constitutive theory focuses on deconstructing the "texts" which give rise to the oppressive and marginalizing aspects of social structure and human agency. "Texts" are understood to be the many symbols of communication including speech, the written word, body language, and so on. In line with its affirmative philosophy, constitutive theory then aims to reconstruct these texts or codes from within a "language of possibility," in ways that are local, relational, and contingent. Constitutive theory blends the insights found in phenomenology and ethnomethodology, symbolic interactionism and social constructionism, structuration theory and poststructural theory, Foucauldian discourse analysis and Marxist theory (Arrigo, 1997; Bak, 1999). The influence of these various schools of thought is evident in constitutive criminological praxis.

For example, in the application of constitutive criminology to the plight of the mentally ill offender (MIO) and to the homeless mentally ill, Arrigo (2001, 1999 respectively) extracts four key principles of constitutive thought that are helpful for deepening our understanding of these disenfranchised groups, especially in relation to how they are treated in the psychiatric courtroom and by the larger society of which such citizens are a part. The first principle is the decentered or "divided" subject. This concept is derived from the psychoanalytic semiotics of Jacques Lacan (1977, 1988). In contrast to the modernist perspective that viewed the individual as an autonomous, self-determining, coherent, unified being (i.e., a centered subject), Lacan (1977) viewed the individual as a decentered subject; that is, as one who was not self-directed nor "in control" (Milovanovic, 1994). Lacan (1977) argued that the unconscious mind was structured much like a language, making the subject inherently connected to the discourse one employed to express one's thoughts, impulses, feelings, attitudes, judgments, and the like (Arrigo, 2001). However, the dominant discourse we use to express ourselves "typically speak[s] through us; that is, it represents a stand-in for the 'real' subject whose identity, regrettably, remains dormant, silenced, oppressed" (ibid., pp. 164).

In an illustration relevant to the dilemma for the mentally ill offender (MIO), Arrigo (2001) explains that words or expressions such as "incompetent to stand trial," "psychotic," "guilty but mentally ill," "diseased," "in need of treatment," and "criminally insane" are all used by medicolegal decision brokers (e.g., forensic psychiatrists/psychologists) as a part of a coordinated and specialized language referred to as psycholegal discourse. These phrases carry with them unstated values and hidden meanings and, when they are invoked, they speak *for* the person in question. Thus, when someone is described as "diseased" or "in need of treatment" these expressions carry with them a concealed message that the individual is passive and not in control of his or her life. Thus, following the logic embedded within this language, we should not be surprised when mental health law "experts" contend that if MIOs are to become "normal" (i.e., depathologized) once again, then some sort of corrective state-sanctioned action must be taken (e.g., civil or criminal confinement, forced drug therapy).

The second key principle of constitutive criminological thought is the concept of the recovering subject. Rooted in the social phenomenology of Alfred Schutz (1967), this phrase embodies the notion that although language may speak for and through the subject, people still play a vital role in naming and defining their reality. As Henry and Milovanovic (1996) observe, "[a] constitutive view sees human subjects as active agents producing a dynamic social world which simultaneously produces them as both social and individual agents and as both active and passive identities. Both agents and structure are 'mutually constitutive,' and their actions are both liberating and constraining" (p. 37). In an example relevant to MIOs, Arrigo (2001) comments that while the criminal justice or mental health system may announce the humanity of MIOs as criminally insane, deviant, or diseased, the subject participates in defining oneself as such by participating in activities like being a "consumer" of mental health services. In this way, the human agent, consciously or otherwise, helps to coproduce the world in which he or she lives.

The third key concept of constitutive criminology is its contention that social structure is "a cluster of ideas and images about order and its maintenance, a collection of humans oriented to uphold their version of these images, the reality of the outcomes that follow from actions they take to bring this about, and the potential to transform these images, actions and outcomes" (Henry & Milovanovic, 1996, p. 65). In other words, social structure and, hence, knowledge are created and re-created through language, whether written or spoken. As Arrigo (2001) explains,

> execution of the mentally ill who invoke a right to refuse treatment (Arrigo and Tasca, 1999) is intimately linked to how the prison system and its agents interpret competency, treatment refusal, and mental illness (Arrigo and Williams, 1999). As a constructed text or narrative, the structural response (i.e., execution or stay of execution) is laden with a multitude of meanings anchored in a coordinated language system (i.e., medicolegal discourse), producing circumscribed images about MIOs on death row (prisoners as diseased, deviant, and dangerous) taken to be de facto reality. (pp. 167–168)

This excerpt provides a contextual example of how the mentally ill offender who is sentenced to death interacts with the ideas and images of "competency," "dangerousness," and "mental illness." Certain versions of these ideas and images become concrete entities when a multitude of (institutional) behaviors are organized around them.

For example, consider a judge's decision to postpone a trial so he or she may first determine if the individual is "competent" to stand trial. Or, consider how forensic psychiatrists and psychologists are called upon to provide "expert" testimony in a court of law, and to speak about the presence or absence of mental illness. In both instances, institutional behavior (i.e., postponing a trial; calling in experts) centers around naming and defining "competency," "dangerousness," "mental defect," and so forth. However, these actions when articulated as such, are transformed into a version of reality that signifies the truth about one's identity as mentally ill and how the mental health law system should respond to such citizens in a criminal case. Lost in this scripted process, though, is all the ideological content that informs these circumscribed descriptions: institutional/organizational/cultural values that remain concealed but function as legitimated expressions of power. Having established the way in which social structural forces are formed through language, it follows that the postmodern critique endeavors to make manifest the hidden assumptions and oppressive nature of the words/phrases that are used to manufacture these encoded institutional realities.

The fourth key concept of constitutive criminology is the definition of crime as the power to harm. Bak (1999) explains that in order to understand the constitutive definition of crime, one must first put aside all preexisting conceptions of a legalistically rooted ideology. The perspective envisions crime to be more than just a violation of written laws derived from a societal consensus of norms and values. At the core of the constitutive argument is the conviction "that crime and its control cannot be separated from the totality of the structural and cultural contexts in which it is produced" (Henry & Milovanovic, 1999, p. 7). Therefore, the narrow view of legalistically oriented definitions of crime fail to consider the numerous harms that are produced through human discourse. As the authors contend, crime is not so much *caused* as it is *discursively constructed*. Further, proponents of the perspective argue that unequal power relations built on subtending difference provides the foundation from which to redefine crime as harm. Of particular concern to constitutive criminological theorists are those disenfranchised, disempowered, and marginalized persons who have had their voices denied and their desires quashed (Barak & Henry, 1999). As such, from the constitutive perspective, crime is defined as "the expression of some agency's energy to make a difference on others and it is the exclusion of those others who in the instant are rendered powerless to maintain or express their humanity. . . . Crime, then, is the power to deny others their ability to make a difference" (Henry & Milovanovic, 1996, p. 116).

Crime takes two forms within constitutive criminological theory: harms of reduction and harms of repression. "Harms of reduction occur when an offended party experiences a loss of some quality relative to their present standing" (Henry & Milovanovic, 1996, p. 103). For example, an individual may experience the loss, reduction, or denial of their dignity (and humanity) following a biased-motivated assault or rape (Barak & Milovanovic, 1999). In an example relevant to the mentally ill offender, "when psychiatrically disordered citizens are thwarted in their request to be found not guilty by reason of insanity [NGRI] because of their difference (Arrigo, 1994) or are found guilty but mentally ill in spite of their difference (Arrigo, 1996), then they experience a loss because of who they are" (Arrigo, 2001, p. 169).

According to Henry and Milovanovic (1996), "harms of repression occur when an offended party experiences a limit or restriction preventing them from achieving a desired position or standing" (p. 103). For example, consider how an individual's dignity (and humanity) is repressed when racially motivated hiring practices deny persons or groups employment opportunities to which they are otherwise entitled. Or, in an example relevant to the psychiatrically disordered, consider the situation in which an individual with a mental disability thinks, speaks, and acts differently from others, and then is denied the opportunity to live in a certain neighborhood or in a particular apartment complex (Arrigo, 2001). From the constitutive perspective, "excessive investors" are the perpetrators of both harms of reduction and harms of repression. The victims are all those who are linguistically (and therefore socially) controlled on the basis of their nonnormative, nonhomogenous existences; that is, class, gender, race, sexual orientation, religious, political, or psychological differences (Barak & Henry, 1999; Henry & Milovanovic, 1996).

Consistent with affirmative postmodern philosophy, constitutive criminology aspires to reduce harms of reduction and harms of repression by deconstructing discourse, codes, or texts that promote victimization. It addition, the theory seeks to replace these systems of communication with positional, provisional, and relational languages that are more empowering, inclusive and tolerant of alternative realities and multiple identities. In this way, "[r]eplacement discourse . . . is directed toward the dual process of deconstructing prevailing structures of meaning and displacing them with new conceptions, distinctions, words and phrases, which convey alternative meanings" (Henry & Milovanovic, 1996, p. 204).

THE SUBSTANTIVE DIFFERENCE OF TED KACZYNSKI

Theodore John Kaczynski was born on May 22, 1942, to Wanda and Theodore R. Kaczynski, two Polish immigrants of middle-class status living in Chicago, Illinois. His brother, David, was born several years later in 1950. At the age of six, Theodore John was given an IQ test by a family friend who was a child psychologist. He was reported to have an IQ of 160 to 170 (Graysmith, 1997).[3] As young boys, both David and Ted were taught the importance of educational pursuits; their mother Wanda reportedly enjoyed reading the magazine *Scientific American* to them on the porch of their modest three-bedroom, frame-and-brick home (Douglas & Olshaker, 1996). Aside from their intellectual skills, their father also found great pride in teaching his boys wilderness survival skills. Both Ted and David learned to fish, hunt, and survive off the land.

Kaczynski's intellect developed quickly as a young man. He often spent more time studying than playing with other kids his age. Although he did play trombone in the high school band, his intellectual pursuits left him socially isolated. Kaczynski graduated from Evergreen Park High School in 1958, two years ahead of his class. At the age of sixteen, he went to Harvard on a merit scholarship and graduated in 1962. He then went on to receive his Ph.D. in mathematics from the University of Michigan in 1967, and became an assistant professor at the University of California at Berkeley in July of that year. In June of 1969, Kaczynski suddenly resigned from his position and moved to Salt Lake City. In June 1971, he and his brother purchased a 1.4-acre lot of land in Lincoln, Montana, where Theodore would later build his ten-by-twelve-foot cabin.[4] In June 1978, Kaczynski moved back to the Chicago area and worked as a press operator at Foam Cutting Engineers where his brother David was his supervisor. In July 1978, Theodore began seeing a female coworker at the plant on a social basis. David was eventually forced to fire Theodore in August 1978 after his brother left lewd notes around the office regarding the coworker who ended their short two-week relationship. Kaczynski eventually moved back to Montana to live on his secluded property and in his quiet cabin.

Theodore Kaczynski's "substantive difference" from mainstream society generally can be found in his alternative ways of thinking and, more specifically, in his political beliefs and reclusive lifestyle. Kaczynski's political ideology is best articulated in the 35,000-word essay entitled *Industrial Society and Its Future*. Eventually, this treatise was known worldwide as the "Unabomber Manifesto" and it was published in both the *New York Times* and the *Washington Post*. The manuscript scrutinized technology's encroachment upon privacy and other American freedoms. Essentially, Kaczynski argued that technological society was destroying personal liberty. Some claimed that the antitechnological and pro-freedom themes were unoriginal, merely mimicking the work of nineteenth-century American thinkers like Henry David Thoreau and Lewis Mumford (Mello, 1999).

Among other disciplines, Kaczynski was especially harsh on psychiatry and psychology. He believed that the discipline was used as an attempt to control behavior. As he explained;

> 'Mental health' programs, 'intervention' techniques, 'psychotherapy' and so forth are ostensibly designed to benefit individuals, but in practice they usually serve as methods for inducing individuals to think and behave as the system requires. (There is no contradiction here; an individual whose attitudes or behavior bring him into conflict with the system is up against a force that is too powerful for him to conquer or escape from, hence he is likely to suffer from stress, frustration, defeat. His path will be much easier if he thinks and behaves as the system requires. In that sense the system is acting for the benefit of the individual when it brainwashes him into conformity.) (Douglas & Olshaker, 1996, p. 243)

Kaczynski went on to state that,

> Our society tends to regard as a 'sickness' any mode of thought or behavior that is inconvenient for the system, and this is plausible because when an individual doesn't fit into the system it causes pain to the individual as well as problems for the system. Thus the manipulation of an individual to adjust him to the system is seen as a 'cure' for a 'sickness' and therefore as good. (Douglas & Olshaker, 1996, p. 246)

Kaczynski expressed these thoughts with ominous foreboding. His ideas are reminiscent of the work of Thomas Szasz (1974) and Michel Foucault (1965; 1973). In their respective ways, both proposed that psychic disorders were intimately linked to society's values and were more an issue of deviation from the norm rather than an underlying medical condition.

Another area constituting Kaczynski's difference was his decision to lead a reclusive, unconventional lifestyle. Kaczynski's "back-to-nature" approach to life included living in a ten-by-twelve-foot cabin with no indoor plumbing or electricity, equipped only with a wood stove. It was built in the dense forest landscape of mountainous Montana. His homestead had a large garden in which he grew potatoes, parsnips, carrots, and other vegetables that he liked to trade with neighbors (Mello, 1999). He baked his own bread and hunted deer and elk for food. The photos that littered newspapers and news broadcasts showed the picture of a man who had been living a "mountain man" existence for years.

We note that these behaviors and ideas, although summarily presented, represent a portrait of who the Unabomber was, what he thought, and how he lived. Interestingly, Kaczynski's antitechnology politics, his willingness to kill for them, and his solitary lifestyle would be defined by others as the substance of his mental illness (ibid., 1999). However, at this juncture, having provided an overview of the key concepts of constitutive criminology and having offered some brief remarks about the substantive difference that Kaczynski embodied, we now consider how the Unabomber, media agencies, and the court appointed defense attorneys interacted to (mis)inform one another about the criminal case, resulting in an aura of "injustice" for the defendant.

COPRODUCING THE "MAD GENIUS"

The four principles of constitutive criminology (i.e., the decentered or divided subject, the recovering subject, the constructed nature of social structure, and crime as the ability to harm) further our understanding of the legal events surrounding the Kaczynski matter and the subsequent failure of the criminal case to advance the administration of justice. From the constitutive perspective, the coproduction of the defendant's humanity as a "mad genius" occurred through the interactive effects of the Unabomber's own speech, thought, and behavior, mass-mediated images about Kaczynski, and attorney characterizations regarding the defendant. As we contend, this cocreated reality fostered both harms of reduction and harms of repression for the defendant. Preliminarily, we note that the exploration of discourse emanating from these three sources is not intended to be exhaustive. Indeed, many more institutional forces and examples of discourse could be described. However, from our perspective, the examples chosen are the most salient.

Kaczynski's Contribution to the Production of His Own Identity

Evidence that Kaczynski embodied the decentered or divided subject can be found in his 35,000-word essay, *Industrial Society and Its Future*, and excerpts from his twenty-two-year-long journal. In these writings, Kaczynski expressed his intense hatred for industrial society, its ability to control human behavior, the way it made him feel about himself, and what it did to his life. In this way, the treatise exemplifies Lacan's (1977) notion of subjectivity. Although Kaczynski wrote his Manifesto in the third person as if authored by an organized terrorist group, it is unmistakably a narrative of his own life. In one such example from his Manifesto, Kaczynski wrote about what he called the "power process" (Douglas & Olshaker, 1996). He believed that individuals acquired a sense of self-esteem, self-confidence, and a sense of power through having a goal and making an autonomous effort to attain the goal. Although industrial society does provide for some trivial freedoms, it subverts the individual's ability to accomplish his or her true desires. The consequences of this imposition are boredom, demoralization, low self-esteem, inferiority feelings, defeatism, depression, anxiety, guilt, frustration, hostility, sleep disorders, and so on.

Kaczynski's manifesto subtly explains how his ability to acquire power in his own life was subverted by industrial society. As he explained "[t]he system has to force people to behave in ways that are increasingly remote from the natural pattern of human behavior . . . It isn't natural for an adolescent human being to spend the bulk of his time sitting at a desk absorbed in study. A normal adolescent wants to spend his time in active contact with the real world" (Douglas & Olshaker, 1996). Presumably, this was a chapter taken from his own life, a brilliant young man who had become socially isolated and bitter toward his parents because they had encouraged him to stay at his desk and study science and technology instead of fulfill his desire to spend time with others (Mello, 1999). Kaczynski articulates his frustration with being the divided subject in a journal entry dated January 21, 1978:

> Our Society allows us great freedom to do nothing or to dream or to play games. But I consider these trivial freedoms and have little interest in them. What I want is the opportunity to make the practical decisions affecting the physical conditions of my own existence. For example: consider the risk of worldwide famine. Probably a small risk at present, so that modern society probably gives me better assurance of food supply than I could give myself as a primitive hunter-gatherer. But that's beside the point. As a primitive I would have the right to deal with the problem myself and make my own decisions regarding it. As it is, the system makes all the decisions for me and I can do nothing about it. Another example: the system makes all the decisions influencing air pollution (and noise pollution!) And it galls me that I can do nothing to change these decisions. All practical decisions are made by the system. I want personal autonomy in making such decisions. But that is impossible in a technological society. (Waits & Shors, 1999, pp. 285–286)

This excerpt demonstrates Kaczynski's belief that society prevented him from having autonomy, self-determination, and self-direction over his own life. In effect, industrial society forced him to feel the social isolation, anger, frustration, and sense of revenge toward the agents of industrial society (i.e., scientists and psychologists). His decision to lead an autonomous, reclusive lifestyle, and effect revenge against enemies (i.e., agents of technological society) was his attempt to retake control over his own life.

In another example, Kaczynski expresses disdain for both society and himself after deciding to quit his job and relinquish his place in society. He wrote;

> One thing that our society demands is that you have a recognized place in the system. By quitting my job, I've made myself again an outcast, a good-for-nothing, a bum—someone who "respectable" people can't view without a certain element of suspicion. I can't feel comfortable in this respect until I get away into the hills again— away from society. (Waits & Shors, 1999, p. 272)

Although Kaczynski expressed some control over his life by choosing to quit his job and moving into the hills, it is clear that he was angered by the way in which society perceived him as being an outcast, a good-for-nothing, a bum, someone to be viewed with suspicion.

As the recovering subject, Kaczynski helped to shape his own identity as being "mentally ill" in a number of ways. For example, Dr. Sally Johnson's (1998) psychological evaluation of Kaczynski revealed that he had sought out assistance from the mental health care community on a number of occasions. Apparently, the first such instance was while he was attending the University of Michigan. After several weeks of experiencing feelings of insecurity regarding his sexuality, Kaczynski made an appointment to see a psychiatrist at the university's health center. He reported that while in the waiting room he became anxious and was humiliated at the thought of discussing his personal feelings with the psychiatrist. Once he began the session, Kaczynski claimed that he was experiencing depression and anxiety over the possibility of losing his deferment and being drafted into the military. The psychiatrist indicated that these feelings were normal, considering the situation in Vietnam. Kaczynski recalled leaving the office feeling rage, shame, and humiliation over his attempt to see a psychiatrist regarding his feelings.

Kaczynski's second contact with the mental health care system was not until the spring of 1988. At this time, Kaczynski contacted a local therapist regarding insomnia and his renewed interest in establishing a relationship with a woman. His first session with the therapist went well and he expressed a desire to continue; however, he decided that he could not afford her fees. He then contacted the Mental Health Center in Helena, Montana, requesting that he be assigned a therapist or counselor that he could correspond with by mail. The facility indicated that this could not be arranged and, apparently, Kaczynski ceased his efforts to seek treatment. In 1991, Kaczynski contacted a general practitioner in Lincoln, Montana, regarding insomnia. The doctor prescribed him a bedtime dosage of Trazadone. He soon stopped the medication because of its side effects and contacted another mental health care center, this time in Great Falls. He asked the facility to recommend a psychiatrist, but failed to follow through on making an appointment. In October 1993, he contacted the director of the Golden Triangle Community Mental Health Center concerning his insomnia. Kaczynski asked for a psychiatrist that he could consult with at a reduced fee. Again, he failed to follow through with an appointment. This final attempt marked the last voluntary contact Kaczynski had with the mental health care community.

Another way in which Kaczynski contributed to the production of his own identity as "psychiatrically ill" was in his refusal to be evaluated by mental health professionals during the pretrial criminal proceedings. This decision was based on his fear that he would be declared mentally ill. Even before his arrest, Kaczynski predicted that, if captured, his work would be dismissed as the crazed ruminations of a "sickie." In his journals, Kaczynski remarks that "many tame, conformist types seem to have a powerful *need* to depict the enemy of society as sordid, repulsive, or 'sick' " (Finnegan, 1998, pp. 54–55). He even makes note of the old Soviet practice of suppressing dissidents by labeling them as mentally ill. Initially, this fear of psychiatry was understood to be a manifestation of a phobia. The psychiatrist hired by the defense to act as a liaison between the legal team and Kaczynski on mental health matters explained this phobia. As the psychiatrist, Dr. David Foster, observed, "[a]n essential component of Mr. Kaczynski's brain disorder is his deeply ingrained fear of being considered mentally ill. In Mr. Kaczynski's perception, psychiatrists seek to eliminate free will and personal autonomy by creating a population that is wholly compliant with the needs of an omnipotent system. A significant feature of Mr. Kaczynski's illness is his pathological fear and compulsive aversion to evaluation by psychiatrists" (as cited in Amador & Paul-Odouard, 2000, pp. 367–368). The prosecution responded to this strategy by demonstrating that, on several occasions, Kaczynsi did attempt to meet with psychiatrists.

This issue was momentarily resolved when a report prepared by Dr. Xavier Amador, a schizophrenia researcher from Columbia University, was submitted to the court as expert testimony on behalf of the defense. Dr. Amador summarized the essence of the report as follows: "[Kaczynski's] refusal to be evaluated and put on a mental illness defense can more easily be understood in light of the research literature on insight. In most cases involving people with schizophrenia, severe deficits in illness awareness and the irrational compulsion to prove one's 'sanity' despite life threatening consequences, are a consequence of brain dysfunction rather than manipulation or defensiveness" (Amador & Paul-Odouard, 2000, p. 364). Dr. Amador explained that he believed Kaczynski's failure to realize his own mental illness was a result of neurological dysfunction similar to that of anosognosia in neurological disorders. The circular nature of both Foster's and Amador's reasoning was troubling to the court. Essentially they were saying that Kaczynski's refusal to accept his mental illness was, in itself, evidence of his mental illness

(Finnegan, 1998; Mello, 1999). Nevertheless, Judge Burrell accepted both of the explanations and the defense's request to have the option of mounting a mental defect defense for Kaczynski (i.e., 12.2 b defense).

The Media's Contribution to the Production of Kaczynski's Identity

Media coverage of the Unabomber case seemed to explode when the eighteen-year manhunt came to an abrupt end in 1996. As pretrial proceedings began to materialize, 75 news organizations congregated in a parking lot near the Sacramento courthouse. The site was affectionately referred to as "Club Ted" (Mello, 1999). Many of the agencies seemed to buy into three main points: (1) Kaczynski was a paranoid schizophrenic; (2) hence, his lawyers acted properly in attempting to raise a mental defect defense; and (3) Kaczynski was responsible for the interruptions of his case (ibid.).

The depiction of Kaczynski as mentally ill began almost immediately after his arrest. Pictures of his disheveled, unkempt appearance with wildly long hair and overgrown beard, littered newspapers, magazines, and evening news reports (Glaberson, 1998b; Klaidman & King, 1998). Convinced that a mental defect defense was the only way to avoid the death penalty, Kaczynski's defense attorneys and his family worked together to wage a media campaign to paint a vivid picture of a complex idealist who was helplessly mentally ill (Finnegan, 1998). On May 26, 1996, an interview with David Kaczynksi ran in the *New York Times*, detailing his brother's life history and bouts with mental illness (Johnston & Scott, 1996; McFadden, 1996). As David reported, "I think that truth from my point of view is that Ted has been a disturbed person for a long time and he's gotten more disturbed" (McFadden, 1996, p. 1). On September 15, 1996, only six months after Kaczynski's arrest, his family went on *60 Minutes* (Hewitt, 1996) to explain that their relative's actions were the result of mental illness and not the result of evilness or a criminal mind. They acknowledged that Ted's psychological state had deteriorated over the past several years to a point of serious disturbance. Wanda Kaczynski explained that when her son was nine months old he suffered a severe allergic reaction for which he had to be hospitalized for a week. He was kept in isolation and denied any meaningful contact with family. She indicated that when she brought him home, he was not the bouncing, joyous baby she remembered; he had become emotionally "flat," like "a little rag doll." As she later explained, this was the beginning of a lifelong pattern of withdrawal for Ted Kaczynski.

After his discharge from the factory, Ted moved back to Montana where he and his brother maintained correspondence by mail. David explained that Ted's letters had become increasingly hostile and withdrawn. Concerned, David and his wife, Linda, showed the letters to a psychiatrist. Linda stated that "The psychiatrist advised us that Ted was mentally disturbed—seriously disturbed—and that not only was he disturbed but that there was a possibility of violence" (Hewitt, 1996). At one point, David and Linda even contemplated having Ted involuntarily committed. It was David who alerted the FBI that his brother might be the Unabomber (Gibbs, et al., 1996; Graysmith, 1997). This was a decision with which the brother struggled a great deal (Glaberson, 1998a).

The media blindly accepted the image of Kaczynski as mentally ill; however, it also seemed to put its own spin on his paranoid schizophrenic persona. In an article from the *New York Times,* Cooper (1998) wrote "Theodore J. Kaczynski, the hermit standing trial on charges that he is the Unabomber, has told his defense team that he believes satellites control people and place electrodes in their brains. He himself is controlled by an omnipotent organization [that] he is powerless to resist, he told the lawyers. So it was with some reluctance that they [his lawyers] finally agreed last week not to mount an insanity defense" (p. 5). Finnegan (1998) adamantly disputed these statements, saying that they were a collage of fragments from various sources. Furthermore, if indeed they had been said, they certainly would have been protected under the attorney-client privilege. Nevertheless, Finnegan's comments did not stop the cocreation of Ted's disturbed humanity. In a later article published in the *New York Times,* Glaberson (1998b) wrote, "[t]he shift in public image, which began with Mr. Kaczynski's arrest for carrying out an 18-year campaign of bombing that killed 3 and injured 28, accelerated after his lawyers said he was a delusional paranoid schizophrenic who believes people have electrodes implanted in their brain" (p. 6).

Finnegan (1998) also draws attention to another example of how Kaczynski's paranoid schizophrenia was accepted and propagated by the media. An article in *Newsweek* stated that new developments in genetic and brain research have enabled psychiatrists to better diagnose mental abnormalities. As the author of the piece noted, "[m]ental health, in this new view, is a continuum. At one extreme might be a Ted Kaczynski, the Unabomber suspect described by his brother's lawyers as obsessive-compulsive, out of touch with reality, delusional, antisocial and paranoid. At the other end of the spectrum lie what are usually considered normal, even wonderful, human differences" (Begley, 1998, p. 52). This statement speaks about Kaczynski as if his mental illness had become a proven fact; that his behavior was undeniably the result of someone who had been extremely emotionally disturbed. Moreover, the author speaks of one polarity of the mental health continuum as indicative of normality, including "wonderful" differences; however, the other end of the spectrum, the polarity to which Kaczynski apparently was assigned, was nothing short of twisted and deranged.

The media regarded Ted's courtroom behavior (i.e., his persistent requests to find new counsel, his refusal to see court-appointed psychiatrists, etc.) as the product of a "manipulative and sinister mastermind." As one journalist wrote, "[t]he two Theodore Kaczynskis are painted in the court papers filed by the defense and prosecution. One is a brilliant but pathologically shy man ravaged by mental illness; the other is a cunning and calculating killer who murdered with malice aforethought" (Associated Press, 1997, p. A10). Other news commentators went even further to ascribe cunningness and deviousness to the defendant. "Pundits and prosecutors indignantly suggested that Kaczynski had once again outfoxed his pursuers. 'I think he's creating chaos and enjoying it,' says former assistant U.S. Attorney Donald Heller. Kaczynski's mind has a devious turn; the Unabomber sometimes taunted his victims" (Klaidman & King, 1998, p. 24). Whether Kaczynski's actions were the work of a "mad genius" or the result of someone who had fallen victim to a terrible mental illness, the print and electronic media painted a vivid, disturbing, and haunting portrait of who he was. We submit that it was this image, mediated by language and its ideological content, which coproduced the reality of the Unabomber.

The Defense Team's Contribution to the Production of Kaczynski's Identity

Kaczynski's defense team acted quickly in creating an image of him as "mentally ill." During the pretrial proceedings, they utilized the assessments of mental health professionals, submitted a notice to the court indicating that they intended on offering expert testimony concerning Kaczynski's mental condition, and, finally, announced to the press their intention of offering his ten-by-twelve-foot cabin and reclusive, primitive lifestyle as evidence of his mental illness.

According to Dr. Sally Johnson's (1998) report, one of the first mental health professionals to evaluate Kaczynski was Dale Warson, Ph.D., who administered a battery of psychological tests. The results of the battery were not made available; however, they were interpreted and expanded on by two other defense experts, Ruben Gur, M.D., and Karen Froming, Ph.D. After conducting an evaluation on June 15 and 16, 1996, Drs. Ruben and Raquel Gur concluded that Kaczynski met the diagnostic criteria for schizophrenia. In February of 1997, Dr. Froming, a psychologist retained by the defense, interviewed Kaczynski and completed additional neuropsychological testing. Dr. Froming also scored a Thematic Apperception Test (TAT) Kaczynski had taken while a student at Harvard. The psychologist reported that Kaczynski was indeed suffering from paranoid schizophrenia. The linchpin for Froming's diagnosis was that the defendant's antitechnology politics were delusional in nature (Finnegan, 1998; Mello, 1999). Dr. David Foster, a psychiatrist retained by the defense, evaluated Kaczynski in late 1997. He also concluded that the defendant suffered from paranoid schizophrenia, and believed that Kaczynski had an aversion to psychiatrists based on his interaction with and his refusal to see previous mental health professionals who shared their diagnoses with him. Finally, Dr. Xavier Amador's declaration concerning Kaczynski's lack of insight into his paranoid schizophrenia was used as evidence, indicating that he suffered from the disease.

The prosecution also retained its own "experts." The opinions of these specialists were incongruent with those who were hired by the defense. They saw no evidence of delusions[5] and believed Kaczynski's behavior fell within the Schizoid or Schizotypal range of personality disorder. One of the individuals reported that the results of the neuropsychological testing were not specific to a diagnosis of schizophrenia. Nevertheless, the opinions of those "experts" retained by the defense were taken to be valid and, hence, informed the defense's decision to utilize a "mental defect" strategy.

In June of 1997, Kaczynski's lawyers filed a notice to the court, pursuant to the Rules of Criminal Procedure, stating their intention to present expert testimony concerning the defendant's mental condition (Mello, 1999). Although Kaczynski did initially agree to this notice, he claimed that he was unaware that his legal team planned to use the testimony as a platform to launch its "mental illness" defense strategy. Essentially, the notice or rule is designed to reduce interruptions of the justice process by insuring that the government (i.e., prosecution) has fair warning to arrange opposing testimony concerning a defendant's mental status. The text of the rule is as follows:

> Rules of Criminal Procedure: 12.2 (b). Expert testimony of defendant's mental condition. If a defendant intends to introduce expert testimony relating to a mental disease or defect or any other mental condition of the defendant bearing upon the issue of guilt, the defendant shall, within the time provided for the filing of pretrial motions or at such later time as the court may direct, notify the attorney for the government in writing of such information and file a copy of such notice with the clerk. (United States Code Service, 1999, p. 601)

What is pertinent about the defense's filing of this notice is the language used in the text. Words and phrases such as "mental disease or defect" convey the presence of something pathological, demented, or bad. As Williams (1998) states, this labeling process "not only denies or invalidates the existence of the mentally ill as citizens, but re-legitimates the abrogation of their essential being (i.e. their subjectivity or desire) in the courtroom" (p. 181). By filing this notice, Kaczynski's attorneys already marginalized his existence and, in effect, set the stage for others to do the same.

In late October, Kaczynski's attorneys began making plans to have his one-room, plywood, ten-by-twelve-foot cabin transported from the wooded mountains of Montana to downtown Sacramento. They intended to show the jury the crude conditions in which Kaczysnki had been living as further proof of his mental illness. In an interview, Quin Denvir was quoted as saying "We feel the cabin represents some of the best evidence of Mr. Kaczyski's background and functioning. . . . It's very important for the jury to understand the conditions under which this Harvard Ph.D. and former mathematics professor was living" (Hubert, 1997, p. 1, A1). Denvir went on to say that "[t]his is not an A-frame in Tahoe. . . . This is the rural equivalent of living in a box or out of a shopping cart. This is a very grim way of living." When asked if the living conditions spoke to Kaczynski's mental state, Denvir replied, "It speaks to everything about him. . . . You simply cannot understand Mr. Kaczynski unless you know how he was living."

In an interview with the Associated Press, Denvir was also quoted as saying, "The cabin is 10-by-12 feet and 13 feet tall. It had no running water, no electricity, no toilet—not even an outhouse. And the irony was that a quarter-mile away [there] was electricity and water that he could have hooked into" (Deutch, 1998). In the same interview, Judy Clarke explained that "[Kaczynski's] only heat in the Montana winters was from a potbellied stove. . . . And he slept on a piece of plywood with a layer of foam on top." Denvir interjected, "It barely had a window. It was very dark, very cramped and crammed with stuff. And he lived there for almost 25 years" (Deutch, 1998). The defense intended to show the jury the dark, grungy, isolated cabin and to ask the question: "Would anyone but a certifiable lunatic choose such a primitive abode?" (Finnegan, 1998).

What is unclear about these accounts is how Kaczynski's lawyers came to equate living a "back to nature" lifestyle with mental pathology. However, what is clear is that they (deliberately) neglected to put aside their own views on what a "normal" or "acceptable" lifestyle amounts to. Moreover, it is evident that they failed to appreciate the beauty that Kaczynski saw in the tranquil forests, majestic mountains, and cascading rivers of Montana. In an excerpt taken from his journal, the Unabomber wrote:

Today I had the most wonderful morning I've had for a long time. At this beautiful dark, densely wooded spot, the Wisp began calling me, so I followed it to an oxen meadow. I slowly climbed to the top of the mountain through this strip of magic meadow. . . . At the top of the mountain I looked down on the ridges below and contemplated the sight for some time. Then I climbed down through the Douglas Fir parks, over the meadow strip again, and sat for a while looking at the blue lupine and yellow flowers of some plant of the composite family, both of which dotted the meadow. Then I climbed back down to camp, looking at the plants. Only 2 jets passed, and those when my walk was nearly over, so that I was able to forget civilization and the threat it poses to these wonderful solitudes. Thus I was able to drink in the things that I saw with full appreciation. This gulch is a glorious place. It has a special magic. I never get tired of seeing these fine old parks of Douglas firs around here. (Waits & Shors, 1999, p. 10)

To be sure, Kaczynski was a man who loved the wilderness. He probably could not imagine why anyone else would want to live in any other place.

Kaczynski's belief that technological society rendered him incapable of controlling his own life, his voluntary efforts to seek mental health treatment, the news-making campaign launched by his family to depict him as disturbed, the media's conviction that he was a paranoid schizophrenic, the alternative characterization of Kaczynski as a "conniving and scheming" mastermind, the filing of a 12.2 (b) notice in order to mount a "mental defect" defense, and the legal team's intentions to use his reclusive, minority lifestyle as evidence of psychiatric disorder, all significantly contributed to the identification of Kaczynski as a "mad genius." Indeed, as Mello (1999) summarily explains, "[i]n the American mind, the complexity that is Theodore Kaczynski has been encapsulated by two words: 'paranoid schizophrenic'" (p. 53).

Following constitutive criminological theory, the discourse that was used to coproduce the identity of the Unabomber rendered him a decentered or divided subject. In an attempt to reclaim, recover, and validate his own deeply felt reality, Kaczynski articulated a logic (i.e., passionate disdain for mental health treatment and psychiatry more generally) that unmistakably contributed to his own victimization. Moreover, the institutional and organizational systems of which he was a part and from which his identity was coshaped (e.g., the media, the legal apparatus, the mental health system), constructed an image of who he was informed by his speech, thought, and behavior. This image was steeped in the logic and language of medicolegal science, with all of its embedded and unspoken ideological content, producing a unique, though marginalizing, coordinated system of communication (i.e., psychiatric [in]justice). As we explain in the following section, this coproduction of the Unabomber, through the interaction of agency/structural dynamics and through the instrumentation of language, fostered the discursive manifestation of crime perpetrated against Theodore Kaczynski.

KACZYNSKI AND HARMS OF REDUCTION AND REPRESSION

The crimes committed against Kaczynski can be understood in terms of being both harms of reduction and harms of repression. As described above, media agencies, the criminal justice system, and the defendant set the stage for the enactment of such crimes by those who wielded power over his life. For example, after being denied a change of counsel and following a failed suicide attempt, Kaczynski felt that he had no other recourse but to exercise his Sixth Amendment right to represent himself. After making the request, Judge Burrell ordered a competency examination to determine if Kaczynski was competent to stand trial and whether he was up to the task of self-representation.

In the evaluation, Dr. Sally Johnson (1998) described her impression of Kaczynski as suffering from Paranoid Type Schizophrenia, episodic with interepisode residual symptoms (provisional), and Paranoid Personality Disorder with avoidant and antisocial features (premorbid) (APA, 1994). However, she described the schizophrenic portion of her diagnosis as being provisional because of the limited duration of the interview period. Essentially, Kaczynski's psychotic symptoms would come in peaks and valleys, described as episodic. For example, she claimed that at various times in his life Kaczynski suffered from delusions that were persecutory in nature, in which he believed that he was maligned and harassed by family members and modern society. Dr. Johnson explained that although Kaczynski had experienced many of the characteristic signs and symptoms of schizophrenia, he would have to be evaluated while undergoing a "peak" in order to make a full diagnosis.

Despite the historical and residual presence of mental illness, Dr. Johnson believed that Kaczynski was competent to stand trial. As she observed:

> Mr. Kaczynski has superior intelligence; he has the ability to read and interpret complex writing, he can contribute to review of documents; he has a full understanding of the roles of the various court personnel; he understands the charges against him and potential penalties if found guilty; he appreciates the nature of the proceedings and understands the likely sequence of events in a trial. . . . He recognizes that continuing to utilize [his lawyers] in his defense would provide him with a higher level of representation than self-representation. He continues to wish to make the crucial decisions in his case, even if they could lead to less likelihood of a more lenient outcome. (Johnson, 1998, p. 45)

Regardless of Dr. Johnson's declaration, Judge Burrell essentially stripped Kaczyski of his constitutional right to self-representation. A decision that both the prosecution and the defense disagreed with strenuously (Associated Press, 1998). Understandably, the prosecution feared that the denial would not withstand the appeal process and would invalidate a conviction (Finnegan, 1998). Mello (1998) speculates that Burrell may have feared that

Kaczynski would fill the courtroom with "lunatic ravings" similar to the way in which Colin Ferguson did in his trial (Arrigo & Bardwell, 2000; Bardwell & Arrigo, 2002). Linking this analysis with the perspective of constitutive criminology, the action of Judge Burrell represented a harm of reduction because it denied Kacynski his Six Amendment right based on unfounded concerns for what the "mad genius" might do in a criminal court of law.

Relatedly, a crime was committed against Kaczynski when his request to mount a defense based on his political ideas was rejected because his legal team believed it would inevitably result in his own courtroom demise. In this case, Kaczynski's defense attorneys manufactured a harm of repression against the accused. Indeed, through the language and imagery they employed, the identity of the Unabomber was discursively constructed. As a consequence, he was insidiously and forcefully denied the opportunity to stand trial as a man with unique ideas and principles (i.e., to make a difference). Instead, these ideas and principles were psychopathologized, consistent with the language and value system of psychiatric justice. As Dr. Johnson (1998) described it:

> [Kaczynski] wanted to present himself as [a] rational person with a point to make; a decent person who felt cornered; as socially vulnerable; in some ways a victim personally and via the system; an individual who had his back against the wall; a person who lived a beautiful life in the woods; and a person whose psychiatric disorder could serve as a mitigating factor. . . . [Furthermore, he wanted to] dispute the descriptions and "facts" of the information provided by the media and his family. (p. 37)

Kaczynski's legal team prevented him from taking a position against his detractors, consistent with his own belief system, life choices and impassioned behavior.

Interestingly, when asked if he understood the difference between representing the client's best interests versus representing the client's expressed interest, Kaczynski replied that representation should support a client's expressed interest (Johnson, 1998). Not only did he understand this distinction, he recognized that, on the matter of his criminal case, his values and those of his lawyers were vastly different. Indeed, Kaczynski's defense team inflicted their own belief system on him, depriving him of his unique and individualized brand of humanness. As Mello (1998) aptly stated,

> Kaczynski's attorneys apparently viewed their essential role as saving their client's life by any legal means necessary—to save him in spite of himself. Although they conceded again and again that Kaczynski was mentally competent to stand trial, his lawyers saw it as their

decision—not their client's decision—to stake their client's life on a defense based on mental defect—a defense that he found reprehensible on many counts, not the least, one would think, being that it was in direct conflict with the Unabomber's manifesto. (p. 26)

Although Kaczynski valued his life, it appears that he cherished his integrity, honor, and principles more than his will to live. As he explained to Dr. Johnson (1998), thwarting the psychiatrists' efforts to denigrate and dismiss his political and lifestyle choices as the product of a mentally ill or deranged citizen would, in itself, be a "symbolic victory" over technology. Kaczynksi was prepared to benefit from this success even if it meant that his life would be terminated. Regrettably, the harms of reduction and repression perpetrated by Judge Burrell and his legal team respectively, deprived him of the very opportunities that otherwise would have given meaning, purpose, and voice to his "different" identity.

REPLACEMENT DISCOURSES:
IMPLICATIONS FOR THE FUTURE

Replacement discourses have been described as possible avenues through which new conceptions, distinctions, vocabularies, and meanings can be articulated that convey empowering, inclusive, multiple, and alternative realities of sense making and truth telling. These languages of possibility are a substitute for discourses or texts that restrict, oppress, marginalize and alienate those who are different. Henry and Milovanovic (1996) offer a number of strategies for replacement discourses with the goal of reducing harm (Sanchez, 1999).

One such strategy is to intervene at the generative sites of discursive production. In this instance, the constitutive criminologist is charged with challenging the dominant discourse propagated by the mass media and making alternative views publicly accessible (Barak, 1993; 1999). The criminologist acts as the expert; he or she sheds light on the way in which language can distort images, can misrepresent victims and/or offenders, and can (and does) contribute to the creation of stereotypes that reflect an inaccurate and incomplete portrayal of crime. These insights can be applied to the Kaczynski case. For example, research that contradicts and clarifies the common misconception that political terrorists are "mentally ill" could have helped to deter the media and the criminal justice community from characterizing and depicting Kaczynski as a "mad genius" (Silke, 1998). In this instance, a replacement discourse, juxtaposed against the language used to describe Kaczynski, might have enabled the public, pundits, and politicians to (dramatically) rethink the relationship between crime, psychiatric disorder, and political dissent.

Another technique in support of the replacement discourse agenda, includes confronting the print and electronic media more directly. In this case, the criminologist functions as the provocateur (Barak, 1993). As applied to the Kaczynski medicolegal dispute, this would have meant challenging the media's uncritical acceptance of the psychiatric assessment of the Unabomber. In addition, it would have included exposing the mental health community's tendency to pathologize beliefs, lifestyles, thoughts, and behaviors, especially those that are different from normative articulations or expressions of the same (Arrigo, 1996, 2002). Another strategy employed by constitutive criminologists who seek to promote languages of possibility and replacement discourses is to reject the notion that crime and victimization can be overcome by state sponsored violence. Instead, "punishment" should work toward the betterment of humanity through peacemaking, conflict mediation, and dispute resolution (Pepinsky & Quinney, 1991). Peacemaking criminology aspires to building relationships between victims and offenders within tense, contradictory, discordant and fractious situations (Pepinsky, 1999). It entails bringing people back into the fabric of social relationships built on mutual respect and friendship. Dispute resolution works to reduce conflict through communication, cooperation, and third party intervention (Folger, Poole, & Stutman, 1997).

Kaczynski never had the opportunity to tell his story on his own terms in the courtroom. Instead, his attorneys endeavored to save him from himself in a desperate attempt to avert the death penalty (Mello, 1999). Implementing the principles of conflict mediation and dispute resolution could help make peace with crime, retrieve the humanity of the Unabomber, and restore justice to society. Clearly, isolating and restricting Kaczynski within the confines of his prison cell for the rest of his life accomplished none of these more emancipatory goals.

Although the recommendations we have identified are purely speculative and clearly provisional, they illustrate how constitutive criminology could facilitate the reduction of harm generated by those who are "excessive investors" in power. In other words, reframing the discourse used to talk about, respond to, or solve crime is as important to understanding this phenomenon as are the behaviors themselves defined as acts of criminal wrongdoing. Furthermore, the suggestions listed above represent contextual and tangible examples of how the insights of constitutive criminology can be meaningfully applied to future high profile legal cases. This is especially important at the crossroads of criminal justice and mental health when the disciplines of law and psychiatry speak for and about defendant's identified as disordered, diseased, and dangerous. In the final analysis, when the coproductive forces of individuals and institutions manufacture and sustain criminal identities, then justice is not only deferred for a citizen but it is forever denied; one's voice is silenced, one's identity is homogenized, one's difference is territorialized, and one's humanness is vanquished. Regrettably, this was the experience of Theodore John Kaczynski.

NOTES

1. The FBI would eventually designate the case code as "Unabomb" because the first two incidents had been *u*niversity-related and the second two incidents were *a*irline related. The name "Unabomber" was derived from this designation (Douglas & Olshaker, 1996).

2. Kaczynski wanted to hire Tony Serra, a defense attorney who had become popular for his representation of political dissidents from groups like the Black Panthers, White Panthers, and the Symbionese Liberation Army (Finnegan, 1998).

3. An IQ score above 140 is superior.

4. Interestingly, David would live in a similar cabin he built in Texas before returning to Illinois to marry his high school sweetheart.

5. A delusion can be understood as a "false belief based on incorrect inference about external reality that is firmly sustained despite what [almost] everyone else believes, and despite what constitutes incontravertible and obvious proof or evidence to the contrary" (Johnson, 1998, p. 41).

REFERENCES

American Psychiatric Association. (1994). *Diagnostic and Statistical Manual of Mental Disorders*, 4th ed. Washington, DC: Author.

Amador, Xavier & Paul-Odouard, Reshmi. (2000). "Defending the Unabomber: Anosognosia in Schizophrenia." *Psychiatric Quarterly* 71 (4): 363–371.

Arrigo, Bruce A. (1994). "Legal Discourse and the Disordered Criminal Defendant." *Legal Studies Forum* 18(1): 93–112.

———. (1996). *The Contours of Psychiatric Justice: A Postmodern Critique of Mental Illness, Criminal Insanity, and the Law*. New York: Garland.

———. (1997). "A Review of Stuart Henry and Dragan Milovanovic's *Constitutive Criminology* and Alan Hunt's *Exploration in Law and Society*." *Theoretical Criminology* 1: 392–396.

———. (1999). "Constitutive Theory and the Homeless Identity: The Discourse of a Community Deviant," (pp. 67–85). In S. Henry & D. Milovanovic (eds.), *Constitutive Criminology at Work: Applications to Crime and Justice*. Albany, NY: SUNY.

———. (2001). "Transcarceration: A Constitutive Ethnography of Mentally Ill Offenders." *The Prison Journal* 81 (2): 162–186.

———. (2002). *Punishing the Mentally Ill: A Critical Analysis of Law and Psychiatry.* Albany, NY: State University of New York Press.

——— & Bardwell, Mark C. (2000). "Law, Psychology, and Competency to Stand Trial: Problems with an Implications for High-Profile Cases." *Criminal Justice and Policy Review* 11 (1): 16–43.

——— & Tasca, Jeffery J. (1999). "The Right to Refuse Treatment, Competency to Be Executed and Therapeutic Jurisprudence: Toward a Systematic Analysis." *Law and Psychology Review* 23: 1–47.

——— & Williams, Christopher R. (1999). "Chaos Theory and the Social Control Thesis: A Post-Foucauldian Analysis of Mental Illness and Involuntary Civil Commitment." *Social Justice* 26 (1): 177–207.

Associated Press. (November 30, 1997). "Two Faces of Kaczynski Confront Jurors: Unabomb Suspect Is Painted as Cold Killer and Mentally Ill." *Boston Globe,* pp. A10.

———. (January 22, 1998). "Sides Back Kaczynski's Right to Represent Himself in Court." *Boston Globe,* pp. A10.

Bak, Andrew. (1999). "Constitutive Criminology: An Introduction to the Core Concepts" (pp. 17–36). In S. Henry & D. Milovanovic (eds.), *Constitutive Criminology at Work: Applications to Crime and Justice.* Albany, NY: SUNY.

Barak, Gregg. (1993). "Media, Crime, and Justice: A Case for Constitutive Criminology." *Humanity and Society* 17 (3): 272–296.

———. (1999). "Constituting O.J.: Mass-Mediated Trials and Newsmaking Criminology" (pp. 87–110). In S. Henry & D. Milovanovic (eds.), *Constitutive Criminology at Work: Applications to Crime and Justice.* Albany, NY: SUNY.

——— & Henry, Stuart. (1999). "An Integrative-Constitutive Theory of Crime, Law, and Social Justice" (pp. 152–175). In B. Arrigo (ed.), *Social Justice/Criminal Justice: The Maturation of Critical Theory in Law, Crime, and Deviance.* Belmont, CA: Wadsworth.

Bardwell, Mark C. & Arrigo, Bruce A. (2002). *Criminal Competency on Trial: The Case of Colin Ferguson.* Durham, NC: Carolina Academic Press.

Begley, Sharon (January 26, 1998). "Is Everybody Crazy?" *Newsweek,* 50–52, 53–55.

Cooper, Michael (January 4, 1998). "The Client's Always Right. Even If He's Not." *New York Times,* p. 5.

Deutch, Linda, Associated Press. (November 10, 1998). "Kaczynski's Sparse, Remote Cabin May Spare Him, His Lawyers Hope." *Houston Chronicle.*

Douglas, John & Olshaker, Mark. (1996). *Unabomber: On the Trail of America's Most-Wanted Serial Killer.* New York: Pocket Books.

Finnegan, William. (March 16, 1998). "Defending the Unabomber." *The New Yorker,* 52–63.

Folger, Joseph P., Poole, Marshall S., & Stutman, Randall K. (1997). *Working through Conflict: Strategies for Relationships, Groups, and Organizations,* 3rd ed. New York: Longman.

Foucault, Michel (1965). *Madness and Civilization: A History of Insanity in the Age of Reason*. Translated by R. Howard. New York: Pantheon Books.

———. (1973). *The Birth of the Clinic: An Archaeology of Medical Perception*. A. M. Sheridan Smith. New York: Pantheon Books.

Gibbs, Nancy, Lacayo, Richard, Morrow, Lance, Smolowe, Jill, & Van Biema, David. (1996). *Mad Genius: The Odyssey, Pursuit, and Capture of the Unabomber Suspect*. New York: Warner Books.

Glaberson, William. (January 5, 1998a). "Heart of Unabomb Trial is Tale of Two Brothers." *The New York Times*, p. A12.

Glaberson, William. (January 18, 1998b). "Rethinking a Myth: 'Who Was that Masked Man?'" *The New York Times*, p. 6.

Graysmith, Robert. (1997). *Unabomber: A Desire to Kill*. Washington, D.C.: Regnery Publishing.

Henry, Stuart & Milovanovic, Dragan. (1996). *Constitutive Criminology: Beyond Postmodernism*. Thousand Oaks, CA: Sage.

———. (eds.) (1999). *Constitutive Criminology at Work: Applications to Crime and Justice*. Albany, NY: SUNY.

Hewitt, Don (Executive Producer). (September 15, 1996). "Ted Kaczynski's Family: Understanding the Family's Reasons for Turning in the Suspected Unabomber." *60 Minutes*. New York: CBS Inc.

Hubert, Cynthia. (October 24, 1997). "Defense Wants to Bring Cabin to Sacramento." *Sacramento Bee*, p. 1, A1.

Johnson, Sally. (January 16, 1998). "Psychological Evaluation of Theodore Kaczynski." *CourtTV.com*. Available on-line: www.courttv.com/trials/unabomber/documents/psychological.html.

Johnston, David & Scott, Janny. (May 26, 1996). "Brother Talks of a Painful Decision." *New York Times*, p. 1, 25.

Klaidman, Daniel & King, Patricia. (January 19, 1998). "Suicide Mission." *Newsweek*, 22–25.

Lacan, Jacques. (1977). *Ecrits: A Selection*. Translated by A. Sheridan. New York: Norton.

———. (1988). *The Seminars of Jacques Lacan, Book II: The Ego in Freud's Theory and the Technique of Psychoanalysis 1954–1955*. Cambridge: Cambridge University Press.

McFadden, Robert D. (May 26, 1996). "The Tortured Genius of Theodore Kaczynski." *New York Times*, p. 1, 22–25.

Mello, Michael. (1999). *The United States of America versus Theodore John Kaczynski: Ethics, Power and the Invention of the Unabomber*. New York: Context Books.

Milovanovic, Dragan. (1994). *A Primer in the Sociology of Law*, 2nd ed. Albany, NY: Harrow and Heston.

Pepinsky, Hal. (1999). "Peacemaking Primer" (pp. 52–70). In B. Arrigo (ed.), *Social Justice/Criminal Justice: The Maturation of Critical Theory in Law, Crime, and Deviance*. Belmont, CA: Wadsworth.

Pepinsky, Hal, & Quinney, Richard (eds.). (1991). *Criminology as Peacemaking* Bloomington, IN: Indiana University Press.

Sanchez, Lisa. (1999). "Sex, Law and the Paradox of Agency and Resistance in the Everyday Practices of Women in the 'Evergreen' Sex Trade" (pp. 39–66). In S. Henry & D. Milovanovic (eds.), *Constitutive Criminology at Work: Applications to Crime and Justice*. Albany, NY: SUNY.

Schutz, Alfred. (1967). *The Phenomenology of the Social World*. Evanston, IL: Northwestern University Press.

Silke, Andrew. (1998). "Chesire-Cat Logic: The Recurring Theme of Terrorist Abnormality in Psychological Research." *Psychology, Crime & Law* 4, 51–69.

Szasz, Thomas. (1974). *The Myth of Mental Illness*. New York: Harper & Row.

United States Code Service (Lawyers ed.). (1999). *Federal Rules of Criminal Procedure* (Rules 1–13). Charlottesville, VA: Lexis Law Publishing.

Waits, Chris & Shors, David. (1999). *Unabomber: The Secret Life of Ted Kaczynski*. Canada: Helena Independent Record and Montana Magazine.

Williams, Christopher R. (1998). "The Abrogation of Subjectivity in the Psychiatric Courtroom: Toward a Psychoanalytic Semiotic Analysis." *International Journal for the Semiotics of Law* XI (32): 181–192.

Chapter 5

The Diminishing Sanctity of Youth

Contributions from General and Family Systems Theory

Jeffrey L. Helms and Bruce A. Arrigo

Overview

The discipline of juvenile forensic psychology has turned a blind eye toward the impact of its work products, particularly with decisions affecting youth. Oftentimes, the reasoning put forth by the field is the need for "objectivity." However, a truly "objective" work product and system of justice would result in an adherence to the principles associated with General Systems Theory (GST) (von Bertalanffy, 1968). This chapter looks at several key concepts associated with GST (e.g., entropy vs. negentropy; closed vs. open systems; homeostasis; adaptation), and considers how the juvenile justice system and its agents violate these tenets in such a way as to negate the critical period of adolescent identity development. In addition, the Bowenian theoretical perspective (Kerr & Bowen, 1988) is detailed both as a GST-sensitive approach and as a potentially useful lens through which to configure a more humane model responsive to adolescent identity development. However, in order to appropriately situate the theoretical material, the chapter begins with a brief review of the statutorily defined purposes of the juvenile justice system within the United States. This review tells us a great deal more about this system's impact on the lives of adolescents and their families and/or communities.

The Juvenile Justice and Court Systems: Purposes on Paper

While various forms of legislation were introduced throughout the United States in the nineteenth century to humanize the law in its interactions with children, the major "break" in the justice system's dealings with children did

127

not come until the end of that century.[1] In 1899, Illinois passed the Illinois Juvenile Court Act of 1899. This act purportedly was motivated by several principles:

- Juveniles should not be held as culpable as adults;
- The juvenile court system should be predicated on (re)habilitation rather than punishment;
- Disposition of youth would be based on their special situations; and
- The new system would avoid the punitive and formalized attributes of the adult system. (Siegel & Senna, 2000)

Along with this motivation came the British doctrine of *parens patriae*, touted as the basis for not only separate justice but also intervention into the community systems of which the youth were a part. At that time, the rhetoric of the court was based in the *parens patriae* concept whereby youth, even delinquent youth, were viewed as in need of protection and rehabilitation. The courts and jurists traditionally viewed adolescents in general from within this framework (Bernard, 1992; Feld, 1999). Some court workers (e.g., judges) extended this view to highly individualized interaction with those youth who appeared before them (e.g., visiting the youth's home and school). This enabled the child, family, and community at large to view the judge as a sort of confidant and mentor to the process of raising the adolescent, especially when things did not go smoothly. As a result of how efficiently the system functioned at the time, no one believed in or even gave much thought to "rights" for juveniles within the justice system. Indeed, youths were seen as in need of protection, not rights. Additionally, little thought was given to what impact the development of the juvenile courts and their jurisdiction would have over the adolescent and his or her community and family. Simply stated, the belief held at the time (and the one maintained to this day) was that the community and the adolescent's family had failed to appropriately provide for the youth. This failure obviated the adolescent's indiscretions thereby undermining or eroding the child's prospects to mature into a productive member of society.

By 1910, thirty-two states had followed Illinois's lead and had developed juvenile court systems (Snyder & Sickmund, 1999). Just two states lacked such a system by 1925. In that year, the Standard Juvenile Court Act was issued. With its revision in 1959, the Act declared that the purpose of the juvenile court system was to issue "care, guidance, and control that will conduce to his welfare and the best interest of the state, and when he is removed from the control of his parents the court shall secure him care as nearly possible equivalent to that which they should have given him" (as cited in Snyder & Sickmund, 1999, p. 3).

Over the course of the next hundred years since the establishment of the first juvenile court, the view of juveniles and their "needs" have changed quite dramatically in this country.[2] The pendulum has swung from the rhetoric of rehabilitation and protection to retribution and punishment. This dramatic transformation is best depicted in the considerable variation among the states and how they define the purpose of the juvenile court system. Some states declare their purpose in explicit statutory language while others simply mention the existence of the juvenile courts. Many statutory purpose clauses have been substantially revised and amended to purportedly reflect the change in the adolescent population over the last hundred years (i.e., viewing them as more culpable). Still others have remained basically unaltered since the 1950s and 1960s (Griffin, 2000). Notwithstanding these differences, the present purpose clauses appear to fall into one of the following five categories:

Clauses Reflecting the Balanced and Restorative Justice (BARJ) Model

According to Griffin (2000), fifteen states have statutory language reflective of the BARJ theme. The BARJ model or theme advocates that attention be given to three primary interests: community safety, individual accountability to the victim(s) and the community, and competency development (i.e., development of the skills necessary to become a productive member of society) (Office of Juvenile Justice and Delinquency Prevention [OJJDP], 1998; Zehr & Mika, 1998). While the jurisdictions that have adopted the themes associated with BARJ vary in language (e.g., substituting terminology like treatment and rehabilitation for competency development), the more important difference comes in the way in which they emphasize each of the three BARJ components with some opting for accentuating the accountability and public safety dimension (Bazemore & Umbreit, 1995). Furthermore, as Griffin (2000) notes, several jurisdictions have incorporated language into their BARJ-consistent purpose clauses that is tailored specifically to the child's welfare. Despite limits with implementation, Bazemore (2000) points to a continuing need to pursue this model in theory and practice, especially if the goal is to address the needs of various stakeholders.

Clauses Reflecting the Standard Juvenile Court Act

As previously mentioned, although the original Standard Juvenile Court Act was issued in 1925, it appears that the most influential version was prepared in 1959 by the National Council of Juvenile Court Judges, the National

Probation and Parole Association, and the U.S. Children's Bureau (Griffin, 2000). The stated purpose delineated in the Act was that children brought to the attention of the juvenile courts should receive the guidance necessary to help them comport their behavior to the best interest of the State and to their own welfare. This purpose also acknowledged the need to secure care as closely equivalent to that of adequate parenting, should the child be removed from their parents' custody. Nine states adopted this purpose and are still working under this clause. Seven others have elements of the Standard Juvenile Court Act (Griffin, 2000).

Clauses Reflecting the Elaborate Legislative Guide

In 1969, the Children's Bureau (now the U.S. Department of Health and Human Services) issued the *Legislative Guide for Drafting Family and Juvenile Court Acts*. According to Griffin (2000), six states followed the guide closely while six other states had language similar to what appeared in the *Guide*. The four purposes delineated by the *Guide* were as follows:

a) To preserve the unity of the family whenever possible and to provide for the care, protection, and wholesome mental and physical development of children coming within the provisions of this Act;

b) Consistent with the protection of the public interest, to remove from children committing delinquent acts the consequences of criminal behavior, and to substitute therefore a program of supervision, care and rehabilitation;

c) To achieve the foregoing purposes in a family environment whenever possible, separating the child from his parents only when necessary for his welfare or in the interests of public safety;

d) To provide judicial procedures through which the provisions of the Act are executed and enforced and in which the parties are assured a fair hearing and their constitutional and other legal rights recognized and enforced. (Children's Bureau, 1969, p. 1)

Clauses Reflecting Retribution and Public Safety

Griffin (2000) reports that six states can be generally characterized as falling within the category of purpose clauses that emphasize retribution and public safety. These statutes accentuate community safety, deterrence and punishment, and juvenile accountability. While some states have incorporated other language that seems consistent with some of the other clauses mentioned above, the ones that fall into this category can be seen as having a "tough on juvenile crime" stance as their primary purpose.

Clauses Reflecting Best Interests of the Juvenile

The states and jurisdictions (roughly 4 altogether) that fall into this category principally emphasize a traditional child welfare posture for their juvenile court systems. On the surface, these clauses appear to be more consistent with the original intent behind the bifurcated justice system. Ostensibly, humanizing the law for juveniles is the cornerstone of these state statutes.

However, as the next section discloses, the "best interests" purpose clauses, along with the BARJ model, the Legislative Guide, and the Standard Juvenile Court Act, considerably fail to be responsive to the needs of adolescents in their rhetoric. Moreover, as the subsequent section delineates, the retributive/public safety purpose clauses are actually quite consistent with the current *zeitgeist* of juvenile justice (i.e., diminishing the prospects for healthy adolescent development). This is because they stress a punitive approach to addressing wayward youth.

GENERAL SYSTEMS (AND RELATED SYSTEM) THEORIES

More youth today than ever before in the history of our country or, more specifically, since the advent of the juvenile justice system, are embroiled in the tangle of delinquency hearings, waiver to adult court, and removal from home and community. At the same time, they are being severely and persistently punished. As a result, it is imperative that we investigate the limits of our thinking, especially with respect to the identified statutory purposes for the juvenile justice system. While most courtroom personnel and testifying forensic psychologists simply adhere to the above-touted tenets in their particular jurisdiction, the reality is that by doing so, they perform a disservice for many youths in the process (Feld, 1999). In particular, the legal perspective on children, informed by the various tenets and purposes proposed through state statutes, has only further alienated children, jeopardizing the sanctity of one of the most important developmental transitions in life; namely, adolescence. The following vignette,[3] developed throughout this chapter, poignantly and succinctly captures this problem.

> I first met Doug nearly seven years ago. At the time, he was only 14 years old. Our first meeting took place in the juvenile detention center. I acutely remember how distraught and dejected he looked.

"I'm going to miss the football game tonight at school. My coach will never let me back on the team. Those are all the friends I got. What am I gonna do?" Unfortunately, there was not much I could offer or do at that point. The "wheels of justice" were already turning (in the direction of alienation from peers, family, and social supports and away from healthy development).

The period of adolescence has been misunderstood by a system that, in some cases, endeavors to statutorily champion this developmental stage. Clearly, on its own, this verbal advocacy is insufficient to ensure the solemnity of this developmental period. Thus, a different perspective on the juvenile justice system is needed. Cases like Doug are not unique. The limits of the adolescent court system make it abundantly clear that it is unable to appropriately respond to the best interests of children funneled through its various treatment/punishment institutions.

There are a myriad of perspectives within the psychological field that can address some of the issues regarding juvenile justice and mental health. This notwithstanding, the majority of the prevalent theoretical orientations operate in a vacuum. For example, while the cognitive perspective convincingly has been shown to alter the "patient's" belief systems to match the dominant culture, the "patient" is treated almost exclusively without the benefit of community presence and familial support. Additionally, when many family-oriented theoretical perspectives (e.g., Haley's Strategic Family Therapy and Minuchin's Structural Family Therapy) are utilized, the focus is predominantly on restoring "traditional" family hierarchies and alleviating symptoms without addressing core issues. Again, this excludes the larger issues at stake in terms of the community and society in which the adolescent lives and develops.

General Systems Theory (GST) appears to be one conceptual model that does not operate in a vacuum (von Bertalanffy, 1968). Admittedly, it is a bit of an oversimplification to suggest that one psychological model can reconfigure, on its own, the serious limits of the juvenile justice system and its understanding of adolescent identity development. However, GST does provocatively advance the dialogue regarding change within the system. Thus, what it proposes represents more of a template or springboard from which future theoretical, empirical, and policy analyses can occur. As such, the following GST tenets (von Bertalanffy, 1968) and other GST-sensitive theories (Becvar & Becvar, 1993) are delineated. While certainly not exhaustive, the presentation of these principles will help shed light on how the current operation of the juvenile justice system precludes healthy adolescent development.

Recursion

According to Becvar and Becvar (1993), recursion is inherent in all healthy systems. It regards "people and events in the context of mutual interaction and mutual influence" (Becvar & Becvar, 1993, p. 68). The statutory purpose clauses previously identified are arguably recursive in that juveniles who become part of the court and treatment systems can affect their own outcomes by succumbing to the will and doctrines imposed on them (i.e., Do what we say, and you will be fine.). However, this is not truly the case. The unidirectional influence of the juvenile system forestalls and precludes this recursive effect (Arrigo & Schehr, 1998). Indeed, the system is not influenced by the individual; but, rather, by the social (and political) pendulum that swings between the philosophies of (re)habilitation and punishment, seemingly without concern for the individual being affected (Bernard, 1992; Feld, 1999). If a more mutually interactive and influential effect were present in the current system, there would be a collective effort that acknowledged the contributions from all participants equally (e.g., Bazemore & Walgrave, 1999). Instead, the current model is linear (i.e., unidirectional), producing cause-effect outcomes and encounters that fail to embrace a more dynamic, interactive component to understanding the youth, the family, the community, and the adolescent's presumably misguided behavior (Bazemore & Schiff, 2001; van Ness & Strong, 1997).

> Over the course of the next couple of weeks after we first met, Doug continued to request the opportunity to "explain" what happened as well as "make things right." By the point of arrest, however, Doug was incapable of communicating with those in authority. This was perpetuated by his attorney who advised him as well not to "explain" the circumstances leading up to his arrest.

Feedback

Feedback is intimately and inexorably connected to recursiveness. According to Becvar and Becvar (1993), feedback is the "process whereby information about past behaviors is fed back into the system in a circular manner" (p. 70). This feedback loop allows self-corrective mechanisms to work (e.g., homeostasis as described by von Bertalanffy, 1968). From its inception, the juvenile court system has relied on various data to assess its effectiveness, especially in the context of curbing adolescent delinquency. The result of this data processing or this information feedback has not produced self-corrective strategies to attain homeostasis. Instead, much of this data has been disregarded or, worse, has been supplanted by influences from outside the system (i.e., societal pressures to "get tough on juvenile crime"). These influences are not based on a "true" internal process of information feedback. Instead, they are external to the system's organic operation. Admittedly, the flow of information from outside can tell a system something about its perceived (or real) health; however, feedback loops refer to the internal operation of information or data processing.

> After Doug's first hearing regarding the alleged offense, I had the opportunity to speak to his attorney about how the hearing went. Doug's attorney reported that the judge refused bail and ignored pleas from the football coach and Doug's mother to release him to their custody, even under a stringent monitoring program. According to the attorney, the judge said that the family and community could not be trusted to care for the child.

Boundaries

One of the key ways to know when a boundary has been crossed is to assess whether, and to what extent, the level of information exchange has been diminished. Sharp reductions indicate that a boundary has been violated. This is true of both input and output information. The current system of juvenile justice has completely disregarded this basic tenet. As a result, it is a misnomer to think of it as a system at all. Instead of there being a recursive feedback process that responds to the internal flow of information on how effectively it is working, the juvenile justice system mostly has relied on external input (i.e., society's feedback) regarding its effectiveness. As external to the system, this input is limited and, therefore, cannot be based on correct or precise information. Indeed, reforms in the juvenile justice system are not fueled from *within*; rather, they are fueled from *without*. As it presently functions, the juvenile justice system does not respond to its own deficits from the recursive, internal feedback it receives but, rather, from the external suprasystem of which it is a part (i.e., society). Once again, the result is an ineffectual method for dealing with youth who have apparently "transgressed" against society.

Relatedly, and perhaps more importantly, are the boundary violations that occur by the juvenile justice system in relation to the family and community of which the adolescent is a part. The operation of the juvenile justice system routinely displaces the primacy of the family/community/kin system boundary. In doing so, it attempts the impossible and, not surprisingly, does so with problematic results. Indeed, to supplant the family and community by disrupting the boundaries of that system for an adolescent, defiles and negates the all-important role that this network assumes in the youth's life. While various state juvenile justice jurisdictions/courts clearly stipulate that their purpose is not the dissolution of the family and community, the reality speaks for itself. Between 1987 and 1996, court-ordered residential (out-of-home) placements rose 51 percent to a total of 159,400 in 1996 (Snyder & Sickmund, 1999). For a system that purports to want to strengthen communities, this only reinforces the belief that the system destroys community.

> For the next 4 months, Doug attended school inside the detention facility. At the beginning of his time there visitors from his community came often (relatively speaking). His mother's church minister would visit about once a week and sometimes bring his mother with him. His mother got to the facility about once or twice a week. I got there once a week. As the months passed, visits occurred less frequently. Eventually, I routinely became his only regular visitor. Because his mother did not have a car or money for the bus, transportation prohibited her from coming more often. Admittedly, it was only 3 or 4 miles to the facility. However, that distance became greater when his mom had to bring his younger brothers with her to the visits. Once, when they made the trek, they arrived too late for visitation hours. Another time, the guard on duty refused to let Doug's mom and his two brothers visit him. The guard also told her she could not leave her sons in the waiting room unattended. As a result of these complications, Doug began writing to his mom in order to keep in touch. The family did not have a phone.

Morphostasis/Morphogenesis

A system's predisposition toward stability is called morphostasis, and a system's tendency toward growth and change is called morphogenesis (Becvar & Becvar, 1993). In healthy systems, both morphogenesis and morphostasis are present and necessary. Without their presence and activity, a system cannot survive, cannot evolve. However, when one of these conditions is predominant, there is a lack of stability and well-being.

In the juvenile justice system, the dynamic equilibrium between these forces is at best continually unsettled and, most often, is in such a constant state of flux that it negates the possibility of adaptive change while simultaneously inhibiting any semblance of stability. In the absence of a dynamic equilibrium, the creativity necessary in a healthy system is subject to if not immersed in fear and anxiety. This disequilibrium comes at the expense of those adolescents already entangled in the system. The disarray that follows in the wake of an unbalanced system translates into society's lack of invest-ment in changing the system, especially since the benefits of reform are not immediately recognizable. Individual members of the system are reluctant to adapt because stability is significantly lacking. Furthermore, prospects for growth are encumbered (if not thwarted) because the system itself is stuck, relying on outdated methods, inefficient practices, and bureaucratized procedures that make meaningful, structural, sustainable change appear insurmountable.

> During the course of our sessions, Doug's attitude toward the juve-nile justice system became quite apparent. When queried about his distrust and seeming paranoia about the workings of the system, it became obvious that these feelings were based in his personal his-tory. Doug's father had a record of cocaine use and was caught with 4 separate bags of rock cocaine (i.e., "crack"). Although identified for personal use, Doug's father was sentenced to 25 years to life in prison for the distribution of crack cocaine pursuant to the statutes relating to the quantity of the substance. The fact that this was the father's first offense or that in reality the cocaine was for private use did not factor in as mitigating evidence. Doug continually feared that this type of situation would happen to him. As he explained it, "If it had been a white guy and powder, he wouldn't have gone to prison." Codifying penalties for the sake of "fairness" created stabil-ity at the expense of Doug's family.

Openness and Closedness

For any system to function adaptively, it must screen out or permit new infor-mation. The degree to which a system screens out or permits new informa-tion is the systems' openness and closedness (Arrigo & Schehr, 1998; Becvar & Becvar, 1993). In order to be adaptive, a system must have an appropriate balance between openness and closedness. When this balance is not appro-priate for a given situation, the system disintegrates. Disintegration occurs when too much information is allowed in—resulting in an enmeshment with another system—or it occurs when an insufficient amount of information is allowed in—resulting in a loss of adaptive connectedness to the environment.

    Historically, the juvenile justice system has demonstrated both open and closed tendencies. Unfortunately, however, it has done so in inappropriate ways. The effect of having an inappropriate balance between these two func-tions creates a reaction to the environment that is not in the best interest of the (juvenile justice) system or the individuals (i.e., adolescents) brought to the system's attention. Indeed, the system's overresponsiveness to the external environment (i.e., the public's concern for the state of juvenile delinquency) transforms the system into a political entity, eroding or undermining those organic or intrinsic principles that would otherwise permit the system to experience higher ordering and adaptiveness. This is especially the case in relation to the system's true constituents (i.e., adolescents).

Entropy and Negentropy

For closed or open systems, entropy abounds. Similar to the instance of evolution itself, without a dynamic balance between appropriate openness and closedness, maximum disorder and disintegration occur (von Bertalanffy, 1968). "By allowing in either too much information or not enough information, the identity and thus the survival of the system are threatened [entropy]. On the other hand, [when there is an appropriate balance] the system is in a state of negentropy . . . it is tending toward maximum order" (Becvar & Becvar, 1993, p. 74). The very survival of a system depends on accepting input that is appropriate. Unfortunately for most systems (including the juvenile justice apparatus), the adaptive knowledge necessary for negentropy to occur continues to be lacking.

Repeated efforts by state legislatures and courtroom settings to adhere to the legal needs of the adolescent (e.g., right to counsel, right to know charges, right to cross-examine witnesses), ensnare or hamstring the operation of the juvenile justice system. While some commentators believe that these adult rights guaranteed to adolescents are fundamental and inalienable (e.g., Feld, 1999), the juvenile system's general inability to appreciate the cognitive deficits that some youth possess in relation to these liberties (Ackerman, 1999; Grisso, 1981), demonstrates that it is not an open system. It is not sufficient that a system is open and closed *sometimes* to input; rather, it is absolutely imperative that it appropriately balances these states for its own health and generative potential.

> Not only was Doug distrustful of the system itself (due in part to what had happened to his father), but also he was distrustful of his public defender. Simply put, Doug said that the attorney was one of "them," part of the system. As a result, Doug refused for the most part to utilize his attorney effectively, putting his situation in further jeopardy.

The tenets and concepts delineated above are widely regarded in the GST field as foundational to the maintenance and growth of all healthy systems (Becvar & Becvar, 1993; von Bertalanffy, 1968). Moreover, proponents of General Systems Theory assert that utilizing these basic principles unifies and restores deteriorating systems. However, in the case of the juvenile justice apparatus, the application of these insights and their potential to make the system itself more adaptive have yet to be considered. While various states adopt different purpose clauses in their juvenile justice statutes, at best these statutes superficially comply with the GST tenets. The question that remains is where to go from here and what to do. Even though it would be quite easy to suggest that the juvenile justice system adopt and implement GST concepts, the reality is that this is more complicated than it first appears. However, there is one particular system's perspective that not only adheres to the principles set forth by GST but also explains how the developmental period of adolescence could be best understood. This perspective is called Bowenian or family systems theory (Kerr & Bowen, 1988). Family Systems Theory (FST) is significant in that it can be used to reorganize the juvenile justice system so that it is reoriented to the formative experience of adolescent identity development. In this way, FST also helps make youths socially productive individuals.

CONTRIBUTIONS FROM THE BOWENIAN THEORETICAL PERSPECTIVE

As discussed in previous sections of this chapter, statutory purpose clauses say one thing yet their implementation suggests an entirely different reality. In addition, both the statutes and their reality fall woefully short of adhering to basic systems principles. In order to move the juvenile justice system closer to the core principles of GST, the Bowenian theoretical perspective is described. Unlike several other family systems theories (e.g., Strategic and Structural family systems theories), the Bowenian model respects and integrates the larger context of the family (e.g., extended family and society) into its approach, without losing sight of the individual. Typically, this is not the case with many other (if not most) family-oriented theoretical orientations. As a result, the utility of this perspective is evident in how it addresses the interests and needs of the individual, family, community, and society, without diminishing any of the participants.

The presentation of Bowenian family systems theory is a useful lens for viewing the developmental period of adolescence. In addition, it functions as a filter, allowing for the identification of practical interventions that ultimately serve the best interests of society. To demonstrate the utility of Bowenian family systems theory, its basic tenets are delineated. These tenets are mindful of GST and the comments outlined above pertaining to this theory. As such, the section that follows demonstrates how both theories (GST and FST) are assimilable for purposes of exploring the juvenile justice system and adolescent identity development.

Chronic Anxiety

To be sure, there can be no understanding of any individual or system without a proper understanding of anxiety and its nature. According to Bowen, chronic anxiety is the "emotional and physical reactivity shared by all [and] the responses . . . are automatic rather than mediated by the cortex" (Friedman, 1991, p. 140). Anxiety is produced from the competing forces of individuation and togetherness. Individuals with little chronic anxiety or those who can deal effectively with the anxiety that is present are able to assess their lives based on a personal evaluation of the circumstances as opposed to the pushes and pulls of others toward togetherness and alignment. When our anxiety is low, our cognitive processes are allowed to function optimally; when our anxiety is high and there is a lack of differentiation (a concept described shortly), our cognitive processes take a back seat to emotionality. An example of this within the juvenile justice system is the politicization of responses to adolescent difficulties. Instead of soundly reasoned responses that ensue from optimally functioning cognitive processes, emotionality overcomes these processes. As a consequence, rash decision-making takes place, negating healthy development for those affected. To be clear, this tenet does not champion intellectualization or rationalization to the exclusion of emotion. Instead, it advocates for differentiation.

> One of the options presented to Doug over the course of his entanglement with the juvenile justice system was to participate in an adolescent boot camp. The "get tough on juvenile crime" sentiment popular during the time openly and genuinely welcomed this untested program. Notwithstanding its lack of justification—especially in terms of efficacy—the major limitation to the program was removal from the community. The specific boot camp program made available to Doug was in a neighboring state. His family would never get to see him.

Differentiation

Friedman (1991) describes the Bowenian concept of differentiation as the ability to manage the forces of individuality and togetherness. Obviously, people differ in their ability to do this and, as a result, can be seen on a continuum of differentiation (sometimes referred to as the scale of differentiation). At high levels of differentiation, people are able to effectively deal with the anxiety experienced in relation to others, while simultaneously acting or responding based on their own evaluation of the situation. At lower levels of differentiation, a person is consumed and dictated by the force of togetherness;

a force that impedes separate thought or emotion. For those who act out of higher differentiation within their relationships, the "penalty" may include the removal of support or, in the extreme, total ostracism (Kerr & Bowen, 1988). Certainly, the stakes can be high in specific situations. Indeed, they are comparable to those experienced by policy makers who display "progressive" thinking in our legislatures.

For the highly differentiated person, while continual activity based on this type of individuation proves satisfying, it can also produce alienation from the public at times. For adolescents who become ensnared in a system that is predominantly (if not exclusively) based in emotionality and the forces of togetherness associated with lower differentiation, they have little maneuverability other than to meld with these forces. In these instances, the hope is that these children at some point may be able to shed the trappings of the system. Moreover, for the "juvenile delinquent," the process is akin to emotional abuse. Indeed, the care that is available is conditioned on sanctioned behavior (i.e., punishments or restrictions) rather than on creative, generative, pro-social conduct. The latter tendencies value and validate individuality, uniqueness, difference; adaptive and human characteristics that represent a sign of healthy adolescent development.

> Doug (and his attorney) rejected the boot camp scenario due in large part to the continued separation it would entail from his family. Instead, his attorney suggested the possibility of an intensive community-based program in which all possible social supports would be garnered for Doug. This program would allow Doug to return to his community, school, and family. As part of the proposal, Doug and his family would continue their sessions with me and would address the issues that brought Doug to the attention of the justice system. Doug would also be required to substantially contribute to the growth of his community in the form of service to his church, community center, or school. The prosecutor rejected the plan. It involved immediate placement back into the community without any significant period of incarceration.

Multigenerational Transmission Process

The multigenerational transmission process entails the waxing and waning of differentiation throughout the course of a family's history (Kerr & Bowen, 1988). The way in which this process works is quite straightforward. Individuals align themselves in marriage and in relationship with others of similar levels of differentiation and beget children that function at similar levels. This process continues across generations unless interrupted by a member of the family system that begins and *continues* to function at a higher level of differentiation. Since functioning at a higher level is quite difficult in the face of pushes and pulls toward togetherness, it is an arduous task to accomplish. Instead of functioning at the higher level, most people will resort to decreasing the chronic anxiety they experience through other processes (e.g., triangulating and emotional cutoffs, which are described elsewhere in this chapter).

For the juvenile justice system, the multigenerational transmission process unfortunately serves as its best ally for the status quo and its worst adversary for change. Since morphostatic processes abound in the system, it is unlikely that morphogenesis can be present as well. Recall that the overrepresentation of the one force therefore creates a dynamic disequilibrium. As such, this imbalance is a significant sign of dysfunction in the system since both are necessary for healthy development. Unfortunately, adolescent courts and related adjudication/treatment facilities engulf the youth in their respective multigenerational transmission processes (e.g., steadfast adherence to due process protections, bureaucratic procedures, inefficient methods). This is similar to a family's unwillingness or inability to allow for differentiation. In summary, the overall result for the system is the same: change, growth, and creativity are thwarted. When new practices are proposed or when novel insights are recommended, they amount to little more than old wine in new bottles (Bernard, 1992).

> For Doug, the multigenerational transmission process occurred from two perspectives. The first and most obvious is the parallel to his father's life, given that Doug was entangled in the justice system. The second relates to the prosecutor's rejection of a community-based placement for Doug. At the time that his case was brought to the attention of the juvenile justice system, the pendulum already had swung significantly in the direction of retribution. As such, there would be little (if anything) that could persuade the prosecutor or the courts that redemption in this instance was possible. The fact that it was an election year also did not help. The "get-tough-on-crime" mantra made certain that morphostatic forces would prevail.

Triangles

Because tension abounds in relationships of all kinds (especially in the family system), it comes as no surprise that individuals have developed coping strategies to deal with this tension. One principle strategy explored in the

Bowenian theoretical perspective is triangles. Kerr (1981) reports that when the chronic anxiety becomes too much for any two individuals in relationship to endure, triangulation occurs. In essence, the anxiety present in the dyadic exchange is divided into thirds by the absorption of another party. In families, this often involves children or one's in-laws. Regardless of who becomes triangulated, the dissipation of this anxiety to the third person is unproductive in the long term. This is because the original relationship now has an "outsider;" an individual who merely functions to bind or solidify the chronic anxiety. In this way, the individuals in the dyad avoid or forestall the hard work of dealing directly and effectively with their tension, impeding prospects for higher levels of differentiation that they would otherwise enjoy.

Inviting a third party into one's relationship with another in an attempt to mediate, dissipate, or extinguish the anxiety within the original dyad, considerably and deleteriously violates the systemic tenet of boundaries described earlier. When this violation occurs, nothing truly creative, healthy, or self-corrective can follow. The third individual is now part of the family's emotional process as opposed to a differentiated outsider. The breaking of the boundary destroys or undoes what is called the "crucible-effect" of the family. This concept as well as effective ways to intervene without disrupting the boundaries (e.g., therapy) will be described later. However, it is painfully obvious that the juvenile justice system has involved itself in the affairs of the family system and, consequently, is responsible for the triangulation that ensues. Originally, while this may have been proposed as an effective intervention strategy based on a commitment to objectivity and fairness, the reality has proven otherwise. Indeed, at best the juvenile justice system has disturbed the delicate boundaries of the family and, at worst (and more than likely) has damaged the community fabric of which the family and the adolescent are intimately a part.

> The only involvement that Doug had in the juvenile justice system prior to his current situation was a "beyond parental control" petition. Doug had been breaking his curfew and showing up late for school at the beginning of the academic year. The school counselor advised his mom to issue the petition so that she would not get into trouble, given her son's truancy. Once the petition was issued, a representative from the local human service agency began visiting the home. According to the mother, it was very humiliating because it made "me feel like I was a bad mother and that I couldn't control my son." The mother reported that by the time the petition had been ordered, Doug was back into the swing of school and had not broken curfew. However, the human services representative refused to disengage from the case and continued "providing services" for the next six months.

Emotional Cutoffs

Another way that anxiety and tension are bound (and not effectively addressed) within relationships is through emotional cutoffs. Papero (1990) defines an emotional cutoff as a means of dealing with the attachment to one's family and to one's relationships. Emotional cutoff is perhaps best illustrated in the example of individuals sharing a home but not a life together. Typically, people voice the sentiment implied in this concept through expressions such as "needing personal space." In actuality, personal space is not what they need. In order to function adaptively (given that we are a social species), it is necessary for us to relate. Avoiding or reducing our inherent sociability through emotional distance, preempts recursion and feedback. Again, these concepts are indicative of healthy systems. Without the give-and-take of exchange endemic to being human, differentiation cannot proceed and it certainly cannot succeed. At best, the emotional cutoff thwarts the process; at worst, it leads to lowering differentiation. In other words, in order to thrive, people must remain connected to others through meaningful interactions and relationships.

The juvenile justice system severs and destroys this healthy connectedness when separating adolescents from their families and communities via incarceration, foster care, and group home placement. Admittedly, one could argue that these system interventions do not necessarily impede connectedness. Indeed, there are other mechanisms for contact (e.g., visitation, telephone calls, letter writing). However, the reality is much different. In the everyday world of juvenile justice, connections of this sort are limited. Adolescents are removed from their environments and families, making their natural supports inaccessible. It is not uncommon for children to be placed great distances from their communities. For adults, this may simply tax their emotional connectedness to their family. For adolescents, their attachments to community and family are still developing. Indeed, these fragile, tenuous relationships are still developing in many instances. Thus, the forced distance only weakens the attachments and initiates emotional cutoffs.

> Doug's attorney worked hard to get the prosecutor to allow him to remain in his community and with his family. After much postadjudication "compromise," Doug received a disposition of confinement until the age of majority (i.e., 18 years old). In particular, he was sent to a local adolescent offender facility (aka juvenile prison) in the same county in which he lived. The facility was approximately fifteen miles from his family and his community. In essence, the disposition cut Doug off from his family for the next four years. In the wake of postadjudication, I lost contact with him. Although on several occasions I tried to set up times to meet with Doug at the

facility, I was continually rebuffed by the warden who explained: "we have our own psychologist here that can treat him."

The concepts put forth by Bowen and Bowenian theorists suggest that first and foremost the family is key to the healthy and adaptive development of the adolescent. Unlike most other theoretical orientations, the Bowenian family systems perspective encourages connectedness to the systems in which we are all embedded. It addresses the "vacuum" left by other conceptual models or perspective by moving the process of differentiation to the forefront. Admittedly, even with support from the community and larger society in which one lives, the period of adolescence can be difficult. Unfortunately, through the administration of the juvenile justice system and its courtroom activities and treatment facilities, society has not only impeded the process of differentiation but has initiated and supported unhealthy interventions with families. Drawing on Bowenian family systems theory, these questionable methods include emotional cutoffs, triangulation, and maladaptive binding of chronic anxiety. In the next section of this chapter, the FST concept of a crucible is discussed. It is a useful method for meaningfully addressing these very weighty concerns.

THE CRUCIBLE

According to Schnarch (1991), a crucible "is a highly nonreactive ("refractory") vessel in which a transfiguring reaction takes place . . . [T]he final desired result is not merely an additive mixture of ingredients; there is a catalytic process that creates a qualitatively different final product" (pp. 158–159). In the notion of a crucible, one must understand that the vessel already *contains* the necessary ingredients. The crucible does not allow for the dissipation of the contents outside of the vessel. The properties associated with the crucible are an apt metaphor for the relationship system of the family. They also represent a basis for understanding how "outside" ingredients (i.e., the juvenile justice system) impinge on the vessel.

At first glance, the crucible of the family (as well as the community) does not appear to fit the definition posited by Schnarch (1991). Most professionals and "objective" outsiders readily label many attributes and activities of the family and community as "reactive" and not "nonreactive." Time and again with our communities and families we witness physical and emotional strife. Corrupted dialogue, hurt feelings, spiteful interactions, and vengeful attitudes—both perceived and real—occur with alarming frequency according to the outside observer. However, what is not seen is the very rare circumstance wherein an individual is ostracized permanently from the family or community. The strife is contained within the boundaries of the system, within the crucible of the family and community.

Additionally, this strife and the aberrant behavior that is sometimes associated with it, is, at its core, consistent with GST and related system theories, particularly the notion of reorganization. When a system is interrupted as in the case of an individual who moves toward higher (or lower) differentiation, the system has an opportunity for growth and adaptation. Indeed, when left to function on its own in this capacity, there will be a higher order and negentropy will follow. When outside intervention or encroachment occurs, it precludes the transition to a higher order, to increased complexity, to self-organization. In short, its natural evolution has been preempted or halted. Recursion, feedback, and morphostasis/morphogenesis have been impaired. Indeed, external ingredients destroy the crucible.

The case of Doug amply demonstrates the potentially devastating impact of outside forces. We will never know what creative and healthy healing could have occurred in his life because the externally mandated interventions availed to Doug and his family resulted in separation. While certainly consistent with the punitive response to juvenile crime, this approach did not thoughtfully consider or explore options that encouraged the family, the community, and Doug to address the socially defined difficulties he was facing as an adolescent.

The point here is not about eliminating outside involvement. Indeed, it is just the opposite. Remember, striking a delicate balance between openness and closedness is essential for a system if it is to optimally function. If a system is inappropriately open or closed, it is subject to disintegration. Thus, the introduction of any new ingredients into the crucible must be wisely considered. For example, if the key reason to add an ingredient into the crucible is to dissipate the anxiety by spreading it to more participants (e.g., third parties), the crucible has transgressed its organic boundaries and is inappropriately open. Furthermore, if the principle reason not to add another ingredient into the crucible is based on fear and anxiety, the vessel again does a disservice to its boundaries and is inappropriately closed (e.g., consider the vessel's closedness to creativity and differing perspectives). This is not to suggest that the crucible and the dynamic equilibrium present in a system are tenuously fragile. Rather, there are wide parameters for inclusion and exclusion of ingredients into the family and community crucible. It is the strongest vessel there is; stronger than any socially or statutorily sanctioned system (e.g., the juvenile justice system).

As I think about Doug in retrospect, I have this curiosity. I am curious about what would have happened if the monetary resources expended on his adjudication, removal from the home, and subsequent incarceration had been allocated instead to the family in terms of assistance. When I think of assistance that would respect the family and community crucibles, I come up with the same thing: community and home-based care. Appropriately allowing support-ive "outsiders" into their family and community to help identify already available resources seems like a logical way to begin. Roger-ian-like education (i.e., genuine, empathic, and unconditional posi-tive regard) about the developmental experiences of adolescents also would be provided, instead of propaganda on the vicissitudes of life and the viciousness of the time. However, another part of me ques-tions whether any "outsider" was needed. As previously mentioned, maybe this was a phase for Doug, and self-correction would have taken place (like it did with the curfew and truancy issues). Unfor-tunately for him, the juvenile justice system desecrated the family's crucible.

Following the logic of Bowenian FST, the bottom line is that when left to its own devices, a family, with community and "tribal" connections present, will prosper and continue the negentropic processes of increasingly higher individuation among its members. In other words, the family system is not simply equipped to deal with these issues of growth and development because of its amorphous and dynamic equilibrium. Instead, through evolutionarily significant adaptive selection it is equipped to deal with its growth and devel-opment, and the dynamic equilibrium that it experiences is a part of that process.

PROVISIONS FOR THE ADOLESCENT AND A JUST SYSTEM

According to Marsha Levy-Warren (1996),

> adolescence is a period in life in which critical psychological changes occur. It is a time when character, a person's customary way of being in the world, crystallizes, and identity, the stable sense of who a person is, forms. It is the time that a fundamental psychological issue—achieving an independent identity, rooted in family but reaching out to the world beyond—is confronted and resolved. (p. xii)

From this passage it is clear that adolescents are not simply pre-adults but rather have special developmental milestones that must be met. In a just soci-ety, community, and family, the work of adolescence occurs in a relatively seamless fashion. Unfortunately, and as noted previously, there are impingements on the attainment of these milestones. These encroachments subsequently impede the adolescent's healthy development, forestalling (or thwarting) the child's ability to become a productive and responsive adult member of society. So what can be done to obviate the impact of these external interruptions and to increase prospects for justice? This final section provides some insight into several possible avenues for change, especially for those practitioners who come into contact with adolescents as a part of their work duties. Additional comments address the future role of society in these matters.

Professional Intervention

As noted at the outset of this chapter, those professionals involved with the juvenile justice system have ignored the effect of their work on those whom they serve (i.e., adolescents). Because of this, the deterioration or destruction of a key transitional stage in life course development takes place for these children. Thus, generally speaking, change begins by adhering to the previously delineated principles devoted to GST, Bowenian Family System Theory, and allied system theories. In order to comply with these principles, several steps are strongly recommended:

Think before you act. Prior to intervening, evaluating, and "preventing," consider carefully whether the proposed action bolsters the crucible that already exists in the community, or whether it is a perturbation on the system that hastens entropy. The latter effect was the case with Doug.

Respect the process of adolescence. While adolescence can be a tumultuous period for some youth, the reality is that most reflect on that time, perceiving it to be full of opportunities for growth and learning. Stifling the process (e.g., removal from the family, out-of-community placements), not only severs or undermines the existing attachments but also destroys many important opportunities for the adolescent to learn how to contain his or her anxiety within the family/community network, and to appropriately and healthily work through those difficulties. In Doug's case, supports were available within his community (e.g., family, extended kinship network, church, school). Unfortunately, the juvenile justice system did not take advantage of internal and more organic resources.

Remember the process of differentiation. Testing social mores and norms is an appropriate adolescent behavior. To censor or quash the creativity that comes from the occasional imbalance between morphostasis and morphogenesis does a disservice to the adolescent and to the youth's growth as a responsible citizen. Doug's truancy and home curfew difficulties were self-corrected prior to any outside intervention.

Consider your own motives. Many times professionals working with adolescents tend to intervene hoping that the child will not make the mistakes they themselves made during adolescence. This is a poor reason to intervene in a person's life. Indeed, this is the point at which the professional needs to recognize his or her own inability to cope and to contain self-anxiety. In these instances, pursuing professional assistance for oneself is strongly recommended. Certainly there are times when professionals, the adolescent's family, and the community are concerned about a particular child or behavior. Providing a holding environment (i.e., a crucible) that is respectful of boundaries is different than approaching the situation in a spirited, save-the-world mentality. To be sure, adolescents have been (successfully) maneuvering developmental milestones far longer that the juvenile justice system has been around.

Advocate for the youth's resources. Inherent in the youth's community and family are strengths that can be accessed. Accessing these strengths not only bolsters the family crucible but also teaches the adolescent an important lesson about coping with the difficulties of everyday life. Doug's mother genuinely tried to be supportive and present when he was incarcerated. However, completely unnecessary impediments imposed by those in charge (e.g., not letting his brothers in to see him) interfered with the salubrious effects of the crucible. Doug had resources that he could have employed; however, he was denied full use of those resources.

Educate your colleagues. The wealth of expertise that professionals have is of consequence for the juvenile justice system. It is imperative that one utilizes one's expertise to the advantage of all adolescents. Attempting to maintain a purportedly superior analytic and objective stance only cheapens the profession. Moreover, it is detrimental to the youth involved. Judicious passion that comes from a place of care and respect can work.

Adopt and base your findings and opinions in systemic thinking. Most professionals are leery of doing this. As mentioned in the previous recommendation, objectivity is not a "removed" stance. Objectivity is about basing your findings in the true nature of forensic psychology. Remember, forensic psychology emerged out of a conviction that the law could be humanized for those who became entangled in it (Arrigo, 2002). Theoretically speaking, culturally and community-sensitive recommendations that adhere to the principles set forth in systemic thinking (in particular, the Bowenian perspective), not only form a solid foundation but also a basis out of which adolescents can thrive into adulthood. If this foundation had been valued by all participants in Doug's situation, there would have been a different outcome. Indeed, the language utilized in the courts and in the discussions of possible dispositions would have been based on how to preserve the crucible of the family, engage the family resources, and support Doug's differentiation as an adolescent.

Encourage morphogenesis. Growth, change, and creativity are the hallmarks of adolescence. The imbalance that will inevitably occur can be fruitful for both the family through the multigenerational transmission process and the individual through increased differentiation. There is no need to worry that the imbalance will be too severe to be corrected or that the dynamic equilibrium will be forever compromised. There is a natural recursiveness that occurs. The practitioner's job is to simply help the adolescent and family be open and responsive to the feedback. Doug was responsive to this feedback when he returned to school and made his curfew.

Societal Interventions

Prior to his death, Murray Bowen suggested that the emotional processes found in the family can and do run parallel to the emotional processes in society (Bowen, 1985). He went so far as to say that "there is evidence that the political-legislative process is more emotional reactiveness than logical thinking, and that much legislation is more of a 'band-aid' type of legislation directed at symptom relief than at underlying factors" (Bowen, 1985, p. 273). Hence, there is the need for higher societal differentiation. Based on the GST and FST tenets described throughout the chapter, the following remedies are suggested for how best to address the juvenile justice system and, more generally, society's response to adolescence.

Reconstitute the juvenile justice system. At no point since its inception has the juvenile justice system even approached a systems theory—sensitive model. While it has adopted purpose clauses that can be configured to support some of the tenets of systems theories, it has fallen woefully short in implementation. Moreover, while legal gains have been made at times to adjust the system toward a fair process for juveniles (e.g., the bestowal of adult due process rights), many adolescents do not comprehend or appreciate the adjustments. The time spent by society on adjusting an unjust system could be better utilized elsewhere.

Strengthen the crucible. The time spent by legislatures and the public-at-large on the "rampant" juvenile delinquency problem could be easily transferred to strengthening the crucible of adolescence. Meaningful investments of time and resources in family and community support services could facilitate this. This is not synonymous with disrupting the family system. Instead, it equates with a provision of resources (without strings) that allow the families and community systems to deal more effectively with adolescents in their process of individuation.

Establish systems services. When the multigenerational transmission process produces generational misfortune in the form of lower differentiation, systems services that are community-sensitive, rather than punitive-based, can (and should) be accessed. The goal here is to increase individuation and family differentiation. We can only speculate what would be different had this happened in Doug's situation.

Honor adolescents and adolescence. To honor adolescents as the future leaders of our communities and society only makes good sense. Doing this is a more difficult process; however, it is not insurmountable. Steps can be implemented that reinforce the community's systemic boundaries. This will allow a zone of safety for the youth to experiment in healthy (and possibly unhealthy) ways, without damaging their future prospects (e.g., labeling them delinquents or offenders). By honoring them in this way, society is saying that adolescence is a time of wonderment and self-discovery. It is a time for one to explore one's comfort zone and push it farther outward, developing lifelong healthy coping strategies when confronted with the chronic anxiety that we all encounter, at one time or another.

Legislate. Admittedly, this country is legislative-prone. However, as previously mentioned, most legislation is emotionally reactive. Instead of being based in the cesspool of emotional reactivity, legislation has the ability to be cerebrally oriented; that is, to be thoughtful and informed. Proper legislation can help effectively balance (or better yet help each community and family balance) the forces of togetherness and individuation.

CONCLUSIONS: BRINGING IT BACK TOGETHER

Although difficult to imagine, the truth is that eventually self-correction for the atrocities perpetrated against the adolescent population will occur, and adaptive self-organization will follow. Unfortunately, these autopoietic changes will not transpire soon enough to prevent the significant damage that the adolescents of today confront and the ones of the near future will confront. Until that point occurs or until that process begins, societal regression (entropy) will continue unabated. Current statutory "purpose clauses" within various state juvenile justice systems do not adhere to the basic tenets that all systems (and their agents) must abide by if they are to function effectively and are to be adaptive. Instead, the juvenile justice system negates those principles; these are guidelines that ensure a just society. Substantially reconfiguring the juvenile justice system so that it adheres to principles that would produce (or at least not impair) health is unlikely. As a result, the focus needs to shift away from the reconfiguration of societal mechanisms (i.e., the juvenile justice system), to a focus on the developmental process that, if left unencumbered, will become fruitful on its own. At most, a strengthening of the community/family/relationship crucible can be attempted. Paradoxically, however, this strengthening would entail less statutorily codified procedures but would involve more reverence for the developmental period of adolescence.

The word *diminishing* suggests that at one point the developmental period of adolescence was a sanctuary for growth, creativity, wonder, experimentation, investigation, individuation, and unencumbered identity develop-ment. However, the reality is that this probably has never been the case in the history of our nation and those of many others. This does not negate the pos-sibility of increasing the sanctity of youth through the measures noted throughout this chapter; but it does support Bowen's (1985) belief that the current trend is entropic. Through community-family involvement, as well as political and legislative action, society must continually ask itself whether it wants to differentiate to a higher level of order and reinitiate negentropic forces for the developmental period of adolescence. Hopefully, the answer to this question will occur before more generations of adolescents slide further down the continuum of differentiation. Debates on and discourse about issues such as this are precisely what Arrigo (2002) has encouraged. The next task is to apply the insights of GST and Bowenian FST to relevant areas of juvenile forensic psychology research, policy, and action.

NOTES

1. For a more detailed review of the history of childhood and adolescence with respect to their legal status, the reader is referred to Feld (1999).

2. For more detailed analyses of these changes, the reader is encouraged to review the edited volume by Fagan and Zimring (2000) and the text by Bernard (1992).

3. All comments pertaining to the case of Doug are based on the therapeutic interventions and the advocacy actions of the first author.

REFERENCES

Ackerman, M. J. (1999). *Essentials of Forensic Psychological Assessment.* New York: John Wiley & Sons.

Arrigo, B. A. (2002). "The Critical Perspective in Psychological Jurisprudence: Theo-retical Advances and Epistemological Assumptions. *International Journal of Law and Psychiatry* 25, 151–172.

——— & Schehr, R. C. (1998). "Restoring Justice for Juveniles: A Critical Analysis of Victim Offender Mediation." *Justice Quarterly* 15(4), 629–666.

Bazemore, G. (2000). "Rock and Roll, Restorative Justice, and the Continuum of the Real World: A Response to 'Purism' in Operationalizing Restorative Justice." *Contemporary Justice Review* 3(4), 459–477.

——— & Schiff, L. (2001). *Restorative Community Justice: Repairing Harm and Trans-forming Communities.* Cincinnati, OH: Anderson Publishing Co.

——— & Walgrave, L. (1999). *Restoring Juvenile Justice: Repairing the Harm of Youth Crime.* Monsey, NY: Criminal Justice Press.

———— & Umbreit, M. (1995). "Rethinking the Sanctioning Function in Juvenile Court: Retributive or Restorative Responses to Youth Crime." *Crime & Delinquency* 41(3), 296–316.

Becvar, D. S. & Becvar, R. J. (1993). *Family Therapy: A Systemic Integration,* 2nd ed. Boston, MA: Allyn and Bacon.

Bernard, T. J. (1992). *The Cycle of Juvenile Justice.* New York, NY: Oxford University Press.

Bowen, M. (1985). *Family Therapy in Clinical Practice.* Northvale, NJ: Jason Aronson.

Children's Bureau (1969). *Legislative Guide for Drafting Family and Juvenile Court Acts* (Children's Bureau Publication No. 472-1969). Washington, DC: U.S. Government Printing Office.

Feld, B. C. (1999). *Bad Kids: Race and the Transformation of the Juvenile Court.* New York, NY: Oxford University Press.

Fagan, J. & Zimring, F. E. (eds.). (2000). *The Changing Borders of Juvenile Justice: Transfer of Adolescents to the Criminal Court.* Chicago, IL: The University of Chicago Press.

Friedman, E. H. (1991). "Bowen Theory and Therapy." In A. S. Gurman & D. P. Kniskern (eds.), *Handbook of Family Therapy: Volume II* (pp. 134–170). New York, NY: Brunner/Mazel.

Griffin, P. (2000). "National Overviews: State Juvenile Justice Profiles." Pittsburgh, PA: National Center for Juvenile Justice. Retrieved March 2, 2002, from http://www.ncjj.org/stateprofiles/.

Grisso, T. (1981). *Juveniles' Waiver of Rights: Legal and Psychological Competence.* New York: Plenum.

Kerr, M. E. (1981). "Family Systems Theory and Therapy." In A. S. Gurman & D. P. Kniskern (eds.), *Handbook of Family Therapy: Volume I* (pp. 226–264). New York, NY: Brunner/Mazel.

———— & Bowen, M. (1988). *Family Evaluation: An Approach Based on Bowen Theory.* New York: W. W. Norton & Company.

Levy-Warren, M. H. (1996). *The Adolescent Journey: Development, Identity Formation, and Psychotherapy.* Northvale, NJ: Jason Aronson.

Office of Juvenile Justice and Delinquency Prevention. (1998 December). *Guide for Implementing the Balanced and Restorative Justice Model* (NCJ No. 167887). Washington, DC: U.S. Government Printing Office.

————. (1999 December). *Juvenile Justice: A Century of Change.* (NCJ No. 178995). Washington, DC: U.S. Government Printing Office.

Papero, D. V. (1990). *Bowen Family Systems Theory.* Boston, MA: Allyn and Bacon.

Schnarch, D. M. (1991). *Constructing the Sexual Crucible: An Integration of Sexual and Marital Therapy.* New York: W. W. Norton & Company.

Siegel, L. & Senna, J. (2000). *Juvenile Delinquency: Theory, Practice, and Law,* 7th ed. Belmont, CA: Wadsworth/Thomson Learning.

Snyder, H. N. & Sickmund, M. (1999). *Juvenile Offenders and Victims: 1999 National Report.* Washington, DC: Office of Juvenile Justice and Delinquency Prevention.

van Ness, D. & Strong, K. H. (1997). *Restoring Justice.* Cincinnati, OH: Anderson Publishing.

von Bertalanffy, L. (1968). *General System Theory: Foundations, Development, Applications,* rev. ed. New York: George Braziller.

Zehr, H. & Mika, H. (1998). "Fundamental Concepts of Restorative Justice." *Contemporary Justice Review* 1, 47–55.

Chapter 6

Recent Perspectives on Penal Punitiveness

Véronique Voruz

Overview

The disconcerting emergence of penal punitiveness as the overarching orientation for the criminal justice systems in both the United Kingdom and the United States is regarded by many as a reaction to the sense of insecurity that permeates the civilizations of late modernity, a period that is often said to be shaped by the decline of state sovereignty. In this chapter I shall present an overview of the distinct interpretations of penal punitiveness elaborated by a number of prominent social scientists. Following this presentation, I shall then argue that the social, economic, cultural, and political mutations identified by these authors remain too narrow. By contrast, psychoanalytic theory affords us the possibility of resituating the emergence of penal punitiveness in terms of the three phenomena that structure the civilizations of late modernity: the predominance of the discourse of science; the ubiquity of anxiety; and a heavy reliance on segregative practices. I draw the argument to a close by arguing that critical criminology, having apprehended penal punitiveness along lines that were drawn by the discourse of crime control, in fact produces the scientific rationality that the latter requires as theoretical support.

This replacement of the power of the individual by the power of a community constitutes the decisive step of civilization. The essence of it lies in the fact that the members of the community restrict themselves in their possibilities of satisfaction, whereas the individual knew no such restrictions. The first requisite of civilization, therefore, is that of justice—that is, the assurance that a law once made will not be broken in favor of an individual. This implies nothing as to the ethical value of such a law.
                                    —Freud, "Civilization and Its Discontents"

A previous version of this chapter was delivered at the annual conference of the American Society of Criminology (Atlanta, Georgia, November 7–10, 2001).

The background affect of policy is now more frequently a collective anger
and a righteous demand for retribution rather than a commitment to a
just, socially engineered solution.

—David Garland, *The Culture of Control*

INTRODUCTION

To an informed audience, the relatively recent proliferation of punitive policies in both the United States and the United Kingdom[1] is no doubt most
familiar. Indeed, these policies have become so frequent as to redefine the
threshold of acceptability in the domain of crime control,[2] particularly with
regard to the rights and dignity of offenders or even would-be offenders. At
approximately the same time, allowing for the slight temporal lag that sepa-
rates theory from practice, a number of academics switched their concerns to
the latest and most unbecoming avatar of modernity. A suitable beginning
was to christen the phenomenon: *penal punitiveness,* a fitting term to encap-
sulate what "law and order" stands for in the "modern" world.

The same familiarity also extends to the thematic incantations that
orchestrate the unfolding of the pervasive rhetoric of insecurity. For in effect,
the failure of traditional responses—essentially those known as *penal welfarism* and *retributivism* (Garland, 2001b, pp. 53–73)—to curtail crime
cleared the way for the relentless enforcement of the twofold and, above all,
opinion-friendly orientation of the contemporary criminal justice system:
incapacitation and *prevention*.[3] Thus today, both these goals are being tire-
lessly hailed as the royal roads to a restored public confidence, with the latter
increasingly presenting itself as a key objective for our governments in devising crime-control strategies.[4]

Broadly speaking, then, criminal justice currently declines itself in two
seemingly unrelated modes. On the one hand, there is a growing tendency to
isolate and neutralize the members of a set defined, with convenient vague-
ness, as representing *dangerous, serious* or *persistent* offenders.[5] This desire to
identify and *incapacitate* the "enemy within" inspired a number of repressive
measures such as mandatory minimum sentences, "three strikes" provisions,
and parole release restrictions, to name but a few in a series of dispositions
designed to remove the undesirable from society with something akin to sur-
gical precision. Not surprisingly, these measures have contributed their fair
share to the unprecedented rise in the prison population of both countries.[6]

The second trend is illustrated by the strong emphasis placed on *prevention* in recent crime control proposals and legislation.[7] However, the type of
prevention foregrounded of late is highly specific. Unlike the welfarism of
yore, and through elective short-sightedness, it solely focuses on the circumstances of the individual offender, thereby heralding the terminal demise of

the collective project of modernity. Indeed, this decidedly individualized approach favors the reform of the criminal by means of his or her responsibilization[8] in lieu of either classical rehabilitation or social reform. As the architects of this approach explain it, responsibilization follows given that existing or previous penal interventions repeatedly have been shown not to work; that is, "nothing works" (Garland, 2001b). In other words, our crime control policies unabashedly ascribe whatever flaw the criminal behavior is predicated on exclusively to the individual offender (Lianos, 2001, p. 20). Thus, the opportunity for correction is equally within the absolute province of the offender. How is this individualized modality of prevention to operate? Quite simply, it functions by way of the detection and monitoring of actual or potential deviance,[9] and with a view to eventually securing the deviant's adhesion to the dominant morality through a process that one may term "ethical reconstruction" (Rose, 2000, p. 334).

The rise of penal punitiveness and the multiplication of control techniques being well documented, this chapter will explore, if somewhat obliquely, what have become riddling questions for many a researcher. These interrogations can take one or more of the following guises. What will be the impact of these punitive, intrusive developments in the field of social control on the future of criminal justice? Are these developments the necessary drawbacks of an efficient struggle against a rising criminality? Or, are there other, more complex forces behind the institution of a "culture of control"? and if yes, what is the nature of these forces? Are they economic, sociological, political, ideological, or cultural? Last, and perhaps most important, *how do the repressive tendencies of our criminal justice systems reflect on the political credos underpinning our liberal democracies?*

Having thus outlined some of the key aspects of a concern that is not only academic—arising as it does from the spreading of *segregative* practices—I will now move on to broach an issue that affords the consistency of a common inquiry to the multiple interrogations listed above: that of the source of "modern" intolerance itself.

ACCOUNTING FOR "MODERN" INTOLERANCE

The following observation, then, is our starting point: American and British attitudes toward crime and criminal justice are currently undergoing a profound transformation, the effects of which are manifest in the insistence of the public on exacting retribution from the criminal, and on being protected *at any cost*. These "righteous demands for retribution," these requests for absolute security, are matched by a marked governmental emphasis on prevention as the new overarching aim of the criminal justice system, and one that is deemed to justify all manners of interference with the private life of offenders.

These broad orientations, which currently structure the discourse of crime control, find a first common point in the source of their momentum: the seemingly unquenchable feeling of *insecurity,* increasingly depicted as the unremitting affliction of industrialized democracies. The second feature shared by theories of retribution, incapacitation, and prevention lies in the legitimizing function they perform. Indeed, such theories supply the discursive material necessary for the cogent unraveling of a rhetoric that affords legitimacy to the task of *segregation.* For in effect, what else is at stake in the current discourse of criminal justice, if not the identification of deviant elements for segregative purposes, be they terrorists, pedophiles, drug addicts, or even repeat property offenders?

As to the common denominator operating in the regrouping of these multiple forms of offending behavior, it is the threat to security that these *visible, antimoral* modalities of deviance incarnate. This threat to security may be in the guise of nonrespect for life, innocence and private property, or in the rejection of work ethics, individual "freedom" of choice and the joys of consumerism. The challenge posed by deviance to the moral consensus of our advanced democracies therefore justifies a ruthless segregation that, in turn, and following the well-known dynamics of group-formation, reinforces the social bond uniting the law-abiding remainder of the community. *Segregation, thus, is what supports the contemporary social bond.*[10]

The segregative nature of these recent developments is, in one form or another, widely recognized in the field of criminology; however, the reactions that they arouse differ wildly. Thus, some are content with analyzing and critiquing the minutiae of penal punitiveness from an empirical perspective, while others concern themselves more specifically with the enigma that they perceive to reside at the core of the present punitive drive. In this chapter, I shall concentrate on the latter enterprise. Accordingly, I begin by reviewing what I consider to be the leading theoretical advances recently made in the endeavor to decipher the seemingly contradictory subtexts that orient the dialectical unfolding of a "culture of insecurity."

The Media, Fear of Crime, Populist-Punitiveness-Loop

An already traditional explanation would pin the responsibility for penal punitiveness on the media. This argument, a classical variation on the social construction theme, unravels along the following lines: first of all, it is said—with the backing of a wealth of supporting evidence—that the media unduly inflate fear of crime by presenting sensationalist accounts of horrific or violent criminal acts. The sensationalist approach of the media is then seen to fuel public demand for zero-tolerance policing, tough-on-crime legislation, truth in sentencing, and preventive measures such as the keeping of registers on sexual offenders against children, class A drug traffickers or, most recently, potential juvenile offenders. Further, in a second moment, the commercial interest of the media in overemphasizing violent and sexual crime is said to be compounded by the reactionary inclinations of a broadly conservative owner-ship. This line of argument concludes by intimating that our politicians, bereft of ideological vision, have taken to fight for the moral high-ground on the insecurity debate for electoral purposes and that, consequently, they do their best to outdo one another in deferring to the public's demands for enhanced security. From such a perspective, media misrepresentation, relayed by political manipulation is, by and large, the main driving force behind the profuse enactment of a series of tough-on-crime policies.

However, this sequential reasoning does not withstand deeper scrutiny. Indeed, even if we were to admit that the public really is as repressive as it is sometimes made out to be, it is evident that no amount of misrepresentation would ever succeed in indiscriminately shaping the public opinion were there not already a propitious ground for feelings of insecurity to flourish. Thus, and notwithstanding the facile attractions of the populist punitiveness analy-sis, it would be unwise not to consider potentially darker origins both for feel-ings of insecurity and the prevailing social treatment of such subjective anxieties—namely, segregation.

Contextual Interpretations of Penal Punitiveness

In recent years, the study of penal punitiveness has yielded a number of highly sophisticated analyses striving to identify the factors orienting a more elusive transformation: that of our civilization. In these analyses, our punitive criminal justice system no longer figures as a self-contained object of study. Instead, it is resituated as a manifestation of the contemporary social processes at play in the ongoing evolution of "modern" societies. In the fol-lowing section I shall discuss some such recent explanations accounting for, on the one hand, the prevalence of feelings of insecurity and, on the other, the generalized acceptance of segregation as a preferred social response to crime.

I will then bring this paper to a close by pointing to the conspicuous absence of a theory of the subject in such accounts, and by sketchily isolating possible lines of future inquiry on the basis of such a theory. Indeed, I would argue that valuable insights are to be gained through the apprehension of the constellation of phenomena gathered under the heading of penal punitiveness from the perspective of psychoanalysis, and this in spite of the discredit incurred by this discipline in certain academic fields. In fact, I consider the advances of psychoanalysis to remain exceedingly relevant for the purposes of making sense of *the dynamics of civilization—and above all, of that of its discon-tents* (see Derrida, 2000)—if only because psychoanalysis does not let itself be arrested by the elemental opacity that lies at the heart of all human constructs.

PENAL PUNITIVENESS IN PERSPECTIVE

I will now delineate the contours of the four distinct approaches that I found to be of interest when studying the specific issue of penal punitiveness. These include the perspectives of: (1) culture; (2) politics; (3) economics; and (4) sociology. Each of these approaches addresses a particular facet of the modernist orientation to crime and its control.

The Cultural Dimension: "A New Collective Experience of Crime"

A recent and most worthwhile contribution to the debate on punitiveness can be found in the concluding volume of Garland's trilogy, entitled *The Culture of Control* (2001b). Indeed, interrogating punitiveness is the book's very *raison d'être*.

Garland initiates his erudite analysis of the contemporary modalities of crime control by presenting a careful genealogy of penal punitiveness, the actuality of which he affirms to be attested to by the presence of twelve distinct indices. Among other indices, these include the prevalence of the figure of the victim, the "decline of the rehabilitative ideal," the "commercialization of crime control," and the "reinvention of the prison" (2001b, chapter I). However, for Garland a mere genealogy of punitiveness would be insufficient; hence, his proposed study of the historical preconditions of the appearance of punitiveness is to include sociological elements as well.

Accordingly, Garland proceeds to argue that recent crime control policies cannot be understood in isolation; that is, as a series of phenomena of concern only to criminal justice. Rather, they are to be apprehended as part of a network of conflicting social and cultural transformations. These transformations, though they play themselves out in other registers, nonetheless paved the way for the progressive constitution of new forms of crime control. Indeed, Garland argues that these other changes gradually shaped the form of civilization he calls "late modernity," and provided the propitious background for the emergence of a culture of control.

There is obviously much more to Garland's analysis, but for the purpose of this chapter, I shall focus on his interpretation of the causes of penal punitiveness. In this respect, Garland's position is that criminology's misconstruction of penal punitiveness is to be ascribed to the failure of its theorists to take account of the part played by individual consciousness in the transformation of social processes. Thus, he states that "too often our attention focuses on the state's institutions and neglects the informal social practices on which state action depends" (2001b, p. 6).

In other words, punitiveness for Garland is not simply an effect of certain changes in the state's response to crime. This is not to say that he disregards changes undergone by the state in recent years. Indeed, these changes are themselves characteristic of late modernity. For instance, Garland refers to the contribution made by rising criminality to the deliquescence of the myth of the sovereign state, insofar as the uncontrollable rise in crime rates exposed the incapacity of the criminal justice system to control crime. The state's patent incapacity to offer security to its citizens brought water to the mill of the liberal project, and validated a further dismantling of the state. In fact, Garland even goes so far as to suggest that if repressive policies are supported and even relished by some policy makers, it is insofar as the use of public force allows the state to reassert its faltering sovereignty (2001b, chapter V).

Yet, although Garland does accord a certain significance to the decline of state sovereignty, penal punitiveness for him is principally consequent on other transformations affecting the social field as a whole. Thus, he clearly indicates his belief in the formation of "a new pattern of mentalities, interests, and sensibilities that has altered how we think and feel about the underlying problem" (Garland, 2001b, p. 6). Again, this quote clearly identifies individual consciousness as the primary locus of social change: for it is the way in which "we think and feel" about crime that is of primary importance, not the conflicting responses of the criminal justice system.

Thus, Garland is foregrounding the significance of the social context in which the culture of control came into being. Being *au fait* with the criticisms heaped on social constructionism, Garland is however careful not to imply the existence of a direct causal relation between the social and the penal field. Instead, he is reminding us that the changing consciousness of social actors plays a crucial part in transforming the *habitus* of criminal justice, this itself being a precondition both to policy making and implementation. As he describes it:

> Structures, and above all structural changes, are emergent properties that result from the recurring, re-iterative actions of the actors who occupy the social space in question. The consciousness of these actors—the categories and styles of reasoning with which they think and the values and sensibilities that guide their choices—is therefore a key element in the production of change and the reproduction of routine, and must be a major focus for a study of this kind. The actors and agencies who occupy the field of criminal justice (. . .) are the human subjects through whom and by whom historical processes are brought about. (Garland, 2001b, p. 24)

The logic that informs Garland's conception of the culture of control should, by now, be readily apparent: our lives in western liberal democracies are shaped by certain conditions that influence social actors' responses to crime. Garland even identifies the social group "responsible" for such changes. In his account, it is primarily the shifting attitudes of the middle-class toward crime that are key to understanding the advent of penal punitiveness. Indeed, this constituency, the foremost supplier of criminal justice personnel, previously pro-welfarism, has now relinquished this mind-set.

In Garland's analysis, the next step is to isolate the precise factual configuration that led to the spreading of intolerance to all classes, as well as the generalization of the sense of insecurity and its consequence; namely, the call for "punitive segregation" (2001b, p. 142). Thus, in an article that slightly predates his book, "The Culture of High Crime Societies" (2000), Garland offers his interpretation of the causal constellation that eventually resulted in the emergence of a culture of control (further developed in chapter VI of *The Culture of Control*, 2001b). In this essay, he asserts that such repressive developments would not have been possible in the absence of a deeply rooted feeling of insecurity. Further, for Garland this feeling of insecurity has genuine causes: a real increase in crime, and more specifically, visible crime. As he explains:

> The social and spatial changes that gave rise to the high crime rates of the 1960s and subsequent decades also, and independently, transformed the middle-class experience of crime. From being a problem that mostly affected the poor, crime (and particularly vandalism, theft, burglary and robbery) increasingly became a daily consideration for anyone who owned a car, used the subway, left their house unguarded during the day, or walked the streets at night. [. . .] And as the tell-tale signs of crime and disorder became more visible on the streets—in the forms of vandalism and graffiti, the incivility of unsupervised teenagers, or the erratic behavior of the newly de-institutionalized mentally ill—fear of crime became an established part of daily existence." (Garland, 2000, p. 359)

Thus, following Garland, if we currently live in a context in which the drive to punish and segregate is so prevalent, this is because we are profoundly marked by "a new collective experience of crime" (2001b, p. 105). In turn, this new collective experience is accounted for by the fact that we live in "high-crime societies." Moreover, our exposure to high levels of visible crime has exposed the state's incapacity to deliver security.

What I have presented here is clearly an abridged account of a single dimension of Garland's complex analysis of the culture of control. However, it is one that will prove sufficient for the purposes of this chapter, which is to isolate and displace the predominant lines of thought in critical criminology's apprehension of the two key phenomena of insecurity and segregation. And indeed, here we may point out that one may rightfully question the critical radicality of a position content to account for the prevalence of punitiveness in terms of a reaction to rising criminality, since this happens to be precisely our governments' contention.

A Political Analysis: "The Government of Insecurity"

In his article entitled "Government and Control," Rose (2000) also takes stock of recent "intelligible shifts in ways of thinking about and seeking to ensure control." Like Garland, Rose acknowledges the necessity to "relocate the problem of crime and its control within a broader field of rationalities and technologies for the conduct of conduct" (ibid., p. 324). Indeed, it is clear that the criminal justice system plays only an infinitesimal part in social control, or in the "government of moral order" (ibid., p. 321).

Moreover, and once again consistent with Garland (2001b), Rose discerns that the contradictory tensions to which the field of crime control are subjected can be accounted for in terms of what I would simply call the dynamics of group-formation. Indeed, the rather classical axes that structure crime control in Rose's analysis are the inclusion of the same and the exclusion of the other, and they are those which Freud (1921) had already perceived to be activated through the function of identification in the constitution of group-identity. As such, it is worth noting that Garland, who orients his discussion around the expressions of *"preventive partnership"* and *"punitive segregation,"* also echoes the inclusion-exclusion polarization of Rose's analysis. Accordingly, it should not prove too bold an extrapolation to suggest that the operational factor at play for both thinkers is the segregative logic that animates crime control practices. And last, we can also note that the logic present in the latest analyses of crime control in fact relies on the function of segregative practices in group-formation, which psychoanalytic theory had long identified as inseparable from civilization.

Rose's (2000) perspective on the "bewildering variety of developments in regimes of control" (p. 321), however, differs markedly from that of Garland (2001b) in at least one key respect. For while Garland articulates his analysis around the pivotal existence of a "real" factor, "a new collective experience of crime," Rose chooses to emphasize the part assumed by morality and ethics in present-day crime control techniques.

Rose encapsulates the multiple and apparently contradictory inventions of modern crime control under the heading of the emergence of programs for the "conduct of conduct." Following Foucault's (1982) work on power, and no doubt inspired by the Deleuzian (1988) interpretation thereof, Rose (2000) chooses to analyze crime control in terms of power relations (p. 322). In other words, and quite schematically, since every individual is at the same time both the object and subject of power, it follows that it is impossible to identify either the *source* of power, a sovereign *agency*, or even a prevailing *intentionality*. Rose's preferred approach thus consists in the deciphering of the assemblage of current risk-management strategies.

Having thus laid down the theoretical premises of his argument, Rose proceeds to construct an analysis of current developments in the field of social control. Being far too sophisticated a thinker to assert that we live in a different era, or that we have made a clean break with modernity, Rose nonetheless affirms the actuality of three indisputable changes in the social field. He then asserts that these transformations, in turn, have had a considerable impact on the practices of crime control.

First, Rose (2000) argues that the ideal representation of the state's function has changed. The state is no longer to be a sovereign agent, "the guarantor and ultimate provider of security" (p. 323). Instead, the new ideal is that the state "should be a partner, animator and facilitator for a variety of independent agents and powers, and should exercise only limited powers of its own, steering and regulating rather than rowing and providing" (ibid., pp. 323–324). Clearly, this conception of the state is bound up with the prevalence of the neoliberal ideology.

Second, Rose (2000) announces the correlative transformation of the social field, which he describes in the following terms:

> [t]here has been a fragmentation of 'the social' as a field of action and thought, a unitary domain more or less coterminous with a national territory and coincident upon a single national economy. In its place we see economic circuits territorialized in other ways, for example in the themes of globalization and localization. (p. 324)

Having thus obligingly corroborated the oft-rehearsed obituary of the nation-state in its two habitual aspects (i.e., the decline of state sovereignty and the challenge posed by globalization to national unity), Rose then proceeds to identify a more original mutation. This third change, for Rose, concerns the function of morality.

The argument proceeds thus: the state, no longer sovereign, has relinquished its monopoly over the "government of moral order" and is now reduced to the residual function of supervising and organizing the actions of multiple, local agents in crime control who are now the prime actors in ensuring the "government of moral order." Crime control, no longer a regal privilege, now falls to the community. This demoted modality of crime control manifests itself in two forms. First, there is a *responsibilisation* of the community for its own security (Rose, 2000, p. 327), leading to the privatization of crime prevention which thrives on the "exacerbation of anxiety" (ibid., p. 328). This privatization of crime prevention, in turn, leads to the development of new commercial sectors, and this development has the effect of reinforcing the individualization of responsibility already foregrounded by the demise of the nation-state. Rose (2000) expresses this idea in the following terms:

> Through this multiplication of expertise in alliance with responsibilisation, the collective logics of community come into alliance with the ethos of individual autonomy characteristic of advanced forms of liberalism: choice, personal responsibility, control over one's own fate, self-promotion and self-government. (p. 329)

In a second moment, the emphasis on individual autonomy attendant to the responsibilization of the community (and of each individual within it) leads to a foregrounding of morality. For in an environment where every single individual is responsible for his or her own security, the "self-steering forces of honor and shame, of propriety, obligation, trust, fidelity and commitment to others" (Rose, 2000, p. 324) inevitably come to be valued.

Rose's (2000) three fold argument can be summed up thus: in view of the decline of the nation-state and its corollary, the responsibilization of each individual for the preservation of the community, we now live in a society where morality is paramount. The prevalence of morality, which replaces faith in the ideal of the sovereign state as absolute guarantor of security, transforms the meaning of deviance. Thus, if criminals are "morally" deviant, it is not so much because they are transgressors, but because they are not taking responsibility for their own well-being. On this score, Rose talks of individuals lacking "competence or capacity for responsible ethical self-management" (p. 333), who are "incapable of exercising responsible self-government" (p. 331), causing a risk to society and whose behavior is to be detected, managed and eradicated.

Finally, Rose (2000) also identifies the two tasks that still fall within the purview of the criminal justice system. These include ethical reconstruction or, alternatively, segregation. Both of these tasks enable the not-so-sovereign state to become sovereign again in the hallowed pursuit of risk-eradication.

On the one hand, the state is in charge of organizing the "ethical reconstruction" (Rose, 2000, p. 334) of the deviant person, where the aim is to enable the individual to achieve "self-reliance" (ibid.), and to remedy a deficiency seen to be an ethical flaw, a failure in personal responsibility. Ethical reconstruction is thus to be distinguished from welfarism, where social and psychological determinants were taken into account. Here, the individual is to be *empowered*, to be *taught freedom*, and to learn how to become self-reliant in a world where individual autonomy is paramount.

On the other hand, and should these attempts at ensuring the future autonomy of the deviant through empowerment prove fruitless, incapacitation and, in the extreme, preventive incapacitation will take over (Rose, 2000, p. 332). Indeed, and though they may no longer be the choice representatives of a sovereign power, "the prison, and penality more generally, have become crucial elements in the government of insecurity" (ibid., p. 336). Individuals that fail to achieve the ethical reconstruction demanded of them will thus be mercilessly segregated. Rose (2000) draws the following conclusion from his argument:

> Those who refuse to become responsible, to govern themselves ethically, have also refused the offer to become members of our moral community. Hence, for them, harsh measures are entirely appropriate. Three strikes and you are out: citizenship becomes conditional upon conduct. [. . . Thus,] the obverse of the responsibilising moral imperatives of welfare reform is the construction and exclusion of a semi-permanent, quasi-criminal population, seen as impervious to the demands of the new morality. (pp. 335–336)

We see, then, that for Rose (2000) the apparent contradictions of contemporary crime control are to be resituated in the broader context of "some rather general mutations and reconfigurations in the rationalities and technologies of government," which he calls "advanced forms of liberalism" (p. 337). The demise of the sovereign state, the responsibilization of the individual (and its corollary the culture of choice) have led to new forms of intolerance. Further, following Rose, it is because the responsibility for one's own security now lies with the community that the anxiety associated with crime and insecurity is more developed. In effect, the ultimate guarantee of security provided by the state is only available as a last resort, and only where the community has failed to protect itself through the private channels of risk-management.

In this analysis, penal punitiveness does not so much stem from moral panics, or a "new collective experience of crime," but from the altered meaning of political subjectivity. We live in a culture of choice, where individual freedom is the crucial virtue, and those who fail to achieve such an autonomous state of being should either be taught freedom or removed from society. As to the contemporary predominance of insecurity and the reliance on segregative practices, they represent by-products of this transformation of the function of the state.

To conclude on Rose's hypothesis, I will identify two problematic aspects in his analysis. First, the demise of the nation-state is not as averred as is frequently made out to be. On the contrary, it seems to me that a most fruitful venture would be to question the forms adopted by national sovereignty at the time of globalization.[11] Second, the function fulfilled by morality in our civilizations needs to be further analyzed. Why indeed should morality offer an effective response to feelings of insecurity? What are the precise dynamics involved in the imposition of morality? Both these fundamental issues are insufficiently explored in Rose's commentary and call for further inquiry.

The Economic Dimension: The Industrialization of Crime Control

In his book, *Crime Control as Industry,* Christie (2000) emphasizes the necessity to take account of the industrialization of crime control techniques when analyzing the evolution of crime control practices. He argues that this industrialization plays a crucial part in the proliferation of preventative and incapacitative strategies. His argument is twofold.

First, he states that imprisonment and other social control devices are in charge of dealing with the unproductive sections of society. Indeed, we now live in an era where unemployment is an unavoidable feature of a profit-ruled economy. Over the past decades, then, a new underclass has taken shape, stigmatized as unproductive. Further, and in view of cuts in public spending affecting most public agencies, the criminal justice system is fast becoming the first port of call for those who find no place in the new flexible economy, governed as it is by the imperative of productivity. Imprisonment, the process of criminalization, provide convenient ways of dealing with the marginalized and the nonproductive. Indeed, they do not require the existence of human service agencies and budgets, which run contrary to the efforts to roll back the welfare-state.

While the political advantage seems clear (i.e., no need to feel guilty about the excluded if they are criminals), the economic advantage is less certain. On this point, Christie (2000) offers the following insight:

> Societies of the Western type face two major problems: wealth is everywhere unequally distributed. So is access to paid work. Both problems contain potentialities for unrest. The crime control industry is suited for coping with both. This industry provides profit and work while at the same time producing control of those who otherwise might have disturbed the social process. (p. 13)

Clearly, then, the interest of industrialized crime control is that it succeeds it extracting profitability, employment, economic growth out of what used to be a financial burden on society (see also Bauman, 2000, p. 211).

Second, Christie (2000) reminds us of the influence of big business interests, prominent mostly in the United States where lobbying for tough law and order policies has become commonplace. Indeed, the privatization of crime control opens very profitable markets: security technology, privatized prisons, advertisements of prison services, insurance markets, and so on. As one Wall Street adviser bluntly put it,

> The beauty of the prison-management business . . . is that incarceration rates are increasing faster than the prison budgets of many states and municipalities. (*Wall Street Journal*, April 10, 1996)

In fact, Christie (2000) is simply drawing a logical inference from the privatization of crime control. The dynamics of capitalism will lead the crime control industry to behave in exactly the same way as all the other sectors that are open to market forces, for "there is a built-in drive for expansion in industrialization." Moreover, the "whole institution of crime control is in itself a part of the system of production . . . it produces control" (ibid., p. 184).

A Sociological Perspective: Capital Anxieties

To conclude this succinct overview on recent theoretical efforts to elaborate a "critical response" to penal punitiveness, I will briefly draw attention to a fourth perspective, the sociological perspective. In particular, I shall refer to yet a third article published in the same special issue of the *British Journal of Criminology*, along with Garland's "The Culture of High-Crime Societies" and Rose's "Government and Control." The sociological perspective is based on the work of Bauman (2000) as delineated in his paper, "Social Issues of Law and Order."

In this article, Bauman (2000) analyzes our liberal democracies in terms of the influence of capitalism on their subjects. He argues that the flexibility of the labor market is a fundamental anxiogenic factor in our industrialized civilizations. As an anxiety-producing agent, the labor market contributes to the development of feelings of insecurity and uncertainty that then become amalgamated with feelings of lack of safety. For Bauman, then, we suffer from what I would term *capital anxieties:* anxieties generated by wild or deregulated capitalism, the political economy favored by neoliberal states.

Bauman (2000) then proceeds to identify the connection between these capital anxieties and penal punitiveness. Thus, he argues that the exponential development of crime control strategies "is, in effect, symptomatic of a failure to face up to the challenge of existential insecurity generated by our social and economic arrangements" (ibid., p. 205). For Bauman, the "present-day law-

and-order obsession" (ibid., p. 220) operates as a mode of containment for the profound existential insecurity resulting from the uncertainty faced by most in the workplace (ibid., p. 213). Finally, and like the other perspectives broached in this chapter, Bauman situates segregation as a consequence of the generalization of insecurity. As he puts it:

> What the sharp acceleration of punishment-by-incarceration suggests, in other words, is that there are some new and large sections of the population targeted for one reason or another as the threat to social order, and that their forcible eviction from social intercourse through imprisonment is seen as an effective method to neutralize the threat, or at least to calm the public anxiety which that threat evokes. (Bauman, 2000, p. 213)

It is also worth noting that Bauman (2000) appropriately identifies what seems to have become a *sine qua non* in recent critical analyses on penal punitiveness, the decline of the nation-state. As he states, "in the world of global finances: state-governments are allotted the role of little else than oversized police-precincts" (Bauman, 2000, p. 216).

In sum, these four analyses—which I believe give a fair representation of the current-day critical theoretical spectrum—respectively highlight distinct aspects of the "culture of control." If they identify slightly different causal configurations leading to the emergence of penal punitiveness, they nonetheless all recognize that this punitive drive is to be understood in connection with a profound sense of insecurity. Moreover, the influence of neoliberalism on the acceptance of segregation as a mode of dealing with crime is also noted by all.

These analyses however fall short of elucidating the true enigma of rising punitiveness. Indeed, they fail to conceptualize the hold that anxiety has on the subject beyond its determination in the socialized, rationalized field of criminal justice and its accompanying critique. Further, I would argue that their ratification of the death of the sovereign state is premature and falls short of a more worthwhile endeavor to identify the axes of *sovereign performativity at the time of globalization*. Indeed, the recent attitude of the United States in the context of the war on terrorism, taken together with the response of industrialized democracies to the anticapitalism movement, is surely enough to at least call into question the oft-heralded demise of the nation-state. Having addressed the question of national sovereignty elsewhere (see footnote 11), in the following section I will examine how a theory of the subject based on psychoanalytic insights could put our apprehension of the phenomenon of penal punitiveness in perspective while also challenging the critical rhetoric that currently informs much of the debate on the matter.

AN INTERVENTION FROM THE
PERSPECTIVE OF PSYCHOANALYSIS

The quotations placed as epigraphs at the beginning of this chapter aptly identify the intimate relationship that exists between law and justice, on the one hand, and the function of the drive in civilization, on the other. In effect, Freud (1930) situates instinctual renunciation as the origin of the sense of justice when he states that: "members of the community restrict themselves in their possibilities of satisfaction [. . .] the first requisite of civilization, therefore, is that of justice—that is, the assurance that a law once made will not be broken in favor of an individual" (p. 284). For his part, Garland (2001b) talks of anger as the "affect" of policy.

It is this connection between what is often cast as the most neutral, disembodied and abstract of all civilized constructions (i.e., law), and what seems most inherently disruptive about the functioning of a civilization (i.e., the drive in its various manifestations of anxiety, aggressiveness, or hatred) which is conspicuously absent in all four preceding accounts. Thus, for my part, I would argue that given the *indissociability* of the supposedly rational constructions of civilization and the subjective affects elaborated therein, psychoanalysis has an important part to play in understanding the contemporary transformations of the social bond. Thus, in what follows, and rather than continuing to dialogue with the four discourses previously delineated, I will now suggest a number of directions for future inquiry.

These, then, are the questions that will inform my subsequent analysis. What, then, is the nature of insecurity? What is it that makes modern subjects so prone to experiencing it? Do the dull refrains of insecurity ceaselessly hummed by media and politicians alike bear any relation to the somber affect that Freud (1930) understood to be a product of civilization—namely, anxiety? And, if current feelings of insecurity can be linked to the primary affect of anxiety, what is it that distinguishes the forms donned by anxiety in our particular civilization from its other possible manifestations? Logically, one must also interrogate the nature of the association between anxiety and segregation. Indeed, in our civilization, it is segregative practices that seem to act as a response to anxiety.

Civilization as Treatment of Anxiety

Clearly, then, if one is to rely at all on psychoanalytic theory to understand the current phenomenon of penal punitiveness and its subtext, the discourse of insecurity, one should begin by defining what anxiety is for psychoanalysis. However, in order to do so, it will prove apposite to begin with the question of culpability.

In his seminal essay on the dynamics of civilization, *Civilization and Its Discontents,* Freud (1930) tried to isolate the origin of the enigmatic feeling of culpability that his patients invariably suffered from, whether consciously or unconsciously. In this essay, Freud notoriously claimed that the sense of guilt was an effect of the repression of incestuous desires enforced by the father on the child by means of the threat of castration.

Faced with the impossibility of accounting for the universal actuality of such a threat, Freud had to fall back on his theory of generalized parricide as a founding moment of civilization. The story is well-known: parricidal culpability is said to have been transmitted from generation to generation, and would account for the child's renunciation both to his sexual desire for the mother and his aggressiveness for the father-legislator. Guilt, then, is a meaningful manifestation of the return of the drive (i.e., sexual desire, aggression, or both) onto the subject, and it returns on the subject as a consequence of a prohibition (of incest, murder, or both). This explanation of the sense of guilt allowed Freud to hold on to his Oedipal theorization of the social bond (for additional elaboration on Freud's theory of parricide see, chapter 3 in this volume).

Admittedly, this is a very summary account of the Oedipal organization. For the present argument, what matters is that for Freud (1930), this organization structures our libidinal investments in civilization. In other words, for Freud the successful Oedipalization of a child will result in the production of a quantum of guilt that will eventually be instrumentalized through the operation of the reality principle and will lead to the community's achievement of certain ethical standards.

However, the theory has also been significantly discredited, especially in view of the questionable status of the Oedipal complex. This is where the work of French psychoanalyst Jacques Lacan becomes relevant to our present purpose. Indeed Lacan (1966) was able to disengage the undeniable importance of the Freudian insights from its Oedipal trappings. For this purpose, Lacan built on an ambiguity that was already present in the Freudian text itself, namely, Freud's oscillation between seeing guilt as an effect of a prohibition or conceiving guilt as the meaningful manifestation of a senseless anxiety.

Indeed, in *Civilization and Its Discontents,* Freud noted the phenomenological similarity between feelings of guilt and the affect of anxiety. At that point in his work, however, Freud had to discount his own observation; for in fact he just had cast anxiety as a by-product of Oedipally structured civilizations. And yet, in his erstwhile essay *Inhibitions, Symptoms and Anxiety,* Freud (1926) had posed that anxiety could in fact be the *cause* of repression rather than the *effect* of repression. In this conception, anxiety is a signal alerting the ego to the fact that further repression needs to be carried out in order to avert an invasion of drive-tension. One can therefore conclude, on the basis of the very Freudian contradictions, that anxiety could very well be at the origin of repression, whereas guilt could be seen to be subsequent to repression.

It is this interpretation of anxiety that Lacan (1962–1963) picks up in his Tenth Seminar, *L'angoisse*. Indeed, for Lacan anxiety is not a product of repression but an index of the failure or insufficiency of repression. Moreover, for Lacan, the concept of repression does not refer to the imposition of a supposed Oedipal prohibition, but simply to the process of symbolization of what for each subject is traumatic. In other words, for Lacan repression names the process whereby the subject's anxiety is taken up in discourse and given a meaning, however symptomatic and painful.

For Lacan (1962–1963), the recurrence of anxiety is thus the manifestation of what he called the "real"; or more exactly, what of the real resisted symbolization. From a Lacanian perspective one can then look back at the Freudian Oedipus and deduce that for Freud, the function of Oedipal guilt is to ascribe a meaning to the foundational trauma of being, thereby symbolizing anxiety. The affect experienced in anxiety is therefore of the same nature as the affect experienced in guilt, with the difference that in the case of anxiety, the affect is meaningless—or rather, meaning is only ever secondary in relation to it. Why, then, should anxiety increasingly manifest itself as dissociated from guilt, and therefore appear to be evermore prevalent?

Following Lacan (1995), the resurgence of anxiety results from the progressive "marginalisation of the Oedipal dialectic," or, in other words, from the foreclosure of subjective truth from the locus of knowledge. This resurgence is to be understood in connection with the "correlative accession of the universalisation of the subject proceeding from science"[12] (quoted in Haddad, 1994, p. 212). To be more explicit, Lacan's underlying argument is that while the Oedipal dialectic allowed the subject's truth to find a particular expression, albeit in terms of guilt, science and the universalization of the subject it effectuates effaces particularity from the field of a discourse that reduces all subjective phenomena to cause-effect analyses.

Lacan (1995) further develops his insight as to the waning hold of the Oedipal dialectic and its consequence, "the reshaping of social groups by science" (quoted in Haddad, 1994, p. 212), by stating that this reshaping promotes all forms of segregation in our societies. As he puts it, "Our future as common markets [would] be balanced by an increasingly hard-line extension of the process of segregation" (Lacan, 1995, p. 12).

Anxiety, Segregation and the Criminal Justice System

Bearing in mind Lacan's theoretical advances concerning the pervasive nature of anxiety in our civilization, let us now rephrase our problematization of insecurity in slightly different terms. What, then, is the connection between the decline of the Oedipal organization of civilization and the spreading of segregation? The function of Oedipal theories, the appearance of which are an index of the weakening hold of religion (see Legendre, 1974), is to allow the subject to handle anxiety through the ascription of the meaning of guilt to the return of the drive on the subject, anxiety being the affect associated with such an unmediated return. In turn, it is the "marginalisation of the Oedipal dialectic" that leaves the anxiety arising from the trauma that splits all subjects undialecticized. As such, this anxiety is insufficiently symbolized. Consequently, the meaningless affect of anxiety becomes more liable to attach itself to external threats, including the threat of would-be criminal offenders.

Further, morality, which was singled out by Rose (2000) as an operative factor in the spreading of segregation, can be seen to have substituted itself for religion as the *functional apparatus of civilization for the treatment of anxiety*. And modern morality is heavily supported by the discourse of science. One only needs to think, for example, of the minute classification of sexual perversions or the taxonomy of mental disorders effected by the *DSM IV-R*, or variations of it.

Finally, why would the discourse of science have such segregative effects? Put simply, because science, which arguably replaced religion as the indisputable locus of truth, can only proceed as such by foreclosing the subject as the locus of desire and *jouissance* (i.e., drive-satisfaction) from its discourse (Lacan, 1966). Science indeed cannot allow the expression of what exceeds its own rational constructs. To do otherwise would jeopardize the mantle of truth and knowledge which science carefully, even jealously, guards. Thus, the discourse of science promotes and sustains segregative effects as it names and classifies offenders. Further, while religion and, in its wake, psychoanalysis, accepted the normal occurrence of such "irrational" or, more accurately, markedly particular feelings as anxiety, love, hatred, culpability, or belief, the survival of the discourse of science, as universal cosmogony, requires the rejection of such drive-manifestations in civilization. Hence, the resurgence of the affect of anxiety as meaningless can be seen to be consequent on the incapacity of the scientific discourse to symbolize the traumatic, to listen to the subject's particular relation to the world.

If one were to accept the insightful advances made by psychoanalysis, one could then pose the following sequence. Relatively recent and ongoing modifications in the structure of the social bond have decreased the efficacy of the discourses supporting civilization in ascribing a meaning to the subject's instinctual discontents. Unattached to meaning, feelings of anxiety are then free to be projected onto the "enemy" who is then situated as the unequivocal cause of our anxiety. The logical social response, then, is segregation. The criminal is easily represented as the enemy within: he or she rejects our morality, creates fear of crime, and feeds our anxiety. He or she is the other.

Indeed, those are the mechanisms described by Freud (e.g., 1921, 1930) over and over again, and notably in *Why War?* (Freud, 1933). Thus, in his response to Einstein, Freud perceptively analyzes war as a projection onto the other nation of one's own unresolved feelings of aggressiveness. The other offers an all-too-convincing explanation for feelings of unmediated anxiety, and this projection allows for the discharge of these feelings onto this other. The other, then, irrespective of what makes him or her other, conveniently becomes the *object-cause of our hatred.*

CONCLUSION

In this chapter I endeavored to define the theoretical premises that structure the analytical framework accounting for penal punitiveness which is currently operational in the discourse of critical criminology. In so doing, I isolated a number of recurrent themes: insecurity, anxiety, the decline of state sovereignty, the prevalence of segregation as a response to anxiety, and the call to morality as a legitimizing rhetoric for penal punitiveness.

Following my summary assessment of the cultural, political, economic, and sociological dimensions of crime control, I then proceeded to argue that these recent endeavors declined to theorize the subject. Indeed, while the subject may be the primary locus of social change (Garland), the agent of morality (Rose), a productive cog in the apparatus of crime control (Christie) or the anxious product of wild capitalism (Bauman), the subject itself, including all of its anxieties, hatreds, and aggressivities, is not recognized within the contemporary writings on penal punitiveness. It is seen to be an interactive element in the sociopolitical forces of late modernity, no doubt, but its particularity, its investment in the discourse of civilization, is not accepted as such.

To that extent, I would argue, somewhat controversially, that the language and logic of critical criminology partakes in the scientific rationality of the current penal discourse, and that it therefore *unwittingly participates in the segregative dynamics of the social bond.* Accordingly, and if one is to open up a space for the particularity of the subject in the present-day discourses on law and order, a different modality of intervention is required, and it must be one whose grammar does not abide by the analytical rationalities that operate in the criminal justice system itself.

NOTES

1. For British examples, see New Labour's reform of youth justice, principally effected in the Crime and Disorder Act 1998, and which includes *Local Curfew Schemes* applicable to children below the age of ten, *Parenting Orders* compelling parents to receive weekly educational advice and *Detention and Treatment Orders* which

normalize imprisonment for children aged twelve onward; or its reform of sentencing legislation in the Crime (Sentences) Act 1997, which introduces automatic life sentences for second-time serious offenders as well as "three strikes" provisions.

2. The expressions "criminal justice" and "crime control" will be used throughout this paper as a convenient encapsulation for "a complex set of practices and institutions, ranging from the conduct of householders locking their doors to the action of authorities enacting criminal laws, from community policing to punishment in prison and all the processes in between" (Garland, 2001b, p. vi).

3. This dual orientation structures current New Labour policies. (see John Halliday's recent report on sentencing, *Making Punishments Work*, London: Home Office, 2001)

4. As is immediately apparent in Home Secretary David Blunkett's speech on sentencing reform delivered at the National Probation Service inaugural conference on July 5, 2001. It is also to be noted that both the rhetoric of insecurity and its corollary—intolerance—are gaining ground in other western democracies: in France for example, insecurity was a key theme of the 2002 presidential campaign.

5. A recurrent concept in UK sentencing legislation since its first appearance in the Criminal Justice Act 1991.

6. In the United States, the prison population increased from 218,000 prisoners in 1974 to nearly 2 million in 2001 (see Garland, 2001a), while in the UK, it increased from around 40,600 prisoners in December 1992 to nearly 70,000 at the end of 2001 in the UK (source: *www.homeoffice.gov.uk*).

7. In the UK the reformative ideal is at present embodied in the Crime and Disorder Act 1998. This piece of legislation is inspired by the government's decision to prevent offending by imposing "responsibility" on the young offender and his or her family through a series of combination orders designed to monitor and rectify the offender's (or would-be offender's) behaviour. Furthermore, John Halliday's recent report on sentencing (op. cit.) recommends the adoption of similar measures for the monitoring of the criminal's reforming: for example, in view of the well-documented failure of imprisonment concerning the prevention of future offending, the Halliday report proposes the introduction of an extended period of supervision for released offenders combined with the threat of resentencing in case of breach.

8. Consider New Labour's recent emphasis on restorative justice and reparation, for example.

9. Concerning the form which prevention is to take, *The Guardian* (January 22, 2002) has recently revealed that London's Metropolitan police proposes to create a database of potential offenders including youngsters as young as three who have never been involved in crime but are predicted to be "at risk" of offending by schools or social services.

10. According to the Freudian theory of group-formation, in societies where groups or communities are not held together by means of a shared transference to an ideal, horizontal modes of group-formations will prevail, the latter being a mode of group-formation that operates through the logic of segregation (Freud, 1921).

11. For a development of the question of sovereignty at the time of globalization, see special issue "Law, Sovereignty and the Nation," *International Journal for the Semiotics of Law* (2002, vol. 15-3), guest editor V. Voruz.

12. These quotes of Lacan's are extracted from different versions of the *Proposition* (1995), which is why I am referring to the text in which Haddad analyzes these different versions.

REFERENCES

Bauman, Z. (2000). "Social Issues of Law and Order." *British Journal of Criminology* 40, 205-221.

Christie, N. (2000). *Crime Control as Industry: Towards Gulags, Western Style*. London & New York: Routledge.

Deleuze, G. (1988). *Foucault*. Minneapolis & London: University of Minnesota Press.

Derrida, J. (1992). "The Force of Law: The Mythical Foundations of Authority. In D. Cornell, M. Rosenfeld and D. Carlson (eds.), *Deconstruction and the Possibility of Justice* (pp. 3–67). New York & London: Routledge.

———. (2000). *Les états d'âme de la psychanalyse*, Paris: Galilée.

Freud, S. (1921). "Group Psychology and the Analysis of the Ego." In *Civilization, Society and Religion*, The Penguin Freud Library, vol. 12.

———. (1926). "Inhibition, Symptom and Anxiety." In *Psychopathology*, The Penguin Freud Library, vol. 10. London: Hogarth.

———. (1930). "Civilisation and Its Discontents." In *Civilization, Society and Religion*, The Penguin Freud Library, vol. 12. London: Hogarth.

———. (1933). "Why War?" In *Civilization, Society and Religion*, The Penguin Freud Library, vol. 12. London: Hogarth.

Foucault, M. (1982). "Afterword: The Subject and Power." In H. L. Dreyfus and P. Rabinow (eds.), *Michel Foucault: Beyond Structuralism and Hermeneutics*, Brighton: Harvester Press.

Garland, D. (2000). "The Culture of High Crime Societies." *British Journal of Criminology* 40, 347–375.

———. (ed). (2001a). *Mass Imprisonment*. London, Thousand Oaks & New Delhi: Sage.

———. (2001b). *The Culture of Control*. Oxford: Oxford University Press.

Haddad, G. (1994). "Discourses of Jewish Identity in Twentieth-Century France." *Yale French Studies* 85.

Lacan, J. (1962–1963). *L'angoisse*, unpublished.

———. (1966). "Science and Truth." In *Ecrits: A Selection*. Paris: Seuil. Translated in English in Newsletter of the Freudian Field, 3 (1989).

———. (1995). "Proposition of the 9 October 1967 on the Psychoanalyst of the School." *Analysis* 6, 1–13.

Legendre, P. (1974). *L'amour du censeur: essai sur l'ordre dogmatique.* Paris: Seuil.

Lianos, M. (2001). *Le nouveau contrôle social.*, Paris: L'Harmattan, collection Logiques Sociales.

Rose, N. (2000). "Government and Control." *British Journal of Criminology* 40, 321–339.

Chapter 7

Is Rationalization Good for the Soul?

Resisting "Responsibilization" in Corrections and the Courts

Shadd Maruna

OVERVIEW

A fundamental tenet of much rehabilitation practice is that offenders need to be made accountable for and to accept unmitigated responsibility for their criminal offenses. If unwilling to do so, an individual faces harsh consequences including longer prison stays or the revocation of one's probation. The courts have generally accepted the aphorism that the first step in rehabilitation is admission of one's problem. However, little research supports this notion. Indeed, quite the contrary, considerable evidence seems to suggest that the practice of "responsibilization" in the prison system is actually more likely to stigmatize individuals and generate higher rates of recidivism. To be made liberating, confession must be accompanied by absolution rather than condemnation.

INTRODUCTION

A few years ago, I volunteered to act as an "expert" witness[1] at an Immigration and Naturalization Service (INS) trial, providing testimony on behalf of a Jamaican woman facing deportation. The defendant, whom I will ridiculously call Ms. Kingston, was in court as a result of one of the more draconian laws to be passed in the United States in the last decade—which is, of course, saying quite a lot. The Illegal Immigration Reform and Immigrant Responsibility Act of 1996 subjects long-term, legal immigrants to the threat of deportation for criminal convictions that might have been committed ten, twenty, or even thirty years ago (and that at the time of the conviction were

179

not considered deportable crimes). The *New York Times* aptly describes the impact of this law:

> Like phantoms barreling down from a hazy, distant past, ancient crimes and misdemeanors, sometimes decades old, have been dredged up by investigators at the immigration service to condemn tens of thousands of immigrants to swift and usually irrevocable removal proceedings. The magnitude of the crime is irrelevant. If it is considered an aggravated felony—shoplifting can be an aggravated felony—the immigrant must go. (Hedges, 2000, A1)

In Ms. Kingston's case, in the late 1980s, when she was just under thirty years old, she was paid fifty dollars to carry a small package on a plane from Jamaica to New York. She accepted this incredibly stupid offer and ended up serving over a year in prison for her troubles. Since then, she has married, started a family, and avoided any subsequent run-ins with the law. That is, until the year 2000 when she found herself about to be separated from her family and sent back to Jamaica because of this decade-old offense.

I went to court presuming my role as academic expert was to provide statistical evidence demonstrating how unlikely it was that a forty-year-old mother of two would suddenly revert back to drug smuggling after a decade of crime-free behavior. Instead, the case turned out far more interesting from my point of view. Like a lot of so-called drug mules, Ms. Kingston insists to this day that she did not know what was in that package. She maintains her essential innocence, says she is a good person, a bit naive maybe, but insists that she never had anything to do with the drug business. She made a mistake. From the perspective of the judge in the case, however, this means that Ms. Kingston is still in denial. She has neither admitted responsibility for her crime nor accepted any blame. As such, the judge was not interested in hearing any risk prediction statistics from me that morning. What the judge wanted to know from the visiting academic expert was whether it was possible for a person like Ms. Kingston to really be rehabilitated—to have experienced "genuine rehabilitation" in the term of art for the case—without expressing "sufficient remorse" or taking responsibility for her act.[2]

I was taken back, mainly because this is precisely the question I had been looking at for the last five years in my research on the phenomenology of desistance from crime (see Maruna, 1997, 2001), and I had never imagined the work had any great relevance in the arena of jurisprudence. As it was, I was thrilled to tell the judge that we in criminology and forensic psychology have almost zero evidence to suggest that the internalization of responsibility and remorse for one's past crimes is correlated with desistance from crime—basically because we have so little reliable data on how reformed ex-convicts really think. (The happy ending was that, utilizing a loophole in the otherwise iron clad law, the INS judge did what appeared to be an amazing turnaround and decided not to deport Ms. Kingston, mentioning my testimony in so doing. This appears to be one case in which the less criminological research we have the better.)

This is far from an isolated example of the criminal justice system's longstanding fixation on what might be deemed personal "responsibilization" (Garland, 1997)—or the construction of blame through a process of coerced confession.[3] In fact, most courts "accept without question" the long-standing assumption that acknowledgment of personal responsibility is a necessary precursor to change (Kaden, 1999). In *Gollaher v. United States*, 419 F.2d 520 (9th Cir. 1969), the Court decided that it is "almost axiomatic that the first step toward rehabilitation of an offender is the offender's recognition that he was at fault" (pp. 530–531).

As in Ms. Kingston's case, this presumption can have serious consequences. The admission of one's guilt is very commonly a prerequisite for admission into treatment programs and correctional alternatives, in particular for sex offenders. Moreover, treatment clients who refuse to accept personal responsibility and display remorse for their behaviors are almost assured to suffer consequences in the form of negative reports to the courts and parole authorities. Individuals like Ms. Kingston who are unwilling to accept full responsibility for an offense can even find themselves legally terminated from treatment and punished with probation revocation or extended stays of imprisonment. These consequences can be especially severe in the case of sex offenders[4] mandated to treatment (see Kaden, 1999). Because it is understood to be a necessary part of the recovery process, self-incrimination is thought to be in the individual's best interest.

Indeed, in a watershed 5-to-4 decision (*McKune v. Lile*, No. 00-1187), the U.S. Supreme Court recently ruled that prison rehabilitation programs that require inmates to reveal even previously undisclosed crimes do not violate the constitutional right against compelled self-incrimination—even in cases in which inmates lose privileges for refusing to participate (see Greenhouse, 2002). The case involved an inmate in the Kansas state prison system's Sexual Abuse Treatment Program. As part of the program, inmates must acknowledge responsibility for their crimes and must fully disclose any unreported sex crimes while being monitored by a polygraph device. If they disclose further undetected crimes, they face the prospect of new prosecutions and also face possible perjury prosecutions if they had maintained their innocence in court. Alternatively, if they choose not to participate in the lie detection process, inmates who had worked their way up to less rigid conditions of confinement could be returned to maximum-security cells, with fewer opportunities to earn money, receive visits, or take part in recreation. Writing for a plurality of four justices, Justice Anthony M. Kennedy argued that imposing this Hobson's choice was necessary for rehabilitation and that "States . . . have a vital interest in rehabilitating convicted sex offenders."

Nelson (1996) compares this coercion of therapeutic confessions to the practice of the old English ecclesiastical courts, in which compulsory confessions were justified for an equally charitable reason—to save the accused's soul from eternal damnation. Foucault (1979, 1988) traces the lineage of psychotherapeutic confrontations even further, back to the prescribed monastic rituals of the fourth and fifth centuries of the Christian Roman Empire. Although remorse and confession with their religious connotations are no longer explicitly discussed in "scientific" discussions of corrections, their influence on actual correctional practice never really went away. Duguid (2000, p. 53) writes:

> Remorse, the demand of the first wave of enlightened prison reformers of the nineteenth century, had an oddly unscientific ring to it and was a difficult quality to assess, test for, and evaluate. It was (however) much in the minds of lay members of parole boards and the citizenry in general.

Indeed, Rose (1996, p. 96) calls confession the "most versatile and most transferable" self-technology, arguing that it characterizes "almost all of the proliferating systems of psychotherapy and counseling."

Yet, is confession necessarily good for the soul? In this chapter, I briefly outline the role of responsibilization in the correctional arena. Drawing heavily on Kathryn Fox's (1999a, 1999b) powerful ethnography of a cognitive treatment program, I make the case that rather than following the model of "confession and absolution," that responsibilization rituals more typically take the form of "confession and condemnation." Using the findings from recent recidivism research (Hood, 2002; Maruna, 2001), I argue that instead of being a path to redemption, this sort of responsibilization may become a formula for stigmatization and the self-fulfilling prophecy of recidivism, limiting rather than creating opportunities for alternative life choices for ex-offenders. I conclude by exploring ways in which the focus on personal autobiography and self-reflection in corrections might be more liberating and less stigmatizing.

NO MORE EXCUSES: CONFESSION AND CONDEMNATION

Offender therapy differs from traditional forms of therapy, of course, in that the "client" being served is not necessarily the person receiving the treatment but often some "community" that is to be protected from the person's future behavior. In terms of "what works" in recidivism reduction, meta-analysts like Gendreau, Goggin, Cullen, and Andrews (2000, p. 13) have reached the "inescapable conclusion" that cognitive-based interventions may be the "only game in town." Certainly, cognitive-based programs—with titles like "Reasoning and Rehabilitation" (Ross & Fabiano, 1985), "Mind Over Matters: Corrective Thinking Treatment Model" (Tru-thought, 2000), and "Thinking for a Change" (Bush, Glick, & Taymans, 1997)—have "dominated practice developments" in correctional programming in the United States and internationally (Vanstone, 2000; see also Rex, 2001).

The primary aim of much of this cognitive programming is simple: Offenders need to "accept responsibility" for their actions and stop "making excuses." In *Changing Criminal Thinking: A Treatment Program*, Sharp (2000, p. 2) writes:

> Criminals do not think like law-abiding prosocial people. . . . Criminal behavior is the result of erroneous thinking. Criminals' thinking leads to their feelings, their feelings lead to their behavior, and their behavior reaffirms their thinking. To use the words of Alcoholics Anonymous, the criminal is afflicted with 'stinking thinking,' which includes rationalizing, justifying, excuse-making, blaming, accusing, and being a victim. (see also Walters, 1998; Samenow, 1984)

The solution offered in Sharp's treatment program and others like it is to convince convicts to internalize responsibility for their actions: "We believe that optimum opportunity for success in a treatment program requires that clients be held accountable for all their actions, past, present and future" (3).

Similarly, White and Walters (1989) argue that a mind-set of "disresponsibility," along with self-indulgence and interpersonal intrusiveness, characterizes almost all offenders. They describe the "psychology of disresponsibility" as a "generalized unwillingness . . . to be accountable for (one's) behavior" (p. 258) or "the intellectual process by which a person's actions are attributed to factors other than the person himself" (p. 259). Further, as in many other formulations, White and Walters lay much of the blame for this sense of "disresponsibility" on the shoulders of social science.[5] "As a result of these early sociological theories, which held that environment, society or some other external factor was the cause of crime, we have unknowingly provided the lifestyle criminal with ready made socially sanctioned excuses for his undesirable behavior" (White & Walters, 1989, p. 259).

Walters (1998, p. 67) and others advocate interventions based on "confronting rationalizations with facts and self-deception with feedback." In particular, the "shaming" of offenders through direct confrontation of their character and behavior has reemerged as a leading paradigm in correctional practice and theory. Occasionally attempts are made to shame in a "reintegrative" fashion, as proposed by Braithwaite (1989), but more commonly, the desire is for the "good, old-fashioned" practice of stigmatizing wrongdoers (Abraria, 1994). Massaro (1997, p. 646) writes, "Shame has become in the 1990s what self-esteem was in the 1980s: a blurry psychological phenomenon that is ill understood, but that nevertheless has become a catch word for sweeping social diagnoses and prescriptions."

In the shaming rituals that often take place in group therapy, therapeutic communities, or cognitive skills work, the only acceptable confession is typically one in which the person accepts complete and unmediated blame for an event. These confrontation-based "technologies of the self" seek to "responsibilize" convicts through the ritual of confession, forcing them to "own up" to their past sins and stop making excuses. Instead of assuming that all adult individuals are capable of responsible (or using Voruz's [2000] term "response-able," i.e., accountable for one's self) behavior, "contemporary penal regimes treat this as a problem to be remedied by procedures that actively seek to 'subjectify' and to 'responsibilize' individuals" (Garland, 1997, p. 191). The responsibilization ritual seeks to reorient offender thinking "towards a set of objectives that coincide with those promoted by governing authorities" (Garland, 1997, p. 198).

Thus, far from spontaneous, the "words and rituals that govern these confessions are those prescribed by an authority, albeit one who has replaced the claims of god and religion with those of nature and the psyche" (Rose, 1996, p. 96). Duguid (2000, p. 200) argues:

> Like the Socratic dialogue, the desire to have the object [of a therapeutic interrogation] understand [him or herself] manifests itself in the form of a deception—the real desire is to have the object adopt the understanding of itself that has been prescribed by the examiner. After all, did any of the companions of Socrates really have a chance in one of his dialogues? . . . Hence, the deception is both transparent and despised.

In fact, since its origins in early Christian practices, the confession ritual has always contained elements of a status degradation ceremony. According to Foucault (1988, p. 42), confession traditionally served two, paradoxical purposes: to "rub out sin and to restore the purity acquired by baptism" but also to "show a sinner as he is." He writes, "The greater part of the act of penitence was not telling the truth of sin but showing the true sinful being of the sinner. It was not a way for the sinner to explain his sins but a way to present himself as a sinner" (p. 42). In this process of "ritual martyrdom," Foucault writes "Self-revelation is at the same time self-destruction" (p. 43).

This process is best illustrated in Kathryn Fox's (1999a, 1999b) ethnographic work in a prison-based cognitive treatment program for "violent offenders." In her extensive field-based data, she demonstrates how "the obligation to confess" is used as a form of "cognitive social control" (Fox, 1999a, p. 91). In her study, she found that the "somewhat sociological" accounts used by prisoners to explain the criminal violence they committed in the past, were rejected by the therapists as an example of "criminal thinking" and replaced by "ideology of moral autonomy" (1999b, p. 442). "These accounts are regarded as 'cognitive distortions' by (treatment) program logic and framed instead as evidence of extraordinary pathology" (p. 436). Alternatively, treatment discourse worked to decontextualize inmates' past actions, as in the following passage from Fox's field notes:

> *Pete*: The situation was: I had been drinking, getting drunk, with my girlfriend and she pissed me off, so I went to bed. I was sleeping and my girlfriend punched me in the balls so I broke her jaw. …
> *Facilitator*: We don't need an explanation—like this getting drunk and all that—just what you did: you broke her jaw.

Through these reality contests, convicts are "talked into being" criminal types (Fox, 1999b, p. 440). That is, decontextualizing criminal actions leaves the individual with little choice but to accept the dominant therapeutic discourse of psychopathology (e.g., Hare, 1993), which has an enormous, even cultlike sway over the correctional treatment world. Fox (1999b, p. 442) argues, "Insofar as the act was discussed, dissected, and analyzed out of context, the actor was reconfigured in another context—that of his own violent nature."

Indeed, the following was listed as a "thinking error" in a workbook for a cognitive treatment program for prisoners: "The criminal believes that he is a good and decent person. He rejects the thought that he is a criminal" (cited in Fox, 1999b; see also chapter 10 of Samenow, 1984). Of course, this becomes a catch-22 for treatment participants—if they claim to be decent, that is proof that they are pathological; if they admit to being pathological, that is also proof that they are pathological! (See Fox, 1999b, p. 448 for an ethnographic account of this dilemma.)

Resistance and Reform

Of course, these "technologies of the self" are not iron-clad. Faced with the catch-22 described above, prisoners have only three possible options according to Duguid (2000, p. 200): "The weakest willed take on the self suggested by the state, the clever wear it only as a veil, and the stubborn resist as best they can." In the last of these three options, resistance, prisoners and treat-ment clients "engage with these procedures in a manner which is at odds with that intended by the authorities, putting them to their own uses, or using them as a lever towards their own ends" (Garland, 1997, p. 207).

Extant research suggests that most often, this resistance takes the form of a predictable reaction-formation. Considerable research suggests that direct confrontation is only likely to induce behavior change when the confronting is done "by those whom we respect very highly" (Ahmed, Harris, Braithwaite, & Braithwaite, 2001, p. 32). As this is unlikely to include correctional staff, defiance in the face of confrontational tactics makes perfect psychological sense (see especially Kear-Colwell & Pollock, 1997). In her discussion of "inmates rhetorics of resistance," Fox (1999a) describes several fascinating cases in which participants in a cognitive treatment program choose to face severe consequences rather than accept the criminal labeling of the counsel-ing staff. Describing one such circumstance, she writes, "The facilitators could not comprehend why he would choose not to 'fake it' and become an 'expedient confessor' . . . given the potential consequence of suspension from the group and a stalled prison release" (Fox, 1999b, p. 448).

For some individuals, caught up in a cycle of crime and punishment, this sort of resistance to criminal essentializing and stigmatization might even be essential for the process of self-transformation and reform. In a powerful new study, Roger Hood and his colleagues (2002) find evidence for just such a possibility. In their study of the experiences of 250 persons convicted of sex offenses released from British prisons, Hood and his colleagues found that those persons deemed to be "in denial" by the parole board (about one third of the sample) were much more likely to be rated as "high risk" by the parole board than sex offenders who admitted responsibility for their offense. How-ever, only one of these 'high-risk deniers' was subsequently reconvicted of a sexual offense. This strikingly high rate of false positives suggests that "being in denial" is given more weight as a risk factor by the British parole board than seems to be justified. Hood and colleagues conclude that some of the "deniers" in their sample might have actually been innocent of the crimes they were charged with, but just as important:

> Some 'deniers,' when faced with the stigma of conviction and pun-ishment may not accept their deviant sexual acts as a reflection of their 'real self.' Nor may they wish to associate with those they regard, unlike themselves, as 'real' sex offenders. It is possible that such per-sons may be less likely to become 'secondary deviants,' that is, persons who accept and seek to justify their sexual deviance. (p. 387)

Indeed, Lemert (1951) was clear on this point in his original differenti-ation between primary and secondary deviation. Lemert writes, "The deviations remain primary deviations or symptomatic and situational *as long as they are rationalized*" (emphasis added). An individual does not move into secondary deviation until he or she undergoes "a process of identification" through which the deviant acts are "incorporated as part of the 'me' of the individual" (p. 75). In other words, those who cling most tightly to excuses for their behavior, resisting efforts at "responsibilization," may be the least likely to persist in criminality.

The Liverpool Desistance Study

This is precisely the self-identity process uncovered in the Liverpool Desistance Study (Maruna, 2001). Although not a prospective study like Hood's, the Liverpool study is unique in that it contains considerable evidence about how reformed, former offenders actually think. Additionally, the study contains a comparison sample of active offenders that allows us to better isolate what particular thinking patterns are uniquely associated with the process of self-transformation or desistance from crime.

Most cognitive research in criminology compares the thinking patterns of a sample of "offenders" with the thinking patterns of control group "innocents." In practice, this almost always means comparing a captive audience of prisoners to a similarly captive audience of high school or university student volunteers (e.g., Barriga, et al., 2000; Slaby & Guerra, 1988). The assumption is that if the two groups differ in some ways, then these differences might be the key elements of "criminal thinking" (and hence targets for change in rehabilitative interventions). This assumption is problematic on several levels. First of all, the many problems with using incarcerated individuals as stand-ins for a criminal population (see Polsky, 1969) are magnified in cognitive research, where measures of low self-efficacy, weak locus of control and high levels of frustration are quite obviously distorted by the depravations associated with incarceration. Prison-based cognition may have little relevance to the same person's thinking patterns outside of such a total institution. Second, even if such designs could isolate ways that innocents think different than offenders, this tells us little about where to target interventions with offenders. After all, try as they might, offenders can never become "innocents." The best they can hope to become is reformed ex-convicts, and we know little about how such individuals think.

Unlike "innocents," reformed ex-convicts are faced with the challenge of "making sense" out of a past life that is "experienced as discontinuous, radically changing and full of shame and guilt and that is felt or feared to be worthless" (Lofland, 1969, p. 282). The purpose of the Liverpool Desistance Study was to better understand the cognitive and identity processes through which ex-offenders could "integrate and make meaningful" their discontinuous life trajectories. Our assumption was that understanding how a large sample of reformed ex-offenders actually think would be the best model on which to design rehabilitative interventions. Additionally, we wanted to be able to compare the self-narratives of this group to a contrasting sample of "offenders" in order to isolate what particular aspects of the sense-making process are uniquely related to desistance and which are common to other groups of individuals accounting for criminal pasts. Following Polsky's (1969) admonition, this comparison group (like the desisting group) consisted of ex-convicts who were outside of "captivity" and admitted to being actively engaged in a variety of criminal activities (from drug sales to burglary to armed robbery)[6] with no plans to stop. It is our view that this sample is far more likely to provide insights into "criminal thinking" than a group of prisoners who might not have committed a crime in years.

Participants in both groups took part in an open-ended, life story interview designed to tap into their self-narrative or storied identity. These interviews were tape-recorded and transcribed, then analyzed inductively for emergent themes (see Maruna, 2001). In addition, we sought to quantitatively test a variety of predetermined hypotheses. One of which was the theory that reformed ex-offenders would accept personal responsibility and blame for their past offenses, while active offenders would blame others and rationalize their actions with excuses and justifications.

In order to test this hypothesis, we first extracted around 15 accounts (9 describing negative events, 6 describing positive events) from each of the 89 narratives included in the sample for a total of over 1250 excerpts altogether. Next, we utilized a team of independent coders, blind to the hypotheses and to the group membership (desisting or active) of the speakers (for details of this process see Maruna, 2002). Coders were trained according to Peterson, Schulman, Castellon & Seligman's (1991) CAVE (Content Analysis of Verbatim Explanations) system. This allows for a measurement of accounts on three, salient dimensions: Internal/External, Stable/Unstable, and Global/Specific causes.

Considerable research suggests that individuals who blame personal failings on internal ("It is my fault"), stable ("It is a permanent problem"), and global ("It will affect everything I do") causes will be most prone to depression and other mental health problems. On the other hand, individuals who use external ("It isn't my fault"), unstable ("It was caused by a once-off fluke"), and specific ("It only affected this one thing") explanations for negative life events are most likely to be able to move on with their lives successfully (see Seligman, 1991). According to this considerable body of research, it makes little difference how accurate one's attributions for personal mistakes are. In fact, depressed persons seem for the most part to be more realistic and more accurate in their assessments of their problems than nondepressed people! What matters is whether one interprets these events pessimistically ("I guess I'm just a loser") or optimistically ("I was robbed"). Stan Cohen (2001) summarizes this literature clearly: "Mental health, it turns out, depends not on being in touch with reality, but on illusion, self-deception and denial" (p. 56).

In our analysis of the Liverpool data, we found that this same relationship could be found between the constructive use of cognitive distortion and successful desistance from crime. Highly internal, stable, and global attributions tended to be associated not with reform, but actually with continued offending. Active offenders in the sample tended to begrudgingly accept the labels society had applied to them. An example might be the active house burglar who summarized his life as follows:

> I'm a thief, but if there was some other way, I'd do that. (*pause*) I guess I'm just a thief—no more, no less (male, 28 yrs).

Far from optimistic, the offender narrative can be characterized as condemnation script, with little hope for the future. One interviewee, for instance, said:

> (My ex-wife) said, like, 'If you got off heroin now, I'd come back,' you know, but I'm happy the way I am. I'm just happy to plod along, and I know I've got a habit. I'm at the stage now where I'm resigned to the fact that I'm an addict and I'm going to be an addict to the day I die, and nothing's going to change that (male, 33 yrs).

On the other hand, those who were able to turn their lives around and desist from crime and addiction, were better able to "distort" the often grim realities of their past lives. One aspect of this sort of distortion was a tendency to externalize the blame for their past acts and minimize their own internal deviance. These accounts ranged from "act adjustment" (e.g., "We never really hurt anyone") to "actor adjustment" ("I wasn't ever really as bad as they say"), using Cohen's (2001) framework. The most common story took the shape of what Cohen (2001, p. 62) calls the most "radical" actor adjustment. In these cases, the narrator denied responsibility by "attributing the action to another part of the self that has been disengaged from the 'real' me." Some examples include:

> Then me mum found out what I was doing (heroin use and burglary). She come to the flat and got me, um, brought me home. She knew I had a bad problem. I was a different person, psychologically. I just—*it weren't me* (male, 25 yrs).

I'd always wanted to be clean. Even being around drug addicts all the time, I've always thought meself to be above it. *It weren't me*, kind of thing. I've always thought that even though I was on it—I mean, I didn't look down on anyone but, I mean, I used to look down on meself kind of thing. I put meself down. I hated it. (male, 25 yrs).

Faced with the challenge of incongruity, needing to make sense of a radical life change from an identity as a criminal to a new identity as a father or counselor or provider, the narrators suggest that their past offenses were committed by a "different person"—what Petrunik and Shearing (1988) call "the It" or an internal, but autonomous "not-I" force that is responsible for behavior considered unintentional, unpredictable, and uncontrollable.

I couldn't believe I was doing it, but I still did it, . . . I hated it. I used to think 'I'm worth more than this.' I really thought I was worth more than this. . . . I didn't want to do it but I did. Booze crippled me. It made me into someone that I never liked being, stripped me of everything I had, and it took me to the depths of—it took me down to doing check card fraud (male, 32 yrs).

Their newly reformed selves are the "real me" that had been waiting, all along, to emerge. One of the Liverpool interviewees articulated this perfectly when accounting for his self-transformation:

It was just that, um, I realized that the entire thing had all been an act, my entire life, all me criminal offenses, all me drug taking, it was all a sham. . . . It was just like what it was, was right at the core of me, I am who I am now, who I've always been inside. I've always been intelligent, right, inside. I've always been intelligent, honest, hard working, truthful, erm, nice, you know, loving. I've always like. But it was always wrapped up in so much shit it couldn't get out. Um and it's only now that . . . I've realized that. That that wasn't who I was, I did it all to try and, to try and find out who I was. . . . That's what people I knew were doing, people I looked up to and . . . you know I was just adapting. I used to adapt to me peers, which most people do, but some people choose the right peers (male, 30 yrs).

Although strictly preliminary, the Liverpool findings seem to suggest that personal reform or rehabilitation may itself be a cognitive distortion of sorts. That is, using Albert Bandura's (1989) words, desisting ex-convicts may need to "exhibit self-enhancing biases that distort appraisals in the positive direction" (p. 1177). By contrast, these findings lend support to the suggestion by Kathryn Fox and others that "responsibilization" rituals can have the impact of essentializing and stigmatizing criminal offenders. After all, Fox suggests that in the name of encouraging offenders to take responsibility for their behaviors, corrections personnel insist that prisoners accept "personal, permanent, and pervasive explanations for bad events"—precisely what social psychologists (see Seligman, 1991, p. 77) say leads to depression and self-defeating behaviors.

Contrary to the hypothesis that internalizing shame is the key to deterrence, persistent offenders in the LDS sample seemed to have become "overwhelmed by shame, drowning in feelings of helplessness and an all encompassing loss of self-worth" (Ahmed et al., 2001, p. 328). Indeed, contemporary restorative justice theorists Elizah Ahmed and her colleagues (2001, p. 11) warn that the real variable of interest is not shame, but rather "shame management": "The resolution or management of shame may be as important as whether shame is felt." The rationalizations employed by desisting ex-convicts may emerge out of just this "human need to protect the self" (Ahmed, et al., 2001, p. 327). Although these are means of avoiding responsibility, these accounts also help to protect self-esteem, increase one's sense of personal worth, and reduce anxiety (Northey, 1999). Such self-protection may be necessary in order for offenders to desist. Meisenhelder (1982) for instance argues, "The plan to exit from crime is in large part founded on the sense of the self as noncriminal" (p. 140).

Wayward Cognitivism

The focus on attributions in psychology emerged as part of the wider movement toward a focus on cognition, referred to as the cognitive revolution. According to one of the movement's chief architects (Bruner, 1990, p. 2), the cognitive revolution in psychology was, in its original form, "an all-out effort to establish meaning as the central concept of psychology—not stimuli and responses, not overtly observable behavior, not biological drives and their transformation, but meaning." Central to this phenomenological effort is a constructionist paradigm that holds that human beings are essentially story-tellers, constantly making sense out of the world and their own lives through narrative (McAdams, 1993). These stories then become a sort of guide for intentional actions and future behavior. According to Bruner (1987, p. 15):

> Eventually, the culturally shaped cognitive and linguistic processes that guide the self-telling of life narratives achieve the power to structure perceptual experience, to organize memory, to segment and purpose-build the very 'events' of a life. In the end, we *become* the autobiographical narratives by which we 'tell about' our lives. (italics in original)

Recently, however, the emphasis of cognitive psychology has shifted into "profoundly different" matters "from 'meaning' to 'information,' from the *construction* of meaning to the *processing* of information," according to Bruner (1990, p. 4, italics in original). This shift has opened the door to a pathologizing discourse of "deficits" and "errors," in contradiction to the relativism inherent in the constructionist approach. As Goffman (1961) suggests, there are no true stories or false stories, only good stories (convincing, coherent, acceptable) and bad stories (unbelievable, illogical, unpopular).

Still, the undifferentiated prohibition against excuses, justifications, and explanations in correctional endeavors can only be explained as a misreading of Sykes and Matza's (1957) work and the social cognition research that followed it. Central to the concept of "criminal thinking" is that, as Sharp explains, "Criminals do not think like law-abiding prosocial people." Yet, of course we know that law-abiding people make excuses all of the time and to great advantage. Describing the "normality of denial," Cohen (2001) writes:

> The contrast between deniers and non-deniers assumes that denial is a property of personality rather than situation. . . . But denial is not a stable psychological condition that can be assessed like this. Unless psychotically cut off from reality, no one is a total denier or non-denier, still less either 'in denial' or 'out of denial' permanently. . . . We oscillate rapidly between states. (Cohen, 2001, p. 54)

Indeed, throughout their discussion of "techniques of neutralization," Sykes and Matza (1957) are clear that neutralizations are "extensions of patterns of thought prevalent in society rather than something created de novo." More recently, Hazani (1991) describes neutralization techniques as "universal modes of response to inconsistency" that "reveal universal modes of reduction of disequilibrium that are totally unrelated to guilt or criminality" (p. 137). From a psychoanalytic point of view, Redl and Wineman (1951: 214–215) go one step further and describe the legalistic sounding neutralizations applied by juvenile delinquents, untrained in legal thinking, as "expert manipulation" and "hypertrophically developed (interpersonal) skills in the service of the wrong cause." They conclude that far from suffering from pathological deficits in cognition, "What (delinquents) seem to 'know' about people and how to handle them—including (treatment practitioners)—often puts current research in such matters to shame."

In their exhaustive review of the research on excuse making, Snyder, Higgins and Stucky (1983) conclude that excuse-making is generally an adaptive mechanism for coping with stress, relieving anxiety, and maintaining self esteem. Rationalizing self-narratives—shifting from "I am the problem" to "I am up against a problem"—are therefore used as a means of "depathologizing" (McAdams, 1993) one's self. Indeed, the attribution literature, excuses and justifications are seen as "a type of aligning action indicating to the audience that the actor is aligned with the social order even though he or she has violated it" (Felson & Ribner, 1981, p. 138). By making an excuse or justification for one's behavior, a person is able to make a claim for their status as a normal person. Without such a story, "there exists no means to locate their identity in a shared narrative of common experience" (Singer, 1997, p. 284).

CONFESSION AS DEREALIZATION:
RE-IMAGINING COGNITIVE CORRECTIONS

My argument up to now has been that pathologizing self-protection (in the form of excuses) and holding persons "completely accountable" for their behaviors creates an impossible situation bound to reify normative identities (for offenders, for treaters) and reaffirm the status quo. That is, responsibilization, mandated by court-ordered treatment programs, seems to be somewhat responsible for talking "criminal types" into being (Fox, 1999b). Of course, nothing inherent to the process of confession, itself, makes it a tool of cognitive social control. Indeed, as Rose (1996) points out, nearly every type of therapeutic intervention is based on some form of confessional interaction. Feminist, client-centered, radical, narrative, and postmodern varieties—not to mention almost every self-help or mutual aid collective from Alcoholics Anonymous to the consciousness-raising encounter groups of the 1970s—all rely principally on the guided telling and retelling of a person's self-narrative. Moreover, the deconstructing and reconstructing of one's own narrative through interactions with others is a process each of us engages in whether we call it "therapy" or not. As Foucault (1979, p. 59) reminds us, "Western man has become a confessing animal."

Confession is not so much the issue, then—coercion is. Indeed, divorced from the pathologizing inherent in the focus on "criminal thinking," "cognitive errors," "deficits," and "corrections," the mutual construction of new self-narratives can be a liberating process. Cognitive or narrative therapies have enormous potential for persons in the prison system, as the imprisonment experience represents an existential crisis in most individuals' lives necessitating some sense-making and a search for meaning (Toch, 1998).

Courts and correctional staff need not abandon confessional work. Ward and Stewart (2002) divide offender therapy approaches into "risk management" and "enhancement" models of treatment practice. Whereas the former is geared toward the correctional goal of avoiding harm in the community, the latter is focused on improving the quality of life for treatment clients, and is typically associated with therapy outside of the correctional system. When given the opportunity to choose between the two, Hannah-Moffatt and

Shaw (2000, p. 9) argue that many correctional clients prefer and "respond well to treatment approaches which the cognitive skills literature rejects such as non-directive client-centered counseling and holistic approaches" associated with enhancement-based treatment. In enhancement model therapy, the confession process becomes a means of self-exploration rather than social control. When professional guidance is given, the direction is designed to point toward stories that seem to "work"—ways of understanding that have helped others make sense of similar experiences. The models for achieving this sort of self-understanding, by necessity then, would have to be the stories of fellow transgressors—a practice employed successfully by mutual aid collectives for decades. The modeling would be success-driven and aspirational rather than deficit-focused and correctional. Like therapy offered outside the correctional arena, this would be framed as a voluntary means of self-improvement rather than reprogramming in the name of protecting others. Rather than being prohibitive (e.g., "no more excuses"), such guidance would be explicitly generative of alternate ways of managing one's shame and moving on with one's life.

Such exercises almost certainly involve a complication of the notion of responsibility and blame. For Lacan, for instance, to make sense of a transgression "was neither to forgive nor condemn it, neither to punish or accept it. It was, on the contrary, to 'derealize' it, that is, to restore to it its imaginary, then symbolic dimension" (Roudinesco, 1990, p. 127).

Derealization, in many ways, is the antithesis to the construction of blame central to the courtroom drama of traditional jurisprudence and corrections. Still, an example of a "derealization dialogue" in practice might be found in an ideal restorative justice conferencing. Indeed, the "telling of stories" (Zehr, 1990), by all parties involved in a conflict, is the central activity in a restorative conference. Although the purpose of these rituals involves "shaming" the offense in question, advocates "seek to avoid at all costs (the turning) of a potential restorative process into a blaming contest" (Sullivan & Tifft, 2001, p. 46). Ahmed and her colleagues (2001, p. 45) are clear on this point:

> Indirect methods of confrontation that seek to elicit volunteered remorse (e.g., dialogue where those who have been hurt discuss consequences of an act; *others owning their share in the responsibility;* others telling stories of their remorse for similar wrongdoing in their past) will be more effective in bringing about desistance from predatory crime than direct verbal disapproval of the act (italics added).

Conference participants are not intended to act as a "Greek chorus standing in the background critiquing the process or the person responsible for the harm" (Sullivan & Tifft, 2001, p. 42). Instead, friends and family members of offenders are involved in conferences in order to "accept their collective responsibility for and give their collective attention to the structural conditions of the issue at hand as well as to personal healing matters" (Sullivan & Tifft, 2001, p. 42).

Unfortunately, institutionalizing derealization of this sort is unlikely in the present climate. As Ahmed and her colleagues (2001, p. 329) write, "Safety to acknowledge shame is not on offer through traditional Western rule enforcing institutions." In the present, so-called culture of blame, if a person admits that they willfully and purposefully committed a crime, they would also be admitting that they are the "type of person" who could commit crimes. As Sawyer (2002, p. 7) writes:

> Apologizing implies an admission of wrong-doing, of guilt, and (people) won't accept their complicity. Because they don't want to be sued. It's . . . an extension of the blame culture that makes sorry the hardest word, for fear of legal action. Never say, 'It's all my fault,' because if you do, your insurance won't cough up. And there's something subtler too. To feel genuine remorse about something we've done is to imply that sometimes . . . we choose badly, we come down on the . . . side of the wicked, the cowardly, the nasty, the unpardonable. No one likes to feel like a bad person.

To be effective, then, the decoupling of person and act must take place on this cultural level, rather than an individual level. It is no small irony that making that sort of cultural transformation would likely require breaking through our collective denial as a society. That is, in order to divorce offender confessions from reifying stigma, we as a society need to go some way toward confessing our own shame and responsibility for the levels of crime and victimization we have tolerated, fostered, and endorsed. The blame is ours to spread.

NOTES

1. As someone who has done research on ex-convict success stories, I am occasionally asked to provide assessments regarding how "rehabilitated" an individual may or may not appear for parole hearings and the like. It is not a role with which I am at all comfortable. I agreed to provide testimony in this particular case because the case was being handled on a pro bono basis by an advocacy organization I admire and because the details of the case seemed so extraordinary.

2. Off the record, the defense attorney asked the judge if the court would prefer her client perjure herself by "admitting" full responsibility rather than state what she believes to be true—that there were mitigating circumstances involved in the smuggling episode.

3. Garland (1997) and others use this term more broadly, referring to the general pattern of enlisting individuals in the process of their own control.

4. Interestingly, there are precedents for this special focus on sexual confessions in history. In his discussion of the role of confession in seventeenth and eighteenth century social controls, Foucault (1988, p. 16) notes that "The confession played an important part in penal and religious institutions of all offenses, not only in sex. But the task of analyzing one's sexual desire is always more important than analyzing any other kind of sin."

5. Parallel arguments have been made by symbolic interactionists (e.g., Maruna, 2001; Matza, 1964). In fact, the denial of responsibility is the master account in Sykes and Matza's (1957) "techniques of neutralization" as well. In this literature, it is more typically argued that the determinism inherent in positivist social science provides little hope for individuals caught in the cycle of offending and may contribute to the public stigmatization of ex-convicts and former deviants (see Maruna, 2001, pp. 83–84).

6. It should be pointed out that none of the sample members self-reported having committed sexual offenses or ever being convicted of such crimes. The applicability of these findings to individuals in that situation is therefore unknown.

REFERENCES

Abraria, R. (September 25, 1994). "What Ever Happened to Good Old-Fashioned Shame?" *Los Angeles Times*, p. E1.

Ahmed, E., Harris, N., Braithwaite, J., & Braithwaite, V. (2001). *Shame Management Through Reintegration*. Cambridge: University of Cambridge Press.

Bandura, A. (1989). "Human Agency in Social Cognitive Theory." *American Psychologist* 44, 1175–1184.

Barriga, A. O., Landau, J. R., Stinson, B. L. Liau, A. K., & Gibbs, J. C. (2000). "Cognitive Distortion and Problem Behaviors in Adolescents." *Criminal Justice and Behavior* 27, 36-56.

Braithwaite, J. (1989). *Crime, Shame and Reintegration*. Cambridge, UK: Cambridge University Press.

Bruner, J. (1987). "Life as Narrative." *Social Research* 54, 11-32.

Bruner, J. S. (1987). "Life as Narrative." *Social Research* 54, 11–32.

Bush, J., Glick, B. & Taymans, J. (1995). *Thinking for a Change: Integrated Cognitive Behavior Change Program Training Manual*. Washington, DC: National Institute of Corrections.

Cohen, S. (2001). *States of Denial*. Cambridge: Polity.

Duguid, S. (2000). *Can Prisons Work? The Prisoner as Object and Subject in Modern Corrections*. Toronto: University of Toronto.

Felson, R. B. & Ribner, S. A. (1981). "An Attributional Approach to Accounts and Sanctions for Criminal Violence." *Social Psychology Quarterly* 44, 137–142.

Foucault, M. (1979). *History of Sexuality, Vol. 1*. New York: Pantheon.

Foucault, M. (1988). "Technologies of the Self." In Martin, L. H., Gutman, H., & Hutton, P. H. (eds.) *Technologies of the Self* (pp. 16–49). Amherst: University of Massachusetts Press.

Fox, K. (1999a). "Changing Violent Minds: Discursive Correction and Resistance in the Cognitive Treatment of Offenders in Treatment." *Social Problems* 46, 88–103.

———. (1999b). "Reproducing Criminal Types: Cognitive Treatment for Violent Offenders in Prison." *Sociological Quarterly* 40, 435–453.

Garland, D. (1997). "Governmentality and the Problem of Crime: Foucault, Criminology, Sociology." *Theoretical Criminology* 1, 173–214.

Gendreau, P., Goggin, C., Cullen, F., & Andrews, D. A. (1998). "The Effects of Community Sanctions and Incarceration on Recidivism." *Forum* 12(2), 10–14.

Goffman, E. (1961). *Asylums: Essays on the Social Situation of Mental Patients and Other Inmates*. Garden City, NY: Anchor Books.

Greenhouse, L. (June 11, 2002). "Supreme Court Upholds Program Requiring Inmates to Acknowledge Unrevealed Crimes." *New York Times*, p. A1

Hannah-Moffat, K. & Shaw, M. (2000). "Thinking About Cognitive Skills? Think Again." *Criminal Justice Matters* 39, 8–9.

Hazani, M. (1991). "The Universal Applicability of the Theory of Neutralization: German Youth Coming to Terms with the Holocaust." *Crime, Law and Social Change* 15, 135–149.

Hedges, C. (August 30, 2000). "Condemned Again for Old Crimes." *New York Times*, p. A1.

Hood, R., Shute, S., Feilzer, M., & Wilcox, A. (2002). "Sex Offenders Emerging from Long-Term Imprisonment: A Study of Their Long-Term Reconviction Rates and of Parole Board Members' Judgements of Their Risk." *British Journal of Criminology* 42, 371–394.

Kaden, J. (1999). "Therapy for Convicted Sex Offenders: Pursuing Rehabilitation Without Incrimination." *Journal of Criminal Law & Criminology* 89, 347–391.

Kear-Colwell, J. & Pollock, P. (1997). "Motivation or Confrontation: Which Approach to the Child Sex Offender?" *Criminal Justice and Behavior* 24, 20–33.

Lemert, E. M. (1951). *Social Pathology*. New York: McGraw-Hill.

Lofland, J. (1969). *Deviance and Identity*. Englewood Cliffs, NJ: Prentice Hall.

Maruna, S. (1997). "Going Straight: Desistance from Crime and Self-Narratives of Reform." *Narrative Study of Lives* 5, 59–93.

———. (2001). *Making Good: How Ex-Convicts Reform and Rebuild Their Lives*. Washington, DC: American Psychological Association Books.

————. (2002). *Self-Attributions and the Criminal Career: Beyond Neutralization Theory*. Unpublished paper.

Massaro, T. M. (1997). "The Meanings of Shame: Implications for Legal Reform." *Psychology, Public Policy and Law* 3, 645–704.

Matza, D. (1964). *Delinquency and Drift*. New York: Wiley.

McAdams, D. P. (1993). *The Stories We Live By: Personal Myths and the Making of the Self*. New York: William Morrow.

Meisenhelder, T. (1982). "Becoming Normal: Certification as a Stage in Exiting from Crime." *Deviant Behavior: An Interdisciplinary Journal* 3, 137–153.

Nelson, W.A. (1996). "The New Inquisition: State Compulsion of Therapeutic Confessions." *Vermont Law Review* 20, 951–980.

Northey, W.F. (1999). "The Politics of Denial: A Postmodern Critique." *Offender Programs Report* 3, 17–18, 30–32.

Peterson, C., Schulman, P., Castellon, C. & Seligman, M. E. P. (1991). "The Explanatory Style Scoring Manual." In Charles P. Smith and John W. Atkinson (eds.), *Motivation and Personality*. New York: Cambridge.

Petrunik, M., & Shearing, C. D. (1988). "The 'I,' the 'Me,' and the 'It': Moving beyond the Meadian Conception of Self." *Canadian Journal of Sociology* 13, 435–448.

Polsky, Ned (1969). *Hustlers, Beats, and Others*. Garden City: Doubleday.

Redl, F. & Wineman, D. (1951). "Children Who Hate: The Disorganization and Breakdown of Behavior Controls." New York: The Free Press.

Rex, S. (2001). "Beyond Cognitive-Behaviorism: Reflections on the Effectiveness of the Literature." In A. E. Bottoms, L. Gelsthorpe, & S. Rex (eds.) *Community Penalties: Change and Challenges*. Devon, UK: Willan.

Rose, N. (1996). *Inventing Our Selves: Psychology, Power and Personhood*. Cambridge: Cambridge University Press.

Ross, R. & Fabiano, E. A. (1985). *Time to Think: A Cognitive Model of Delinquency Prevention and Offender Rehabilitation*. Johnston City, TN: Institute of Social Sciences and Arts.

Roudinesco, E. (1990). "Jacques Lacan and Co: A History of Psychoanalysis in France 1925–1985." Chicago: University of Chicago.

Samenow, S. (1984). *Inside the Criminal Mind*. New York: Times Books.

Sawyer, M. (2002). "Why These Days Sorry Really Is the Hardest Word." *Observer Magazine* June 9, p. 7.

Seligman, M. E. P. (1991). *Learned Optimism*. New York: Knopf.

Sharp, B. D. (2000). *Changing Criminal Thinking: A Treatment Program*. Lanham, MD: American Correctional Association.

Singer, J. A. (1997). *Message in a Bottle: Stories of Men and Addiction*. New York: Free Press.

Slaby, R. & Guerra, N. G. (1988). "Cognitive Mediators of Aggression in Adolescent Offenders: I. Assessment." *Developmental Psychology* 24, 580–588.

Snyder, C. R., Higgins, R. L. & Stucky, R. J. (1983). *Excuses: Masquerades in Search of Grace.* New York: Wiley.

Sullivan, D. & Tifft, L. (2001). *Restorative Justice.* Monsey, NY: Willow Tree Press.

Sykes, G. M. & Matza, D. (1957). "Techniques of Neutralization: A Theory of Delinquency." *American Sociological Review* 22, 664–673.

Toch, H. (1998). "Corrections: A Humanistic Approach." Guilderland, NY: Harrow & Heston.

Tru-thought, LLC. (2000). *Just Thinking: Corrective Thinking Workbook.* Roscoe, IL: Tru-thought.

Vanstone, M. (2000). "Cognitive-Behavioral Work with Offenders in the UK: A History of an Influential Endeavor." *Howard Journal* 39, 171–183.

Voruz, V. (2000). "Psychosis and the Law: Legal Responsibility and the Law of Symbolization." *International Hournal for the Semiotics of Law* 13, 133–158.

Walters, G. D. (1998). *Changing Lives of Crime and Drugs: Intervening with Substance-Abusing Offenders.* New York: Wiley.

Ward, T. & Stewart, C. (2002). "Criminogenic Needs and Human Needs: A Theoretical Model." Unpublished paper.

White, T. W. & Walters, G. D. (1989). "Lifestyle Criminality and the Psychology of Disresponsibility." *International Journal of Offender Therapy and Comparative Criminology* 33, 257–263.

Zehr, H. (1990). *Changing Lenses: A New Focus for Crime and Justice.* Scottsdale, PA: Herald Press.

Chapter 8

Prospects for Justice at the Law-Psychology Divide

An Agenda for Theory, Research, and Practice

Bruce A. Arrigo

OVERVIEW

The following chapter reviews and assesses the application chapters previously presented, mindful of how the various authors explored or otherwise commented upon the limits of mainstream (liberal) psycholegal theory, research, and practice. Given this analysis, the chapter also examines how the law-psychology-crime divide could be more consistent with the values of humanism and justice. To this end, I consider several major points of convergence within the application chapters and within the presentation of critical theory entertained in chapter 1 more generally. I conclude by commenting on what work is needed in theory, research, and policy (including education), if the law-psychology-crime movement is to get back to its future of furthering the aims of consumer empowerment, dignity, autonomy, and the like. As I contend, these are the requisite ingredients for advancing the aims of citizen justice and social change, so vital to meaningful, sustainable reform in psycholegal affairs.

INTRODUCTION

Thus far, the purpose of this anthology has been twofold: to document and explore several recent theoretical strains of analysis representing the critical agenda in law-psychology-crime research; and to link a number of these radical approaches to important, practical, and thought-provoking issues in the area of forensic psychology or, more generally, criminal justice and mental health. The introductory chapter identified a number of radical lines of inquiry, receiving considerable attention in the domain of psychological jurisprudence today. The application chapters, utilizing the insights of these radical perspectives or relying on still other approaches not specifically examined within the confines of this anthology, demonstrated the utility of critical analysis for purposes of deepening our regard for pressing controversies at the law-psychology-crime divide. Indeed, topics addressed included the following: anarchism and the violence of mental health decision making; (neo)Freudian theory, parricide and crime in general; constitutive criminology and criminal competency to stand trial; general/family systems theory, juvenile forensic psychology, and adolescent identity development; Lacanian psychoanalysis, critical criminology, and penal punitiveness; and restorative justice, responsibilization, and offender rehabilitation. Although certainly not exhaustive, both the theoretical insights of chapter 1 and the application chapters that followed suggested new and different ways by which to address ongoing problems in law, crime, and society, relevant to the field of psychological jurisprudence.

In this chapter, I examine more systematically both the limits of mainstream (liberal) law and psychology theory, research, and practice, as well as whether greater prospects for justice, humanism, and reform are attainable within the forensic mental health arena. To accomplish these goals, I consider what lessons can be gleaned from the chapters of this anthology. In particular, I question how the forces of ideology and violence have impeded or thwarted the agenda of change, so integral to the founding of the American Psychology—Law Society (APLS) organization and movement established decades ago. As I explain, the theories relied on throughout this volume draw our attention to where and how the traditional psycholegal community mostly has failed to reflect on the way in which its own decision-making logic and system of values has been (and continues to be) responsible, in part, for the limited success of the AP-LS and for the absence of widespread change in the law and social science field more broadly. In addition, by reviewing major points of convergence across the conceptual orientations recounted and developed in the preceding chapters of this book, I identify what important work remains if the call for justice and humanism is to be made real at the crossroads of law, psychology, and crime. Along these lines, I explain how psychological jurisprudence and the radical approaches constituting it, collectively reframe the agenda and recast the debates in forensic psychology, criminal justice, and mental health. Consistent with this analysis, I conclude by commenting on what changes are needed in theory, research, and practice (including education) if sustainable, structural reform is to be meaningfully achieved.

THE LIMITS OF MAINSTREAM LAW AND PSYCHOLOGY: CONTRIBUTIONS FROM THE CRITICAL AGENDA

In this section, specific attention is paid to the failings of traditional psycho-legal theory, research, and practice to advance more completely the aims of citizen justice, collective well-being, and social reform. The "data" for this chapter include the metatheoretical analyses delineated in chapter 1, as well as the insights gleaned from the subsequent applications chapters. Admittedly, it is somewhat difficult to generalize from a limited inventory of "findings," especially when attempting to make a persuasive and cogent statement about the shortcomings of a particular field of inquiry. This notwithstanding, the material described in the previous two portions of this book is suggestive for where and how the mainstream (liberal) psycholegal agenda has spawned an intellectual approach to scholarly law-crime-society endeavors that inadequately addresses the need for systemic, structural change. Accordingly, this section of the chapter delineates the basis on which this conclusion is reached.

Table 1 identifies the various radical perspectives previously explored in this anthology. In addition, these perspectives are linked to the categories of ideology and violence, and the way they operate in conventional psycholegal theory, research, and practice. Again, these determinations were made based on assessing what the insights of the critical agenda are in relation to the mainstream field's epistemological assumptions and value system.

TABLE 1. The Limits of Mainstream Law and Psychology

Categories

Critical Theories	*Ideology* Theory–Research–Practice	*Violence* Theory–Research–Practice
Marxism	Political organization of capital results in alienation and exploitation; users and producers of mental health services accept law's legitimacy to construct identities; these identities create unequal statuses presumed to be natural.	Users and producers of mental health services falsely adopt their class position endorsed by the law; the legal apparatus ensures that those who exercise political and economic power do so at the expense of those with limited power.
Feminist Jurisprudence	Masculine logic of law displaces feminine identities and women's ways of knowing; emphasis on rules and facts incompletely embodies the psychology of women; feminine consciousness to construct juridical narratives is denied or dismissed.	The legal method silences women's voices; patriarchal values are embedded in legal narratives; justice is gendered, valorizing masculine approaches to sense making.

TABLE 1. continued

Categories

Critical Theories	*Ideology* *Theory-Research-Practice*	*Violence* *Theory-Research-Practice*
Anarchism	Law functions as a system of authority; law reduces possibilities for humanity and restricts perspectives on community; the "artificial" limits of law cannot solve human problems because it regulates, coerces, and controls people.	Law's presumed legitimacy denies individual differences; identities are homogenized, human frailties are pathologized, differences are cleansed, justice is deferred.
Postmodernism & Constitutive Criminology	Language structures thought in ways that are not neutral; individuals and the psycholegal systems of which they are a part coproduce a discourse that denies citizens their humanity; harms of reduction and repression abound; system-maintaining meaning displaces individual being.	The discourses of law and psychology are a substitute for the identity and humanity of the subject (e.g., mental health citizens, judges, police officers); linguistic oppression abounds because the manner, flow, and meaning of communication are controlled; knowledge is homogenized and difference is territorialized.
Chaology & General Systems Theory	The mental health and justice systems contain disorder, even though it is organic; artificial policing of human chaos forces citizens to act uniformly; imposed compliance dismisses the natural, life-affirming capacities of people.	The behavior of law forces the tight, rigid control of human conduct; the legal apparatus deprives people of their natural tendencies to adapt and self-organize, notwithstanding extreme levels of organic disorder.
Psychoanalysis	Unresolved insecurity regarding crime and its control means that the offender as other must be segregated; segregation as punishment is a response to unexamined social anxiety defined as offender culpability.	Penal punitiveness as a discursive response to crime control is legitimized, unwittingly, by critical criminology; it has produced the scientific rationality that modern penal intolerance requires as conceptual support.
Restorative Justice	Responsibilization promotes confession without absolution; offender rehabilitation models emphasizing punishment or forgiveness are inadequate; stories that "derealize" the offender-crime relationship must promote self-understanding.	Responsibilization does not make peace with crime or restore justice to society; responsibilization, as offender rehabiliation, is stigmatizing; it does not account for the culture of blame and the presence of societal shame.

There are two notable and interrelated ways in which critical psychological jurisprudence contests the behavior of law, crime, and, by logical extension, society. The first of these is the power of unexamined ideology to shape human affairs and civic life. While this observation is not necessarily new, its affect in the psycholegal sphere is profound. We see this focus on ideology prominently displayed in each of the theories entertained throughout this anthology.

Ideology in Theory-Research-Practice

Marxist psycholegal scholars identify how the political organization of capital disenfranchises people (i.e., leads to alienation and exploitation). Indeed, users and producers of mental health services generally accept, without question, law's legitimacy to construct and codify their identities as "insane," "expert," "dangerous," "healthy," and so on. These identities create unequal statuses, where people (falsely) assume that such divisions are "natural, appropriate, and inevitable" (Schmitt, 1987, p. 54), and where people therefore live, work, and interact accordingly.

Feminist legal criticism explains how the masculine logic of law displaces women's ways of knowing. As critics contend, juridical texts, codes or statutes repress the felt identities of women in various legal practices and institutions and, moreover, dismiss (or deny) feminine consciousness altogether in the construction of juridical narratives. The emphasis on facts, rules, proof, and causes, cornerstones of law's omnipotence (Smart, 1989), incompletely and inadequately embody the psychology of women (Arrigo, 1992, 1995), depriving them of their uniquely lived experiences.

Anarchist psycholegal researchers demonstrate how law, as an entrenched system of authority, cannot solve human problems (Fox, 1993a). Indeed, the law forces closure to possibilities and perspectives that would otherwise promote greater individual autonomy and foster a richer psychological sense of community. Thus, proponents of anarchist theory conclude that the power of legal ideology (i.e., to control, to regulate, to coerce) "is not healthy for people" (Fox, 1993b, p. 106).

Postmodernists, including constitutive criminologists, indicate that legal thought always and already assumes the form of a language that communicates circumscribed desire (e.g., Caudill, 1997; Schroeder, 1998). The desiring voice of the law seeks meaning consistent with its own internal logic, dismissing alternative articulations of it, thereby concealing and repressing the humanity of people (e.g., lawyers, judges, offenders, psychiatric patients, witnesses) (Arrigo, 1996, 2002). In this way, law and legal language are ideological, anchored in specialized values, beliefs, and assumptions that divest subjects of their being (Milovanovic, 1997; Goodrich, 1997). These values are coproduced by people who name, define, or otherwise communicate them as such in various law-psychology-crime contexts.

Chaologists and advocates of general systems/family systems theory describe how order and disorder are natural processes found within all complex systems (Barton, 1994). However, the mental health and justice systems (including the behavior of the juvenile justice apparatus) function to corral human expressions of disorganization, claiming that they are unhealthy for the long-term sustainability of one's existence (Butz, 1997; Williams & Arrigo, 2002a). Thus, law functions to police artificially human chaos (Arrigo & Williams, 1999a), insisting that people mechanically behave like good legal subjects (Williams & Arrigo, 2002b), even when the identity of the person is at stake.

Psychoanalytic investigators of law, crime, and punishment are mindful of the way in which societal responses to offender conduct are linked to power and ideology. Whether in the context of parricide, penal punitiveness, or crime in general, understanding these phenomena entails naming the transgressor as "the other." While this often unspoken, unconscious practice results in segregation or confinement, it does not account for the unresolved feelings (e.g., anxiety, insecurity) that underscore our modern-day culture of intolerance. As such, the legal apparatus uncritically and unreflectively legitimizes social disease, placing responsibility for criminal wrongdoing with the individual and not with the collective (and unexamined) conscience of society.

Advocates of restorative justice recognize that the correctional doctrine of responsibilization promotes confession without absolution, condemnation without understanding. As a model of offender rehabilitation, responsibilization is inadequate because it identifies the individual as the complete and unfettered source of accountability. Following the principles of restorative justice, a more honest and healing model of offender rehabilitation would not simply emphasize punishment or forgiveness because these categories are trite, succumbing to the political rhetoric on what constitutes the moral high ground. Instead, an effective desistance-from-crime strategy would entail the construction of offender narratives that promote self-reflection.

Violence in Theory-Research-Practice

The second way in which the radical psycholegal critique challenges the behavior of law is by emphasizing how it manufactures violence. For the critical agenda, law's violence is not merely an expression of social consequence (e.g., failing to find a defendant competent to stand trial, engaging in biased child custody evaluations, executing the mentally ill); rather, it is a function of how legal thought, logic, imagery, and language symbolically reveal the roots of cultural intolerance (e.g., Sarat & Kearns, 1992). Each critical perspective developed in this anthology distinctively and provocatively draws attention to the phenomenon of law's violence.

Marxist psycholegal theory indicates that users and producers of mental health services falsely (and mostly uncritically) adopt the class position they occupy. These positions are legitimized and enforced by the law. Thus, the law ensures that those who wield economic and political power in the mental health and justice systems (e.g., corporate administrators) do so at the expense of those whose personal and political power is comparatively small (e.g., patients/consumer) (McCubbin & Cohen, 1996).

Feminist legal critics identify the legal method as responsible for silencing the voice of women (MacKinnon, 1991). Embedded within the very syntactical construction of juridical reasoning are patriarchal values and assumptions that subtend women's lived experiences (Bartlett, 1991; Smart, 1995). Excluding female identities in legal analysis means that justice is gendered (Fraser, 1997), privileging and embodying only masculine sensibilities (Arrigo, 1992).

Psycholegal scholars sympathetic to the philosophy of anarchism explain how law's supposed legitimacy repudiates individual differences, assuming that "the rule of law is always superior to nonlaw" (Fox, 1993a, p. 237). When all of human conduct is forced to fit through the needle of the law, identities are normalized, human frailties are pathologized, differences are cleansed, and justice is deferred (Ferrell, 1999). Practices such as civil commitment, involuntary drug treatment, and dangerous predictions abound. To legitimize its behavior, the law, consistent with the logic of the mental health sciences, engages in ontological realism, epistemological objectivism, and theoretical positivism.

Postmodern and constitutive law-psychology-crime researchers indicate that when legal discourse functions as a stand-in, as a replacement, for the identity of the speaking subject, then the person experiences linguistic oppression (Arrigo, 1996, 2002). In the mental health law arena, linguistic oppression amounts to violence. It denies defendants, patients, officers, psychologists, correctional workers, witnesses, and so forth the ability to speak freely, such that the unspoken but felt constraints of a legal code or a courtroom procedure exert dictatorial control over the flow, manner, and meaning of communication (Milovanovic, 1992). As subjects coproduce the language that constrains them, knowledge is homogenized and difference is territorialized.

Psycholegal commentators supportive of general systems/family systems theory locate law's violence in its tight, rigid control of human behavior (e.g., William & Arrigo, 2002a). Forced psychotropic treatment (especially over objection), involuntary civil commitment, determinations of dangerousness, and the execution of mentally disordered offenders illustrate harm not merely in effect but in how the legal apparatus deprives citizens of their natural capacities to adapt and self-organize in the face of extreme levels of disorder (Williams & Arrigo, 2002b). This same dilemma presents itself in the area of juvenile forensic psychology. Indeed, clinical assessments, diagnoses, case reports, and courtroom testimony promote equilibrium or stasis conditions that thwart or undermine variable interpretations in understanding differences in adolescent identity development.

Proponents of the psychoanalytic orientation in forensic psychology and criminology, recognize that law and social control, definitions of crime, and society's urge to punish are rooted in the modernist culture of intolerance. For example, penal punitiveness (i.e., offender responsibilization) emerges as the result of the anxiety and insecurity society confronts in the face of crime perceived as immediate, local, and pervasive. More problematic, however, is the complicitous role of critical criminology. Indeed, it unknowingly establishes the requisite political, economic, cultural, and social scientific grounding that anchors the present-day punitive response to crime and its control.

Researchers supportive of restorative justice and its utility for furthering a social psychology of law and criminal behavior recognize that an effective model of offender rehabilitation must make peace with crime and restore justice to society. Responsibilization condemns and stigmatizes offenders, potentially generating higher rates of recidivism. The culture of blame and the presence of societal shame must be accounted for if the self-reflective, autobiographical narratives generated by recovering offenders are to be meaningful.

PROSPECTS FOR JUSTICE, HUMANISM, AND REFORM: POINTS OF CONVERGENCE IN CRITICAL PSYCHOLOGICAL JURISPRUDENCE

In this section, specific attention is given to the way in which the various radical frames of reference explored throughout this anthology intersect on several noteworthy law, crime, and society themes. In particular, I identify where and how the critical agenda in psychological jurisprudence, represented by the assemblage of theories explored in the first two portions of this book, advances the call for justice, humanism, and reform. This commentary is significant in that it suggests what the future direction of the law-psychology-crime discipline must be if progress in theory, research, and practice is to occur systemically. Similar to the analysis presented in the previous section of this chapter, the data consist of the insights thusfar developed in this anthology. Thus, the observations that follow are mostly provisional, suggesting, rather than resolving, what critical psychological jurisprudence signifies as it seeks to promote change in our scholarly approach to law, crime, and society.

Table 2 lists the specific theories explored in this anthology. In addition, the Table identifies several thematic points on which the various perspectives converge. These points of intersection tell us something more or something other about the nature of law, crime, and society in relation to psychological jurisprudence and its call for critical inquiry.

Table 2 identifies four areas of thematic convergence in critical psychological jurisprudence. These juncture points include the following: (1) the person-world dialectic; (2) demythologizing systems of control; (3) the narrative of crime, justice, and community; and (4) restoration and reconciliation. Admittedly, other domains of intersection could be identified and chronicled (e.g., the goals of science, the meaning of progress); however, as I contend, the themes selected uniquely inform our regard for psychological jurisprudence and its critical potential to further the aims of justice, humanism, and reform. In addition, I note that Table 2 summarily indicates how each theory uniquely expresses its shared commitment to the identified themes. In other words, each radical perspective entertained throughout this anthology endorses the four points of convergence. However, how each critical theory articulates its support for each particular theme differs. Capturing these differences is important as it tells us a great deal more about how critical psychological jurisprudence recasts many of the debates in law, crime, and society.

Elsewhere, I have employed this particular strategy of locating juncture points across various intellectual strains of thought in relation to critical criminological theory (Arrigo, 1999, 2000, 2001). In these instances, I argued that the links among the respective conceptual prisms hinged on identifying existential-humanistic themes, and describing how each radical perspective uniquely embraced or expressed its shared commitment to those areas of intersection. In this regard, I demonstrated how each theme had a corresponding knowledge category or dimension. Thus, for example, the knowledge uniformly at issue with the person-world dialectic is the struggle to be human; the knowledge singularly at issue with demythologizing systems of control is the struggle to be free; the knowledge consistently at issue in the narratives of crime, justice and community is the discovery of one's being and the possibility of one's becoming; and the knowledge that unvaryingly is at issue with the theme of restoration and reconciliation is the belief in redemption. For purposes of investigating the domains of thematic convergence in critical psychological jurisprudence, this same strategy of exploring existential-humanistic knowledge categories will be employed. This decision is based on my previous work in the area (Arrigo, 2000, 2001), especially since I demonstrated how critical criminological theory could further prospects for justice, humanism, and reform in various law-crime-society contexts.

TABLE 2. Critical Psychological Jurisprudence: Thematic Points of Convergence

Critical Theories	Person-World Dialectic	Demythologize Systems of Control	Narratives of Crime, Justice, & Community	Restoration and Reconciliation
	(Struggle to Be Human)	*(Struggle to Be Free)*	*(On Being and Becoming)*	*(Redemption)*
		(Corresponding Knowledge Categories)		
Marxism	exploitation & alienation	class oppression/ emancipation	class conscious reform	classless society
Feminist Jurisprudence	gender & difference	displace male voice, recount women's stories	value subjectivity, process, identity different conceptions of power	contingent universalities
Anarchism	embrace ambiguity	resist all authority, self-governance	value epistemic uncertainty, change & all perspectives equally	community and tolerance
Postmodernism & Constitutive Criminology	power of language	oppression & emancipation in words; agency-structure co-production of harm and liberation	multiple and divergent vocabularies of meaning; replace technologies of control with languages of possibility	multiaccentuated reality
Chaos & General/Family Systems Theory	orderly disorder	multiple, nonlinear outcomes	far-from-equilibrium conditions	bifurcations
Psychoanalysis	unresolved & unexamined societal anxiety	psychic urge to punish, segregate, & confine the "other"	societal insecurity absent a theory of the subject	turn analytical lens inward/outward
Restorative Justice	culture of blame, societal shame	responsibilization condemns and stigmatizes	"derealizing" dialogues	self-understanding, personal autobiography

The Person-World Dialectic

Critical psychological jurisprudence recognizes that struggle is endemic to human social interaction and to ongoing civic life. More profoundly, however, what is at stake in this struggle is the humanity of citizens. Humanity in this context refers to the ability of individuals or groups to express themselves and to shape their identities as they deem appropriate, such that they are not the mere products of social, political-economic, and other control-driven forces.

The Marxist approach to law-psychology-crime embraces this concern for one's humanity. It draws attention to how the material conditions of society (i.e., forms of exploitation in the mental health and justice systems) interact with political-economic presuppositions about human nature (i.e., alienating and disenfranchising persons with mental health disorders). Indeed, to the extent that certain collectives or institutions (e.g., health management organizations, the legal system, the psychiatric profession) exercise regulatory power and control over others (e.g., the poor, users of mental health services), the struggle for individual or group humanity will continue unabated.

Psychologists of law persuaded by the insights of radical feminist jurisprudence embrace and emphasize the humanity of women. As psycholegal codes, actors, institutions, and decisions unfold, the question is whether, and to what extent, these artifacts of culture and society embody gender differences. To the extent that the divergent voices and manifold ways of knowing for women fail to find expression and legitimacy within the "malestream" texts regarding psycholegal thought, all women struggle to experience their humanness.

The anarchist critique in psychological jurisprudence also endorses the humanity of individuals and collectives. This freedom resides in the value assigned to ambiguity, uncertainty, and change, especially in the sundry ways in which these notions are expressed communally through human social interaction. In this regard, people live their differences "without the normalizing and external constraints of regulatory and disciplinary regimes (e.g., the mental health system, the criminal justice apparatus)" (Arrigo, 2000, p. 12). When individual freedoms are in conflict, citizens must work collaboratively and humanely to resolve them. Thus, for example, the imposition of forced psychotropic treatment over objection, involuntary civil commitment, competency restoration for purposes of execution are all social practices that deny individuals their humanity, especially when the freedoms of others are not infringed on or otherwise abrogated.

Postmodern and constitutive approaches to psycholegal inquiry recognize that the person-world dialectic entails an affirmative struggle to be human. The agency-structure coproduction of language potentially limits (if not thwarts) greater opportunities for individuals to express openly the differences that they embody. When individuals, the media, and agents of the legal and psychiatric systems define and shape one's identity (e.g., Theodore Kaczynski) such that the person is transformed into and becomes the marginalizing persona assigned to that citizen (i.e., the "mad" genius unable to *pro se* his criminal case), then the subject's humanness has been vanquished. This is the power of language to foster harm in social consequence.

Chaos and general/family systems theory as appropriated by psychology of law scholars also acknowledges that the humanity of people is at stake in psycholegal decision-making practices. For example, when the mental health, juvenile justice, social welfare, and correctional systems impose a one-size-fits-all order on people (e.g., mandated reporting, waiver to the adult system, removal of children from parents, the death penalty), then these institutions and organizations have failed to comprehend the importance of disorder, spontaneity, and unpredictability in the mapping of human social interaction over time. These chaotic forces are organic and healthy to the long-term sustainability of any organism, including people. To quash such tendencies is to deny people their humanness and to deprive them of their ability to thrive. Thus, orderly disorder more completely explains the nature of people in various social contexts or arrangements.

Proponents of psychoanalysis interested in decisions, actors, rules, and institutions situated at the law-psychology-crime divide recognize that people struggle to be human in the interplay of the cultural, social, and psychic forces that establish or shape individual identities. When society's unexamined and repressed pain (i.e., anxiety) manifests itself as collective insecurity, the humanness of individuals or citizen groups is called into question. Thus, for example, modern-day intolerance for offender behavior locates responsibility for criminogenic conduct with "the other," and finds legitimacy for this punitive practice through the law (e.g., mandatory-minimum sentences, three strikes legislation). However, these correctional responses do not account for the psychic health of the social body; instead, they make offenders casualties of our own nonreflective actions.

Restorative justice efforts to rethink psycholegal thought and action recognize that the person-world dialectic entails an affirmative struggle whereby people seek to retain or reclaim their humanity. Whether as victims, offenders, police agents, correctional personnel, probation/parole officers, or others exposed to the criminal justice and mental health systems, making peace with crime and restoring justice to society are integral to the healing process. A significant feature to this process is the extent to which the culture of blame and societal shame remain largely intact and unexamined, underscoring decisions made at the crossroads of law and psychology, and crime. As long as these conditions go uninvestigated, all people will be at least one step removed from experiencing their full, unfettered humanness.

Demythologize Systems of Control

Institutional control over the freedom of citizens involves a monopoly of power in which state apparatuses discipline, contain, or otherwise corral human consciousness (i.e., speech, thought, behavior). Demystifying such control entails resistance to these disciplinary regimes or mechanisms. Without such contestation, the very identity of citizens is vanquished. Thus, demythologizing disciplinary institutions involves a persistent struggle to be free from such oppression.

Marxist psychology of law researchers resist the control wielded by the criminal justice and mental health systems by demonstrating where and how it fosters class oppression. The contested terrain for this struggle is the psychiatric courtroom, the forensic unit of a prison, the outpatient settings for persons with persistent and chronic mental health disorders, and so on. In these instances, privilege and power serve the interests of those who possess economic and political currency at the expense of those who lack such standing. Devising strategies to emancipate citizens from these inequities is the challenge for Marxist psychology of law scholars.

Psychologists of law sympathetic to the critique of feminist jurisprudence draw attention to how the discourses of law, crime, and society privilege the masculine voice and subtend that of the feminine. Thus, as texts are constructed germane to various psycholegal issues (e.g., battered women's syndrome, rape trauma syndrome, and sexual harassment), the criminal justice and mental health systems exercise control over the identity of women, with debilitating social consequences. Indeed, "women must conform to and comport themselves within a narrowly defined and prescribed horizon of meaning, rendering them essentially powerless to speak, to think, to act, and to be free" (Arrigo 2000, p. 16). Demythologizing these regimes of control means that those narratives that uniquely embody the divergently lived experiences of women must be articulated and legitimized in positional, contingent, and interpersonal ways.

Anarchist psychologists of law recognize that the mental health and criminal justice systems function to artificially police and regulate human conduct. Demystifying their control involves a resistance to fixed codes and inflexible procedures because such practices deny individual differences. In the anarchist tradition, all expressions of state-sanctioned authority are to be debunked and dismantled, especially since containment practices do nothing but erode the personal freedom of citizens to live humanely with others. Thus, the mental health, the criminal justice, the youth service, and the social welfare systems should be disassembled and replaced with local, decentralized, self-governing communities of support and mutual aid where such networks responsibly attend to the needs of citizens as they emerge.

Postmodern and constitutive researchers of law-psychology-crime understand that language and systems of communication are both restrictive and liberating simultaneously. The discourse of mental health law is one such example. Only certain meanings for "mental illness," "dangerous," "responsibility," "insanity," "civil commitment," "criminal competency," and so forth find their way into the lexicon of psychiatric justice (Arrigo, 2002). The organizations that support and sustain these interpretations and the agents or actors affiliated with these institutions who speak about such matters, invoke system-maintaining language to convey meaning at the expense of more liberating alternatives. In other words, the coproduction of mental health law discourse affirms one version of reality, mediated by language, and dismisses all others that do not comport with psycholegal values. This is the presence of linguistic oppression or harm (Arrigo, 1993, 1996). However, to the extent that the words people select to convey thought and to invite action are reflexively and deliberately chosen—even in the face of entrenched resistance from institutional regimes of control—subjects can be emancipated from the dictatorial hold that language wields in their lives (Henry & Milovanovic, 1996).

Advocates of chaos or general/family systems theory in psycholegal research and practice are committed to liberating people from the forces of institutional or disciplinary control in their lives. These systems of regulation and confinement reduce the possible ways in which offenders, victims, judges, police officers, psychiatrists, consumers, attorneys, and so forth interact and relate to one another. The routinized, technical, official, and bureaucratic methods by which courts, hospitals, correctional units, police precincts, and juvenile facilities respond to issues and controversies in forensic psychology and criminology forces individuals into tightly scripted mechanical roles of human social interaction. These predictable, ordered, linear, and coordinated patterns of comportment fail to include the other equally meaningful (and natural) dimensions to our existences. In short, these would include moments of absurdity, inconsistency, randomness, and spontaneity. The importance of these more unpredictable and fluid aspects of our humanity must be responsibly and reasonably positioned within the systems that seek to regulate our lives. In this way, both order and disorder (i.e., chaos) function to enable citizens to maximize their liberating potentials. Indeed, under these conditions people are freed from the artificial constraints that restrict and deny them of their self-hood.

The psychoanalytic approach in law and psychology recognizes the limits of prevailing systems of control and regulation. For example, the present-day urge to punish in the form of segregative or other confinement practices implicates the conscience of society as much as the responsibilization of the offender. However, as a culture, we have yet to examine the unconscious societal motivations or the deep affective undercurrents (e.g., insecurity, anxiety, repression) that result in penal punitiveness. Psychoanalytically demystifying disciplinary institutions entails a deliberate and sustained engagement with the "mind" of society in relation to the legal and criminological policies it seeks to promote. Liberating society from the dark and primal forces that constrain it will help free those citizens who needlessly (and wrongfully) suffer because of our collectively unresolved and latent psychic conflicts.

The restorative justice agenda in law-psychology-crime recognizes that demystifying systems of control involves a struggle for personal freedom and societal well-being. Today, we see this conflict waged in the area of offender rehabilitation and desistance from crime strategies. The emphasis on responsibilization and confession merely condemns and stigmatizes offenders without something more. The challenge is not merely to promote punishment or rehabilitation as legitimate correctional goals because both approaches falsely lay claim to the moral high ground. Instead, restorative justice seeks an approach that derealizes the offense while humanizing the offender, appropriately assigning responsibility for criminal transgression to all parties involved. In this context, the systems of which one is a part and the behavior of the offender are appropriately and proportionately implicated in the process of corrections and rehabilitation.

The Narratives of Crime, Justice, and Community

Proponents of critical psychological jurisprudence recognize that the stories of crime, justice, and community are evolving texts about identity, personhood, dignity, autonomy, proprietorship, and equality. In addition, advocates of a radical psychology of law, crime, and society understand that various political, economic, social, and cultural forces can be embedded within these narrative accounts. Thus, critical psychological jurisprudence seeks to uncover these marginalizing forces and to promote more liberating prospects for citizens. These prospects affirm the humanity and the freedom of the subject. As such, the narratives of critical psychological jurisprudence endeavor to affirm the discovery of one's being and the possibility of one's becoming.

Advocates of a Marxist-based psychological jurisprudence advance the subject's being and becoming by assessing the means, mode, and relations of production in the mental health and justice sectors. Economic change (i.e., eliminating the psychiatric citizen's exploitation) and psychological reform (i.e., eliminating alienation, self-estrangement) manifest themselves when people experience class consciousness. In other words, when mental health system users recognize the ideological distortions to which they are subjected, then they can mobilize and pursue the possibility of personal and group liberation. Thus, the narratives of crime, law, and society in psychological jurisprudence are stories of revolution and reform. These stories challenge mental health citizens and the legal and psychiatric systems to which their identities are connected, to advocate for change consistent with maximizing their freedom and their human potential.

Psycholegal scholars persuaded by the insights of radical feminist jurisprudence emphasize the possibility and discovery of being and becoming for women in various civil and criminal contexts. In these instances the traditional "texts" of mental health law are displaced as they subtend feminine voices and ways of knowing. In their place, narrative accounts that value subjectivity (over objectivity), process (over content), identity and difference (over sameness), and relational (rather than regulated) power are cornerstones to articulating the divergently lived experiences of women. In this way, process dialogue, interpersonal truth, feminine consciousness, and intersubjective knowledge inform the texts of mental health law, retrieving the humanity of women and reclaiming their freedom.

For anarchist psychologists of law, the discovery of one's being and the possibility of one's becoming are central to their critical agenda. The rejection of absolute truth, defiance of authority, and the belief in epistemic uncertainty, signal an alternative vision for justice, humanism, and reform. In psychological jurisprudence, the narratives of crime, law, and society promote difference, ambiguity, and change. Individuals are free to be who they are with others in local, noncentralized, nonhierarchical, and inclusive communal contexts, provided they do not infringe on the freedoms of others. Thus, being and becoming in the anarchist tradition mean that the artificial categories of "mental illness," "offender," "homeless person," "victim," "prostitute," "delinquent youth," and the like can be transformed and reconstituted in ways that affirm the identity and humanity of people, especially when all people, perspectives, and identities are equally valued.

Postmodern and constitutive psycholegal theorists celebrate the being and becoming of individuals. The power wielded by discourse in the narratives of crime, law, and justice is that it often unwittingly marginalizes, alienates, and victimizes. The coproduction of this discourse (e.g., the Unabomer case) only further serves to demonstrate how language can result in harms of reduction and repression, denying people their humanness and their freedom. Advocates of postmodern and constitutive approaches to the psychology of law validate multiple and divergent vocabularies of meaning for different citizens or groups. Thus, the technologies of control and regulation, symptomatic of the narratives found within the legal and psychiatric systems (e.g., criminal competency to stand trial, civil commitment, predictions of dangerousness), need to be replaced with languages of possibility. These grammars, these stories, validate one's right to be, to become, and to make a difference.

Proponents of chaos and general/family systems theory in psychological jurisprudence support the advancement of one's being and the discovery of one's becoming. Recognizing that natural and social systems change, evolve, and adapt, advocates of these critical approaches identify natural instabilities or far-from-equilibrium conditions as important and organic features to the generative potential of people. In other words, fractal, incomplete, contradictory, and disordered tendencies are a natural part of the human condition. Thus, the stories of crime, law, and society must embrace, rather than contain or correct, these healthy inclinations. Indeed, these propensities are so integral to the life force of any system (including people), that imposing manufactured order, tight regulation, and rigid control (e.g., mandated sentencing, compulsory waiver to the adult system, three strikes legislation, forced hospitalization), undermines and undoes one's maximum potential to evolve, to heal, to be.

The psychoanalytic perspective in psychological jurisprudence supports the discovery of one's being and the possibility of one's becoming. The narratives of crime, law, and society (e.g., modern-day penal punitiveness), are steeped in societal insecurity shrouded in collective anxiety, absent a theory of the subject. In order to affirm the humanity and freedom of people, psychoanalytic scholars of psychological jurisprudence maintain that accounts of crime and justice must articulate how the subject's identity (e.g., agency, person-hood, autonomy, dignity) is folded into the language, logic, and thought of conventional psycholegal decision-making practices.

Advocates of restorative justice in psychological jurisprudence affirm the being and becoming of citizens in the narratives of forensic psychology and criminology. Conventional approaches merely promote retributive accounts (e.g., responsibilization) or rehabilitative stories (e.g., forgiveness), without a deeper, more robust, understanding of the mutually implicated role of offenders and society in the criminal act. Proponents of restorative justice in psychological jurisprudence draw attention to "derealizing" dialogues. These efforts demystify the offense and humanize the offender, mindful that a cultural struggle is waged in the contested terrain of the social psychology of corrections and offender therapy. As a recontextual account of transgression, criminals and responsibility, these dialogues redefine how crime desistance and personal recovery can meaningfully occur.

Restoration and Reconciliation

The person-world dialectic, the demystification of control-driven systems, and the stories of crime, justice, and community are three significant and thematic points of convergence in critical psychological jurisprudence. Indeed, they powerfully reshape our understanding of human behavior and social action, especially in the context of ongoing decisions and practices in civil and criminal mental health law. These juncture points, and their corresponding knowledge categories, also inform the fourth, pivotal area of intersection: restoration and reconciliation.

Critical psychological jurisprudence envisions a vastly different approach to crime, law, and society then its mainstream (liberal) counterparts. In particular, "the logic of crime control is displaced, the will of institutional authority is dismantled, and the practice of justice rendering is reconfigured" (Arrigo, 2000, p. 23). The reformist struggle to be human, to be free, and to discovery one's being and becoming means that change is to be anticipated, welcomed, and celebrated. The nature of this change is such that a better life for people is contemplated and a better world in which to experience it is imagined. Thus, prospects for reconciliation and restoration signify that redemption is not only possible but is necessary if the generative potential of individuals and the society of which they are a part is to be achieved.

For Marxist supporters of psychological jurisprudence, the struggle to be human requires that users and producers of mental health services overcome economic exploitation and personal alienation. The struggle to be free involves the liberation and emancipation of psychiatric citizens from their felt sense of class (or group) oppression. The discovery of one's being and the possibility of one's becoming entail class conscious reform in which psycholegal narratives more fully affirm the humanity, dignity, and autonomy of such individuals. This level and type of change yields prospects for individual and communal restoration. Thus, the redemption Marxist proponents of psychological jurisprudence anticipate and celebrate is one that is devoid of class stratification or other institutional mechanisms of inequality.

For advocates of feminist jurisprudence as applied to psycholegal research, policy, and, practice, the struggle to be human entails the validation of gender and difference as crucial components of knowing and experiencing law, crime, and society. The struggle to be free involves displacing the masculine voice privileged in justice and mental health narratives, and the affirmation of the feminine register in these texts. The discovery of one's being and the possibility of one's becoming require that the values of identity, process, subjectivity, and relational power be folded into these narrative accounts. Thus, retrieving the voices of and ways of knowing for women promotes positional and provisional truths, or contingent universalities (Butler, 1992). These are restorative and redemptive moments that affirm the multiplicity of feminine thought, language, imagery, logic, and identity.

For proponents of an anarchist psychology of law, the person-world dialectic and the struggle to be human necessitate that ambiguity be embraced within various institutional contexts and throughout human social interaction. Demythologizing disciplinary regimes of excessive or unwarranted regulation (e.g., the legal and psychiatric systems) means that authority, in all its forms, must be resisted, debunked and dismantled because it limits our freedom and undermines our existence. In the anarchist tradition, the stories of law, crime, and society promote epistemic uncertainty, value change, and cultivate difference. In this way, critical psychological jurisprudence reconciles itself to toleration of all things (except intolerance), such that people are responsible for themselves and others. Thus, prospects for restoration are located in the communities that people inhabit where mutual support, shared governance, and local decision-making, and collective action loosely configure in the redemptive affirmation of all citizens.

For supporters of postmodern and constitutive approaches to psychological jurisprudence, the struggle to be human involves the oppressive and marginalizing force of language to shape individual identities and to circumscribe human potential in various institutional or situational contexts. The struggle to be free entails deconstructing and reconstructing the coproductive role of discourse such that harms in speech (and action) are avoided and languages of possibility are affirmed. Thus, the narratives of crime, law, and justice require that new, alternative, and replacement vocabularies of sense-making be validated, notwithstanding how unfamiliar, unusual, or unconventional they may be. Again, this is because language constrains and represses identities in ways that support system-maintaining declarations. In order to restore the subject, reality must not be anchored in one linguistic scheme. Instead, a variety of grammars, a multitude of "accentuated" versions of truth, knowledge, meaning, identity, self-hood, dignity, and so on must be articulated. This approach retrieves and restores the humanity of citizens otherwise exposed to the brutalizing and totalizing effects of the mental health, criminal justice, social welfare, youth services, and other systems. As such, the possibility for redemption is found within these alternative grammars.

For chaos and general/family systems theorists persuaded by the critical agenda in psychological jurisprudence, the struggle to by human requires that a mix of order and disorder (i.e., chaos) be embraced in various law, crime, and society contexts. Self-expression that is predictably unpredictable represents a more honest, organic, and, therefore, healthy approach to understanding the human condition. The struggle to be free means that multiple, nonlinear outcomes are not only possible but are to be pursued, especially when mechanisms of control (e.g., the juvenile justice system, the mental health system) tightly, bureaucratically, procedurally attempt to regulate people. According to proponents of psychological jurisprudence, informed by the principles of chaos and general/family systems theory, when one's humanity and freedom are maximized, the narratives of crime, justice, and community include the uncertain, spontaneous, serendipitous, dimensions of human social interaction along with the routinized, the coordinated, the predictable. Indeed, the stories about dangerousness, adolescent identity, confinement, criminal conduct, psychiatric disorder, and the like must, by necessity, include inherent instabilities; that is, pockets of incomplete sense-making. Again, this is because far-from-equilibrium conditions are intrinsic to human social behavior. When chaos, fuzzy logic, variation, and randomness are embraced by the psycholegal system, decision-making practices are reconstituted. Local and immediate interventions may appear uneven, fragmented, inconsistent, and even absurd; however, over time, when a system is sufficiently exposed to the principles of chaos and general/family systems theory, "a new semblance of global order spontaneously emerges" (Arrigo, 2000, p. 28). Prospects for redemption are located in these expressions of local instability and global order. These are "bifurcation" points or periods of fluctuation that yield a new, more adaptive order for people, for systems, and for the society of which both are a part.

For psychoanalytic scholars of psychological jurisprudence, the struggle to be human is linked to the unexamined and unresolved anxiety that society harbors, expressed through various law, crime, and justice practices (e.g., parricide, penal punitiveness). The struggle to be free centers on the operation of disciplinary systems (e.g., the mental health apparatus, the correctional apparatus) and the psychic urge to punish, to segregate and to confine the "other." The discovery of one's being and the possibility of one's becoming are jeopardized when the stories of crime and justice are grounded in societal insecurity, absent a theory of the subject. In order to experience restoration, psychoanalytic researchers of psychological jurisprudence assert that the analytical lens must be turned both inward and outward. In this way, redemption is possible when the conscience of individuals and of society are examined.

For advocates of restorative justice in psychological jurisprudence, the struggle to be human entails a focused consideration on the culture of blame and societal shame that promote alienating, victimizing practices. The struggle to be free means that systems of power and regulation need to acknowledge how penal solutions such as responsibilization condemn and stigmatize without fostering absolution. The narrative accounts of crime, justice, and community need to embrace "derealizing" dialogues. These are stories that acknowledge the offense but also humanize the offender, in ways that move beyond the ordinary labels of punishment or forgiveness. These accounts maximize prospects for one to be and to become more than a criminal offender, a juvenile delinquent, a dangerous mentally ill patient, and so forth. Efforts at restoration and reconciliation hinge on the transformation envisioned by restorative justice proponents, linked to these life-altering themes. As such, the possibility for redemption is located in the personal and autobiographical stories articulated and recounted by offenders and others exposed to the mental health and criminal justice systems. These are attempts at self-understanding, introspection, revelation, insight, and meaning. Through these narratives, the person is able to make peace with his or her crime and with the harm and suffering the transgression produced for others. This is the restorative path in which one takes genuine responsibility for one's wrongdoing and, in its wake, experiences genuine forgiveness for oneself.

CRITICAL PSYCHOLOGICAL JURISPRUDENCE:
FUTURE DIRECTIONS IN THEORY, RESEARCH, AND PRACTICE

In this section, I tentatively outline what work must be done if critical psychological jurisprudence is to make real the call for justice, humanism, and reform in law, crime, and society. In particular, I explore where and how future theoretical, empirical, and policy analyses are warranted. Along these lines, I also speculate on what changes are needed in education, classroom instruction, and related training. Admittedly, the initiatives I identity represent a blueprint for change. As such, they should be interpreted as provisional and incomplete at best.

Theoretical Considerations

Based on the comments developed in the previous two sections, humanizing the law entails a deliberate and sustained focus on the struggle people confront when they attempt to establish, through the law, legal identities that do not seamlessly fit into existing institutions, practices, policies, or procedures. Legal psychologists, forensic psychologist, and criminologists—especially those interested in the pragmatics of good theory—need to explore further whether juridical reasoning and logic can, if at all, comport with the psychological values of different citizen groups. For example, whose needs are served by exposing *everyone* in a dispute to the formal or informal machinery of the civil or criminal law when, given the radical critique, legal thought and language invalidate certain ways of knowing and being? How, if at all, do the legal constructs of "reasonableness," "intent," "due process," "insanity," and the like, embody legal ideology and to what extent does this ideology reflect the consciousness of different cultural groups? These and similar questions require greater theoretical attention.

Relatedly, radical psychology of law and crime scholars must articulate a sophisticated theory of justice. Although this volume made several tentative suggestions along these lines (see chapter 1 and the previous two sections of this chapter), no systematic statement about the nature of justice was provided. Admittedly, this was not the purpose of this anthology; rather, the aim was to explain what the critical agenda encompasses informed by several critical (criminological) theories and epistemological assumptions, demonstrating how the radical critique could further the goal of substantial and sustainable change in law, crime, and society. In addition, the purpose of this project was to showcase some of the more provocative and pertinent work presently undertaken by various researchers, supportive of critical psychological jurisprudence. If the radical law-psychology perspective is to assist meaningfully in the process of humanizing legal and criminal institutions, practices, and decisions, then it must develop a detailed conceptual framework, disclosing what its vision of a just society is and how this vision could bring about much needed structural reform. Issues such as these are at the heart of the radical critique and theoretical investigations of this sort must advance the agenda of individual well-being, collective humanism, and widespread change.

Critics of this approach in psychological jurisprudence may take exception to this wholesale assault on the law. In addition, opponents may reject the notion that the rule of law fosters the degree of ideology, violence, and injustice implied throughout this book. After all, the mental health law field has witnessed a number of substantive reforms, resulting, for example, in improved patient care (e.g., the right to treatment, the right to refuse treatment) and access to it (e.g., least restrictive care, least invasive care) (e.g., Perlin, 1999). Further, legal psychologists and criminologists may be skeptical about the radical agenda's capacity to affect structural and long-lasting change, suggesting reform that effectively would come from *outside* the system itself.

These are all valid criticisms and they do present something of a formidable challenge in theory and in practice for critical law-psychology-crime work in the future. However, changing fundamental inequalities in society entails a major departure from mainstream liberal initiatives (Fox, 1993a). "The problems inherent in our justice system cannot be resolved simply by addressing problems within that system" (Roesch, 1995, p. 329). While improvements through the instrumentation of the law arguably can be identified, to what degree have these enactments furthered its already sedimented power to shape the identity of women, minorities, the poor, and the disabled, consistent with the prevailing ideology, logic, and language of the law (Arrigo, 1996, 2002)? Mindful of how legal psychologists have historically neglected to research questions of this sort, Ogloff (2000) sharply criticized the American Psychology-Law Society in his 1999 Presidential Address. As he noted, "for far too long we have ignored sex/ethnic/cultural/ differences and gender roles in the phenomena we study. . . . [T]hese differences have either been ignored or blindly overlooked" (Ogloff, 2000, p. 475). These are important concerns that radical scholars need to investigate as they require more detailed and more thoughtful conceptual work, informed by the insights of psychology.

Research Considerations

The critical perspective in psychological jurisprudence contests the assumption of absolute objectivity in scientific practices. The Marxist and anarchist orientations are extremely skeptical about unbiased and impartial reality construction. Marxists argue that the political economy can shape and manufacture scientific truths (Lynch & Stretesky, 1999), while anarchists claim that science, as an expression of centralized authority, is ill-equipped to explain the contradictions, inconsistencies, ambiguities, and absurdities of the human condition (Ferrell, 1999). The approaches of feminist jurisprudence, post-modernism and constitutive theory, chaology and general/family systems theory, psychoanalysis, and restorative justice dismiss the value of total objectivism (and positivism).

The decry of objectivity in law-psychology-crime research is particularly problematic. As Ogloff (2000) explained, citing Weiner and Hunt (1999),

> The courts and legislatures are less likely to listen to the values of social scientists than to those scientists' empirical findings. It is only when psychology can offer empirically valid and reliable research findings that psychologists effectively block the court's ability to dismiss their arguments on political and ideological grounds. (p. 473)

Although not expressly reviewed throughout this anthology, one research lesson culled from the critical perspective in psychological jurisprudence is the need for greater qualitative inquiries. The attention given to qualitative analysis is significant. Consistent with the presuppositions of the radical agenda, it recognizes how studying people and their behavior is, after all, a human science (e.g., Giorgi, 1973), and that the frailties of living cannot be adequately or completely conveyed in a statistical equation. In fact, such manipulations often distort or conceal the felt dimension of our experiences, rendering them incidental to or contaminating for the purpose of the researcher's investigation. Interestingly, however, the conduct of people and the way in which the law responds to it is, by definition, an intimate and personal reality. Accordingly, and following the radical critique, it is a reality that necessitates richly descriptive, qualitative explanations.

Part of the dilemma for legal psychologists and criminologists (whether testifying in a courtroom, engaging in risk assessment work, studying jury behavior, or participating in other technical matters), is the belief that rigorous statistical analyses produce "facts" that can be assembled together, yielding a "pure" (i.e., nonpolitical or nonideological) science of humanity. However, if nonneutral language always intervenes to construct reality as postmodernists note, and if the researcher's perspective always influences the object of inquiry as chaologists assert, then what degree of scientific objectivity can really be assured? At best, we are left with approximations, "predictions [that] involve only probabilities, statistical regularities, and not certainties" (Best & Kellner, 1997, p. 214). One can reasonably ask if this degree of certainty is sufficient for the demands of justice, especially when someone may be civilly confined, administered forced mind-altering medication, or sentenced to death.

Relatedly, the critical perspective in psychological jurisprudence significantly questions the values implied in objective science. For example, the feminist assault on the legal method challenges masculine approaches to meaning, particularly when sequential thinking, deductive reasoning, and syllogistic logic are esteemed as the pillars of scientific truth (e.g., Arrigo, 1995). The order, regimentation, and detachment implied in this model of understanding, while invaluable in some instances, neglects the importance of narrativity, interpersonal truth, and consciousness-raising, hallmarks of feminine ways of knowing and experiencing phenomena (e.g., Smart, 1995; Fraser, 1997).

Where the theoretical considerations previously outlined suggested that legal psychologists and criminologists reconsider what they investigate in the pursuit of justice, the focus on qualitative analysis as discussed here encourages psycholegal researchers to rethink how they examine the phenomena they study. This shift will not be easy. The contention is not that qualitative inquiry alone can completely address the problems posed in the field. For example, feminist approaches, too, convey hidden values that may not be conducive to an appropriate assessment of psycholegal issues impacting men, people of color, all women, or other constituencies. Thus, there is a useful and vital role for quantitative inquiry. However, following the radical agenda, it is not so serviceable that it facilitates our fullest understanding of *all* psycholegal matters.

Future social scientists need to question the research methods they employ and the assumptions these methods make, in relation to what (and who) they investigate *before* the actual research occurs. In addition, law-psychology-crime studies that evaluate critically the methods of mainstream empirical research must be conducted, particularly in relation to how conventional social scientific inquiries unwittingly include and exclude people's felt sense of identity, agency, meaning, and person-hood in their very syntactical construction. Finally, legal psychologists and criminologists, particularly those who testify, have an affirmative obligation to explain to the legal, correctional, juvenile, mental health, and other communities the nature of their findings from the perspective of justice. What this means is that manifestations of ideology, power, and violence, forces lodged deeply within the psyche of law that thwart human potential, need to be identified, demystified, and rectified so that social well-being and individual autonomy can be ensured, as much as possible, for all parties involved.

There are limits to these research considerations. The psychologist's or criminologist's role as advocate of justice rather than avatar of objective science, a position that substantially moves the prevailing psycholegal paradigm in a different direction, will not be easy to accomplish in practice. Persuading the legal system that part of reforming the law entails a deliberate and sustained focus on where and how juridical practices, institutions, and decisions often and unknowingly undermine prospects for human justice through legal logic, imagery, thought, and language will be difficult. This is definitely not how the legal community presently understands what legal psychologists can offer police, court, and correctional agencies. Consequently, there will be more not less confusion and uncertainty about the appropriate role for forensic psychologists or criminologists in the justice system.

In addition, financial incentives for expert testimony will undoubtedly change. Lawyers skeptical about or suspicious of psychology's capacity to demonstrate successfully how the law potentially manufactures injustices in its assessment of human behavior will lead to accusations of charlatanism and pseudoscience. The inclusion of alternative, and perhaps novel, methods of inquiry in psychological tests, risk assessments, child custody evaluations, and the like, will not be received warmly and will be the source of considerable scientific and legal scrutiny. These are legitimate concerns and future legal psychologists and criminologists, sympathetic to the critical agenda, must thoughtfully, patiently, and clearly explain why their research findings are relevant and what they meaningfully contribute to the justice system. Without this degree of care the value of the radical critique—for law, crime, and society—will be significantly marginalized if not altogether dismissed.

Policy Considerations

Policy begins with education and programs in law-psychology-crime must reevaluate the extent to which justice is central to the classroom and field instruction. Typically, legal and forensic psychology are identified as subspecialities of clinical training and course offerings in these areas are minimal at best (Bersoff, et al., 1997). While joint degree programs in law and psychology produce legally trained clinicians or psychologically sophisticated policy analysts (e.g., Grisso, et al., 1982; Hafemeister, Ogloff, & Small, 1990; Ogloff, Tomkins, & Bersoff, 1996), students take course in such seemingly nonrelated areas as Wills and Estates, Property Law, and Bankruptcy (Wexler, 1990). This produces a disjuncture between the law-psychology relationship, and the overall educational experience regrettably is compromised (Bersoff, et al., 1997).

The emphasis on justice in educating legal psychologists has already been explored in theory and implemented in practice (Arrigo, 2001b). In this model of instruction, students are exposed to a cross-disciplinary but integrative curriculum, taking such requirements as: Theories of Crime; Juvenile Justice Administration; Minority Populations in Forensic Systems; Organizational Behavior; Conflict Mediation and Dispute Resolution; Legal Research and Writing; and Policy Analysis. Where appropriate, these courses are supplemented with the standard fare of required classes in therapy, testing, and research. Thus, the overall instructional model blends conventional forensic psychological instruction and training with the more innovative law-psychology-crime approach described throughout this chapter. Although somewhat new, students have been placed successfully at American Psychological Association Internship sites, and graduates have secured gainful employment as administrators, educators, policy analysts, and clinicians.

As a practical matter, the limits of this educational paradigm have yet to be identified and assessed systematically. Relatedly, the importance placed on justice in the psycholegal sphere has led some prospective students, practicum/internship supervisors, and would-be employers to question how this model produces different and potentially more meaningful outcomes than what clinically trained or dual-degree graduates offer. While several tangible explanations consistent with the thrust of this volume have been delineated (Arrigo, 2001b), their real, sustainable impact has yet to be felt in any appreciable way.

Other areas of policy exploration consistent with critical psychological jurisprudence require considerable attention. The full list of policy domains is just too vast to explore in the remaining pages of this chapter. However, some comments are warranted. In general, the manner in which police, court, correctional, and juvenile systems manage people, organizational units, and programs needs to be reconsidered. For example, to what extent, if at all, do the agencies that employ personnel who work directly or indirectly with persons experiencing persistent and severe mental illness provide training on race, gender, and class inequalities and the context in which these social conditions affect individual conduct? To what extent, if at all, is correctional policy concerning inmate riots and violence filtered through the lens of how the behavior of prisons dynamically interacts with and contributes to the actions of people (Arrigo & Williams, 2000)? To what extent, if at all, is stress reduction training, while in the academy and while on the force, regarded as a necessary and vital skill for saving lives, for promoting recruitment, for retaining quality officers, and for reducing disability claim prospects (Arrigo & Garsky, 2002; Abdollahi, 2002)? These and similar questions are anchored both in psychology and in justice, and critically trained forensic psychologists and criminologists can play an important role in changing the present culture by which we understanding and address them.

CONCLUSIONS

In this chapter I endeavored to accomplish three things. First, given the critical insights delineated in the application chapters found in this volume and given the theoretical commentary outlined in chapter 1, I assessed the limits of mainstream (liberal) law-psychology-crime research. In particular, I explained how the forces of ideology, violence, and power are lodged within conventional psycholegal decision-making. Indeed, each radical perspective drew attention to specific components of these notions and their operation in traditional forensic psychological contexts.

Second, this chapter explained how the critical agenda in psychological jurisprudence advances prospects for justice, humanism, and reform. Here, too, I relied on the radical insights developed throughout the text, and explained how each theory uniquely expressed its shared commitment to four existential-humanistic themes. These themes included: the person-world dialectic; demythologizing disciplinary systems of control; the narratives of crime, justice, and community; and reconciliation and restoration. Furthermore, I explained how each of these points of intersection was linked to a corresponding knowledge category. I examined both the themes and the categories in relation to how the various theoretical approaches explored in this text deepened our regard for citizen justice, collective humanism, and social reform.

Third, I tentatively examined what work remained if critical psychological jurisprudence was to make real the call for change in law, crime, and society. Along these lines, I commented on how future theorizing, qualitative research, and justice policy in forensic psychology and criminology were pivotal to recasting many of the debates in the field. Relatedly, I explained how specific reforms in education, including classroom instruction and field training, could go a long way in recasting the way in which law-psychology-crime practitioners understand and appreciate their work.

The utility of critical psychological jurisprudence, as a unique set of conceptual lenses to employ for mental health and criminal justice research, remains in its infancy. This book moves the academic community one step closer to recognizing its potential for substantial, meaningful, and sustainable reform in various law, crime, and society contexts. The challenge that awaits is to transform the vision of change at the core of this radical critique into purposeful action. In the final analysis, if forensic psychology and criminology are to make real the call for justice identified by its architects decades ago, we can ill afford to postpone or dismiss this agenda. Indeed, to do otherwise would defer (and deny) prospects for much needed structural reform so essential to the radical critique. Moreover, it would legitimize those very systems and institutions of oppression, alienation, and victimization that psychiatric consumers, criminal offenders, at-risk youth, and other disempowered citizen groups confront daily, directly, and deeply.

REFERENCES

Abdollahi, M. K. (2002). "Understanding Police Stress Research." *Journal of Forensic Psychology Practice* 2(2), 1–24.

Arrigo, B. A. (1992). "Deconstructing Jurisprudence: An Experiential Feminist Critique." *Journal of Human Justice* 4, 13–29.

———. (1993). *Madness, Language, and the Law*. Albany, NY: Harrow and Heston.

———. (1995). "Rethinking the Language of Law, Justice, and Community: Postmodern Feminist Jurisprudence." In D. Caudill & S. Gold (eds.) *Radical Philosophy of Law: Contemporary Challenges to Mainstream Legal Theory and Practice* (pp. 88–107). Atlantic Heights, NJ: Humanities Press.

———. (1996). *The Contours of Psychiatric Justice: A Postmodern Critique of Mental Illness, Criminal Insanity, and the Law*. New York/London: Garland.

——— (ed). (1999). *Social Justice/Criminal Justice: The Maturation of Critical Theory in Law, Crime, and Deviance*. Belmont, CA: West/Wadsworth.

———. (2000). "Social Justice and Critical Criminology. On Integrating Knowledge." *Contemporary Justice Review* 3(1), 7–37.

———. (2001a). "Critical Criminology, Existential Humanism, and Social Justice: Exploring the Contours of Conceptual Integration." *Critical Criminology: An International Journal* 10(2), 83–95.

———. (2001b). "A Review of Graduate Training Models in Forensic Psychology: Implications for Practice." *Journal of Forensic Psychology Practice* 1(1), 9–31.

———. (2002). *Punishing the Mentally Ill: A Critical Analysis of Law and Psychiatry*. Albany, NY: State University of New York Press.

——— & Garsky, K. (2002). "Police Suicide: A Glimpse Behind the Badge." In R. Dunham & G. Alpert (eds.), *Critical Issues in Policing* (pp. 609–626). Prospect Heights, IL: Waveland.

——— & Williams, C. R. (1999). "Chaos Theory and the Social Control Thesis. A Post-Foucauldian Analysis of Mental Illness and Involuntary Civil Confinement." *Social Justice* 26(1), 177–207.

——— & Williams, C. R. (2000). "Reading Prisons: A Metaphoric-Organization Approach." *Sociology of Crime, Law, and Deviance* 2, 191–231.

Bartlett, K. (1991). "Feminist Legal Methods." In K. Bartlett & R. Kennedy (eds.). *Feminist Legal Theory* (pp. 393–413). Oxford: Westview Press.

Bersoff, D. N., Goodman-Delahunty, J., Grisso, J. T., Hans, V. P., Poythress, N. G., & Roesch, R. G. (1997). "Training in Law and Psychology: Models from the Villanova Conference." *American Psychologist* 52, 1301–1310.

Best, S. & Kellner, D. (1997). *Postmodern Theory: Critical Interrogations*. New York: Guilford. *of the FDA*. New York: Springer.

Butler, J. (1992). "Contingent Foundations: Feminism and the Questions of Postmodernism." In J. Butler & J. W. Scott (eds.). *Feminists Theorize the Political*. London: Routledge.

Butz, M. (1997). *Chaos and Complexity: Implications for Psychological Theory and Practice*. Bristol, PA: Taylor & Francis.

Caudill, D. (1997). *Lacan and the Subject of Law: Toward a Psychoanalytic Critical Legal Theory*. Atlantic Heights, NJ: Humanities Press.

Ferrell, J. (1999). "Anarchist Criminology and Social Justice." In B. Arrigo (ed.) *Social Justice/Criminal Justice: The Maturation of Critical Theory in Law, Crime, and Deviance* (pp. 93–108). Belmont, CA: West/Wadsworth.

Fox, D. R. (1993a). "Psychological Jurisprudence and Radical Social Change. *American Psychologist* 48(3), 234–241.

———. (1993b). "The Autonomy-Community Balance and the Equity-Law Distinction: Anarchy's Task for Psychological Jurisprudence." *Behavioral Sciences and the Law* 11, 97–109.

Fraser, N. (1997). *Justice Interruptus: Critical Reflections on the "Postsocialist" Condition*. New York: Routledge.

Giorgi, A. (1973). *Psychology as a Human Science: An Existential-Phenomenological Approach*. New York: Harper & Row.

Goodrich, P. (1997). *Law and the Unconscious: A Legendre Reader*. New York: St. Martin's Press.

Grisso, T., Sales, B. D., & Bayless, S. (1982). "Law-Related Courses and Programs in Graduate Psychology Departments." *American Psychologist* 37, 267–278.

Hafemeister, T. L., Ogloff, J. R. P., & Small, M. A. (1990). "Training and Careers in Law and Psychology: The Perspective of Students and Graduates of Dual Degree Programs." *Behavioral Sciences and the Law* 8, 263–283.

Henry, S. & Milovanovic, D. (1996). *Constitutive Criminology: Beyond Postmodernism*. London: Sage.

Lynch, M. & Stretesky, P. (1999). "Marxism and Social Justice." In B. Arrigo (ed.) *Social Justice/Criminal Justice: The Maturation of Critical Theory in Law, Crime, and Deviance* (pp. 13–29). Belmont, CA: West/Wadsworth.

MacKinnon, C. (1991). "Difference and Dominance: On Sexual Discrimination." In K. Bartlett & R. Kennedy (eds.) *Feminist Legal Theory* (pp. 81–94). Oxford: Westview Press.

McCubbin, M. & Cohen, D. (1996). "Extremely Unbalanced: Interest Divergence and Power Disparities Between Clients and Psychiatry." *International Journal of Law and Psychiatry* 19(1), 1–25.

Milovanovic, D. (1992). *Postmodern Law and Disorder: Psychoanalytic Semiotics, Chaos, and Juridic Exegeses*. Liverpool, UK: Deborah Charles.

Milovanovic, D. (1997). *Postmodern Criminology*. New York/London: Garland.

Ogloff, J. R. P. (2000). "Presidential Address to the American Psychology and Law Society. Two Steps Forward and One Step Backward: The Law and Psychology Movement(s) in the Twentieth Century." *Law and Human Behavior* 24(4), 457–483.

Perlin, M. (1999). *Mental Disability Law*. Durham, NC: Carolina Academic Press.

Roesch, R. (1995). "Creating Change in the Legal System: Contributions from Community Psychology." *Law and Human Behavior* 19, 325–343.

Sarat, A. & Kearns, T. (1992). *Law's Violence*. Ann Arbor, Michigan: Michigan University Press.

Schmitt, R. (1987). *Introduction to Marx and Engels: A Critical Reconstruction*. Boulder: Westview Press.

Schroeder, J. L. (1998). *The Vestal and the Fasces: Hegel, Lacan, Property, and the Feminine*. Berkeley, CA: University of California Press.

Smart, C. (1989). *Feminism and the Power of Law*. New York: Routledge.

———. (1995). *Law, Crime, and Sexuality: Essays in Sexuality*. Newbury Park, CA: Sage.

Wiener, R. L. & Hunt, L. E. (1999). "An Interdisciplinary Approach to Understanding Social Sexual Conduct at Work." *Psychology, Public Policy, and Law* 5, 565–595.

Wexler, D. B. (1990). "Training in Law and Behavioral Sciences: Issues from a Legal Educator's Perspective." *Behavioral Sciences and the Law* 8, 197–204.

Williams, C. R. & Arrigo, B. A. (2002a). "Law, Psychology, and the 'New Sciences': Rethinking Mental Illness and Dangerousness." *International Journal of Offender Therapy and Comparative Criminology* 46(1), 6–29.

About the Contributors

MICHAEL P. ARENA, Ph.D., earned his master's degree in organizational behavior and his doctoral degree in forensic psychology from Alliant International University. He is currently employed by the State of California, where he works on a variety of criminal justice-related programs. His major areas of research and practice interest include international/domestic terrorism, juvenile justice, and policing. His published work has appeared in such periodicals as *Professional Psychology: Research and Practice*, *Deviant Behavior: An Interdisciplinary Journal*, and the *Journal of Forensic Psychology Practice*. Presently he is completing a book on identity and the terrorist threat.

BRUCE A. ARRIGO, Ph.D., is Professor and Chair of the Department of Criminal Justice at the University of North Carolina–Charlotte, with additional faculty appointments in the Psychology Department, the Public Policy Program, and the Center for Applied and Professional Ethics. Dr. Arrigo received his Ph.D. from Pennsylvania State University, and holds a master's degree in psychology and in sociology. He is an internationally recognized scholar who has authored more than 100 journal articles, chapters in books, and scholarly essays. These works explore interdisciplinary, applied, and policy topics in criminological theory, law and psychology, and problems in crime and social justice. He is the author, coauthor, or editor of twelve books; including, *Madness, Language, and the Law* (1993), *The Contours of Psychiatric Justice* (1996), *Social Justice/Criminal Justice* (1998), *The Dictionary of Critical Social Sciences* (with T. R. Young, 1999), *Introduction to Forensic Psychology* (2000), *Law, Psychology, and Justice* (with Christopher R. Williams, 2001), *The Power Serial Rapist* (with Dawn J. Graney, 2001), *Punishing the Mentally Ill: A Critical Analysis of Law and Psychiatry* (2002), *Criminal Competency on Trial* (with Mark C. Bardwell, 2002), *The Female Homicide Offender: Serial*

231

Murder and the Case of Aileen Wuornos (with Stacey Shipley, 2004), *Criminal Behavior: A Systems Approach* (in press), and *The French Connection: Rediscovering Crime, Law, and Social Change* (with Dragan Milovanovic and Robert Schehr, in press). Dr. Arrigo was the Editor of *Humanity & Society* (1996–2000) and is founding and current Editor of the peer-reviewed quarterly, *Journal of Forensic Psychology Practice*. He is a past recipient of the Critical Criminologist of the Year Award (2000), sponsored by the Division of Critical Criminology of the American Society of Criminology. He is also a Fellow of the American Psychological Association through the Law-Psychology Division (Div. 41) of the APA.

JEFFREY L. HELMS, Psy.D., received his master's and doctoral degrees in clinical psychology from Spalding University in Louisville, Kentucky. Currently, he is a member of the psychology faculty at Kennesaw State University. He holds licensure as a psychologist in California and Kentucky. His research and practice interests are predominantly in the areas of adolescence and forensic psychology. His published work has appeared in such periodicals as *Aggression and Violent Behavior, Journal of Forensic Psychology Practice, Humanity and Society, Caribbean Journal of Criminology and Social Psychology, and American Journal of Forensic Psychology*. He has practiced within the community mental health arena where his client base was predominantly minority juveniles (and their families) who had become involved in the criminal justice system. He also maintains a private forensic and clinical consulting practice.

SHAD MARUNA, Ph.D., received his doctorate from Northwestern University in Human Development and Social Policy. He joined the Institute of Criminology at the University of Cambridge in 2001. Prior to that, he had been an Assistant Professor at the School of Criminal Justice at the University of Albany, State University of New York. His research focuses on issues of offender reintegration, reconciliation, exclusion, and forgiveness. In 2001, he was awarded the Michael J. Hindelang Award for Outstanding Contribution to Criminology by the American Society of Criminology for his book *Making Good: How Ex-Convicts Reform and Rebuild Their Lives* (American Psychological Association Books, 2001). He is also the coeditor of the anthology, *After Crime and Punishment: Ex-Convict Reintegration and Desistance from Crime* (with R. Immarigeon, 2004).

PHILLIP C. H. SHON, Ph.D., was awarded the doctoral degree (Criminal Justice) from the University of Illinois–Chicago and is Assistant Professor of Criminology at Indiana State University. His research interests include homicide and psychoanalysis, policing, law and society, discourse analysis, and language and law. His published work has appeared in such journals as

Critical Criminology: An International Journal, Humanity and Society, Journal for the Psychoanalysis of Culture and Society, International Journal for the Semiotics of Law, and *Police Quarterly.* Presently he is completing a book on police-citizen encounters based on discourse analysis.

CHRISTOPHER R. WILLIAMS, Ph.D., received his doctorate from the California School of Professional Psychology and is Assistant Professor of Sociology and Criminology at the State University of West Georgia. His research interests include the philosophy of law, the sociology of mental health and deviance, and theoretical criminology. His numerous articles and chapters on these and related subjects have appeared in such journals as *International Journal for the Semiotics of Law, Humanity and Society, Social Justice,* and *Theoretical Criminology.* He is also the coauthor of *Law, Psychology, and Justice: Chaos Theory and the New (Dis)order* (with Bruce A. Arrigo, 2001), and is coeditor of the anthology, *Philosophical Foundations of Crime* (with Bruce A. Arrigo, 2005).

VÉRONIQUE VORUZ, Ph.D., was awarded the LL.B. for the University of Kent (Cantebury) in 1995 and the Ph.D. in law from the University of London (Queen Mary College) in 2002. Dr. Voruz is a lecturer in Law and Criminology at the University of Leicester (UK). The central concern of her research work is to apply insights derived from psychoanalytic theory to political theory with a view to thinking through the evolution of the subject. Her published work has appeared in a number of outlets including, *Social and Legal Studies: An International Journal* and the *International Journal for the Semiotics of Law.*

Index